THE RABBIS,
DONALD TRUMP,
AND THE TOP-SECRET PLAN TO BUILD THE
THIRD TEMPLE

★★★★★ *"[Building the Third Temple] is an act which must be done to complete the redemption of the people of the Bible in the Land of the Bible."*
– Gershon Salomon, Director, Temple Mount Faithful

THE RABBIS, DONALD TRUMP,

AND THE TOP-SECRET PLAN TO BUILD THE

THIRD TEMPLE

UNVEILING THE INCENDIARY SCHEME BY RELIGIOUS AUTHORITIES, GOVERNMENT AGENTS, & JEWISH RABBIS TO INVOKE MESSIAH

THOMAS R. HORN

DEFENDER

CRANE, MO

THE RABBIS, DONALD TRUMP, AND THE TOP-SECRET
PLAN TO BUILD THE THIRD TEMPLE: UNVEILING THE
INCENDIARY SCHEME BY RELIGIOUS AUTHORITIES,
GOVERNMENT AGENTS, AND JEWISH RABBIS TO INVOKE
MESSIAH

CONTENTS

Introduction

PLANET EARTH, WHILE rotating at relatively the same speed as in eons past, nonetheless seems to now rush ahead with exponentially increasing forward movement. Ability to instantly know of events anywhere in the world creates this illusory, anxiety-laden sensation. This generation is speeding into an increasingly dark future.

This is true for the majority of the world's inhabitants, but it doesn't have to be true for those who believe what the Creator of all things has to say about things to come. That Creator is none other than Jesus Christ, whom the Bible says is the very *Word* of God.

> In the beginning was the Word, and the Word was with God, and the Word was God.
>
> The same was in the beginning with God.
>
> All things were made by him; and without him was not any thing made that was made.
>
> In him was life; and the life was the light of men.
>
> And the light shineth in darkness; and the darkness comprehended it not. (John 1:1–5)

Jesus Christ illuminates the pathway through a sin-saturated world where dangerous pitfalls of every sort lurk. His Word tells the believer:

Trust in the Lord with all thine heart, and lean not unto thine own understanding. In all thy ways acknowledge Him, and He shall direct thy paths. (Proverbs 3:5–6)

The believer's pathways toward the future are illuminated through the prophetic Word of God. Many signs are posted along those paths. God's prophets—of whom Jesus, the Son of God, the Second Person of the Godhead, is greatest—foretell things to come with unerring clarity.

The Third Temple, the subject of this book, is one prophetic sign God's Word posts for those who seek truth. That Jewish house of worship is prophetically scheduled to be constructed atop the most volatile piece of real estate on the planet. That rocky plot of earth is feared by world diplomats to present the greatest threat to Middle East and world peace.

Mount Moriah, known as the Temple Mount, is the focal point for adherents of the world's three most prominent religions—Judaism, Christianity, and Islam. Only worshippers within Islam are now allowed to worship upon this promontory at the southern area of Jerusalem. Merely the hint of the other religions' attempt to conduct worship atop Moriah is met with violence from Muslim militants. It seems inconceivable that a Jewish house of worship can ever be built there.

Yet there is more than a concept with the matter of wanting to build a Jewish Temple on Moriah. In the thinking of some, it is as good as already done, and, as the reader will discover, *there is a secret plan by Jewish authorities to make it happen sooner than most know.* The reason is because the God of Heaven has declared that it will be built. His prophetic Word never fails. The nation in the midst of which Moriah sits is absolute proof, in the thinking of those who believe the Third Temple is as good as already there.

Modern Israel is a miracle entity guided by the hand of God through more than 1,900 years of dispersion. The Jewish people endured enemies and persecutions of every description while being reestablished on the very ground where ancient Israel surrounded the Temple Mount. This is proof that God's Word is truth. Bible prophecy foretold that Israel would be destroyed as a nation and removed completely from the land God promised Abraham, Isaac, and Jacob.

Second Temple Trouble

Daniel the prophet clearly prophesied the beginning of the nation's diaspora, or dispersion, that would follow the Messiah's being "cut off," as recorded in chapter 9 of the book called by his name:

> And after threescore and two weeks shall Messiah be cut off, but not for himself; and the people of the prince that shall come shall destroy the city and the sanctuary, and the end of it shall be with a flood, and unto the end of the war desolations are determined. (Daniel 9:26)

Jesus, who gave this prophecy to Daniel centuries before Christ came to die for the sins of the world, foretold this destruction while on the Mount of Olives just before His crucifixion. He spoke to His disciples concerning the beautiful Temple—the Second Temple—atop Moriah at that time.

> And Jesus went out, and departed from the temple; and his disciples came to him to show him the buildings of the temple.
> And Jesus said unto them, See ye not all these things? Verily I say unto you, There shall not be left here one stone upon another, that shall not be thrown down. (Matthew 24:1–2)

The *Second* Temple was built following a previous diaspora, or dispersion, when the First Temple—the one built by King Solomon—was destroyed by Babylonian King Nebuchadnezzar in 587 BC. The construction of that Second Temple is wrapped up in the prophecy of the ninth chapter of Daniel, where the angel, Gabriel, gave the prophet the timeline of Israel's future:

> Know, therefore, and understand, that from the going forth of the commandment to restore and to build Jerusalem unto the Messiah, the Prince, shall be seven weeks, and threescore and two weeks; the street shall be built again, and the wall, even in troublous times. (Daniel 9:25)

There is debate on exactly when the actual fulfillment of this prophecy began. One biblical scholar writes:

> When do the seventy weeks begin? There are four possible decrees which might fulfill verse 25; most commentators narrow it down to either Artexerxes' decree in 458 BC (Ezra 7:11–26) or his decree in 445 BC (Nehemiah 2:1–8). There are also decrees by Cyrus in 538 BC, recorded by Ezra in 1:1–4 and 5:13–17; to rebuild the temple, and by Darius in 517 BC, recorded in Ezra 6:6–12; another decree to rebuild the temple.[1]

The Second Temple, the one Jesus and His disciples viewed from their Mount of Olives vantagepoint, was greatly enhanced in size and beauty by Herod, who was appointed by Rome to rule the region. The Temple had been built by the sixth century B.C. and came to be celebrated as one of the most admired structures of the time.

Just as Daniel and Jesus foretold, Jerusalem and the Second Temple were destroyed.

At the heart of all the tumult surrounding the Temple Mount is an increasing call for the Jewish right to worship there. Muslims already have the right to worship on this site, which is the third most holy in Islam, while it is the first holiest in Judaism. This discrimination generates increased tension and amps up the desire of the religious Jews to be allowed access to it. Further, a growing number of Jews are demanding that a Third Temple be built so animal sacrifice and the ritual worship of Judaism can resume.

Praying, kneeling, bowing, prostrating, dancing, singing, ripping clothes—all are forbidden. Jews must do none of these things, according to the rules set for them when visiting the Temple Mount. The site of the former Temples is located above and behind the Western Wall in the heart of Jerusalem's Old City. The area is under Israeli sovereignty, but the mount—called by Muslims Haram al-Sharif—is controlled by the Islamic Wakf, a joint Palestinian-Jordanian religious body.

The Al-Aqsa Mosque and the golden-crowned Dome of the Rock overlooking the city attract daily crowds of Muslim worshipers to the Temple Mount. Jews may only access the site for four and a half hours a day under Wakf regulations, and, as stated, are forbidden from praying there. Most religious Jews still consider the Western Wall to be the faith's holiest site. But growing demand is gathering political support for the status quo on the Temple Mount to be changed. Jews must be able to pray upon their ancient site of worship, it is argued.

Interest in building the Third Temple continues to increase. One survey to determine attitudes among religious Jews showed that 43 percent supported its construction, compared to 20 percent among the ultra-Orthodox and the national ultra-Orthodox, and 31 percent among secular Jews.

The survey showed that among the Israeli Jewish public, 59 percent favor the demand to change the way things presently are on the Mount. One question on the survey asked if "the state should enforce an agreement on the Mount, similar to one that exists in the Tomb of the Patriarchs in Hebron, which is shared by Jews and Moslems?" Just 23 percent answered no.

The survey's results show a considerable change in attitudes among the religious public within the nation: The direction of thought of the people is toward building the Third Temple on Moriah.

Many groups are trying to rev up talk of building the Third Temple. Some are devoted to reconstructing the ancient objects and vessels necessary to carry out rituals of worship once the structure is built. Training for performing ceremonial acts and worship services is taking place, and even ritual garbs for the high priest have reportedly been recreated and are being stored for the moment worship in a rebuilt Temple is instituted. Preparations for reinstituting animal sacrifice are also well underway, it is reported. Others just as devoted to a Third Temple being rebuilt are engaging in political lobbying and various methods of trying to get the Jewish community to visit the Temple site at every opportunity.

Of course, under current circumstances, any effort to remove the Dome of the Rock and the al-Aqsa Mosque would mean that the more than one-billion-strong Muslim world would launch World War III.

At this point, talk of a Third Temple must remain just talk. However, passion among the Jewish people is building for that prophesied future Temple.

Blueprint Blossoming

Rabbi Chaim Richman is the international director of the Temple Institute, an organization based in the Old City devoted to one purpose—building the third Temple atop Mount Moriah. "Our goal is to fulfill the commandment of, 'They shall make a Temple for me and I will dwell among them,'" says Richman, quoting Exodus 25:8. "The basis of a Torah life is action."

Since the destruction of the Temple in AD 70 by the Roman legions led by General Titus, rabbis have generally taken the position that the rebuilding should not be undertaken until the Messiah comes. They hold that their religious law on the matter is too unclear.

Rabbi Richman and the Temple Mount Institute take a different position. Richman says there are no Jewish legal barriers against rebuilding a Temple, only political ones.

A great concern among those who want the Temple Institute suppressed is that Richman and those within the organization aren't shy about wanting the Dome of the Rock and other shrines of Islam removed from the Temple Mount so the construction can begin. The Institute is devoted to laying the groundwork for that purpose. Under the guidance of twenty scholars who study Temple law full-time, it has put together a blueprint for where the structure will stand and what the vessels will look like. The research and directives have produced items of worship that are replicas of the objects used in the ancient Temples that were destroyed.

Plexiglas cases at the institute's headquarters in the Old City contain forty such objects. A short list of some of those items follows:

- Silver trumpets to be blown by priests
- A wooden lyre
- Long-handled pans—one for collecting blood from small sacrificial offerings and another for large sacrifices such as the Passover lamb
- Vestments with azure weaves, gold thread, and a breastplate with twelve precious stones, to be worn by deputy priests and the high priest, are displayed on mannequins that have beards. (It reportedly took eleven years and more than one hundred thousand dollars to complete the outfits for worship.)
- A massive, twelve-spigot sink with electric faucets—modern technology Chaim Richman says will be permitted to be in the Third Temple
- A golden, two-hundred-pound, seven-branch menorah in a case overlooking the Western Wall

Troubling to many who consider these marvelous recreations for worship is the fact that those of the Temple Institute, unlike other museums displaying articles of worship, intend to remove these objects as soon as possible and begin using them in the Third Temple.

The world's diplomatic community likely views the goings-on at Richman's organization as creating a future trigger for conflict that could bring all-out war in the Middle East. Many Jews who aren't so religious-minded also worry.

Rabbi Richman's passion—obvious from the following excerpt—reflects the strong sense of longing for a return to Temple:

> "All of our outreach here at the Temple Institute is about deepening our feeling of connection—not our feeling of loss, not our feeling of mourning—but our joy with the possibility of our generation being the generation that is leading to the rebuilding of the temple," said Rabbi Chaim Richman, head of the Temple Institute International department in an interview with *Israel National News*.
>
> The Temple Institute website says its short-term goal is to "rekindle the flame" of the temple in people's hearts, and its long-term goal is to rebuild the temple in "our time."
>
> "We consider the rebuilding of the holy temple to be one of the positive commandments. Unfortunately because of the whole long diaspora experience, a lot of ideas crept into our sub-consciousness, and even our consciousness, and there are those that say that the temple is going to come down from heaven, there are those that say that only Mashiach (the Messiah) can build the temple, there are those that say, 'well, the whole idea is just not relevant at all,'" Richman said.
>
> "Our position is really just that our lives are like, on hold. The Jewish people are just a skeleton of what they could be. The whole world is really, totally muted and just completely drained of its vibrancy because we don't have the holy temple. And so what we're really trying to emphasize during these days is to rekindle the anticipation and the beauty and the longing

for having that closer relationship…when the divine presence returns to the world," he added.[2]

With all the plans for the coming Third Temple, which will be built beyond any shadow of a doubt if one believes the Bible, the terrible fact remains. It will be a Temple not of great joy but of great sorrow for the Jewish people. As a matter of fact, the Third Temple will be the *Tribulation* Temple, the one of the time of "Jacob's trouble" (see Jeremiah 30:7). Jesus said it will be the most horrendous time in human history (Matthew 24:21).

But, Jesus, the Jewish Messiah, the Savior of the world, will Himself build a Temple that will be His headquarters throughout His millennial reign. King David will also rule there at the side of Jesus for a thousand years. Jesus will reign as King of all Kings; David, in his resurrected body, will reign as king over all of Israel. Thus, his is called "the throne of David." It will be a time of joy and great glory beyond any mankind has known when Jesus builds that Temple.

> And speak unto him, saying, Thus speaketh the Lord of hosts, saying, Behold, the man whose name is The Branch; and he shall grow up out of his place, and he shall build the temple of the Lord;
>
> Even he shall build the temple of the Lord; and he shall bear the glory, and shall sit and rule upon his throne; and he shall be a priest upon his throne; and the counsel of peace shall be between them both. (Zechariah 6:12–13).

one

Donald Trump, the Rabbis, and the Abomination of Desolation

THOUGH I'M NOT a prophet, I make several incredible predictions in this work, and I might as well get the biggest ones out of the way in the very beginning, so I can then proceed to explain over the course of this tome why I am convinced of something very extraordinary.

It has not been since I and my late investigative partner Cris Putnam accurately predicted the resignation of Pope Benedict XVI one year in advance (naming the very month and year he would retire while writing the best-selling book *Petrus Romanus*) that I've had such a powerful "gut feeling" about something ahead.

This time, however, events set to transpire (soon, in my studied opinion) are much bigger than the *Prophecy of the Popes*.

They are, in fact, earth-shattering, and will accomplish nothing less than altering the course of history. What is about to unfold will set in motion arrival of Antichrist and Armageddon, followed by the Second Coming of Jesus Christ.

During this study, you will learn why I say this and of a secret plan to instigate it by building the Third Temple in Jerusalem. It's happening right now behind the scenes in clandestine negotiations between global powers and religious leaders. These astonishing claims, regardless how incredible they may seem, will be unveiled over the course of this book.

Connected to all this, I will ultimately make the forceful argument that, when the time is right, US President Donald Trump will, as the rabbis in Israel hold, play a key role by speaking in favor of the Third Temple's construction. When that happens, it will ignite the single most important and prophetic event in our lifetime. Unfortunately for those who at first find great joy in the Temple's reconstruction, exuberance will be short-lived and will ultimately cave to terror.

On this order, did you know that:

- The architectural plans for the Third Temple have already begun?[3]
- The Sanhedrin—the nascent tribunal that has styled itself after the Second Temple-era Jewish court—recently instructed Jerusalem mayoral candidates to include in their plans the building of the Third Temple?[4]
- At the close of 2018, the Sanhedrin also invited seventy nations to dedicate the altar for the Third Temple?[5]
- Evangelical Christians and Jews gathered in Jerusalem at the close of 2018 for an interfaith conference aimed at joining efforts to build the Third Temple for inaugurating the "Messianic Era"?[6]
- Freemasons in the US and Israel have been secretly planning for decades to build the Third Temple?
- Jews are increasingly demanding access to the Temple Mount with visions of building the Third Temple?
- In September 2018, a newborn red heifer was certified by a board of rabbis as fulfilling all the biblical requirements for Temple service, a prerequisite for "the biblically mandated process of ritual purification for impurity that results from proximity or contact with a dead body. Because the elements

needed for this ceremony have been lacking since the
destruction of the Second Temple, all Jews today are considered
ritually impure, thereby preventing the return of the Temple
service"?[7] That is, until now.

- A growing number of rabbis in Israel view Donald Trump as a
Cyrus-like figure, whom the God of Israel raised up to initiate
the "Messianic era" and the construction of the Third Temple
(more on this later in this chapter)?[8]

- Saudi Arabia, Jewish religious leaders, and Donald Trump are
negotiating behind the scenes to transfer control of Israel's
holy sites—including the Temple Mount—to the Saudis, to
complete a "peace covenant" that could result in, among other
things, the building of the Third Temple (more on this later)?

- Even some Muslim scholars have come to believe the time has
arrived to build the Third Jewish Temple?[9]

These are just some of the revelations we will examine over the pages
of this groundbreaking work, but suffice to say, since the 1980s, the
Temple Movement has been steadily working in earnest to gather and
prepare the critical elements and to even train the priesthood that will
serve in this new religious complex seated in Jerusalem. The importance
of these efforts throughout parts of the Orthodox Jewish community
and machinations of global political interests will become clearer as we
reveal the Temple's role in what rabbis believe has already started—the
first stage of the messianic process (Moshiach Ben Yosef, or "Messiah
from the house of Joseph"), which is described as the practical and social
precursor to the second stage of the Messiah's appearing as Moshiach
Ben David ("Messiah from the house of David") that includes reinstitution of Temple services for the third and final sanctuary under a Davidic
dynasty.

But, you may say, the Muslim Dome sits atop the Temple Mount
over the very (ancient) spot where Jehovah's Holy of Holies existed, and
thus a Jewish Temple cannot be built, as it would start a world war if

anybody tried to remove and replace the Al Aqsa Mosque, which rests on the far southern side of the Mount, facing Mecca, and/or the Dome of the Rock that currently sits in the middle where the Jews' Holy Temple previously stood.

And yet, there are ways this substantial hurdle may soon be overcome.

For instance, a fault line near Jerusalem has been the cause of a half dozen major earthquakes over the last thousand years and may be strategically located to destroy the Islamic shrines at any point in time. Zechariah 14:3–4 reads:

> Then the LORD will go out and fight against those nations, as he fights in the day of battle.
>
> On that day his feet will stand on the Mount of Olives, east of Jerusalem, and the Mount of Olives will be split in two from east to west, forming a great valley, with half of the mountain moving north and half moving south.

Such a catastrophic event could wipe out the Muslim compound and provide a catalyst for rebuilding Solomon's Temple (or a version of it as a global center for all faiths) under international (perhaps even United Nations) efforts. Recent quake activity throughout the Holy Land (some thirty tremors have shaken Israel this month alone as I write this chapter)[10] indicates that seismic activity could be building toward a prophetic eventuality. Reports in recent years have also featured scientific evidence and geological surveys warning that buildings in the Temple Mount area could be severely damaged if not demolished by an earthquake. The Associated Press, in what sounded particularly prophetic, reported, "Most at risk…is the Old City and the eleven-acre elevated plaza housing two major mosques, including the gold-capped Dome of the Rock. The site is known to Muslims as the Al Aqsa Mosque compound and to Jews as the Temple Mount—once home to the biblical Temples."[11]

It is also entirely possible that an event such as an earthquake would not be required to bring about the dream of a new Temple in Jerusalem.

The Middle East is a powder keg, and war with its missiles and bombs could take out the Islamic shrines in a single hour. Some claim the Muslim structures could even be intentionally targeted during a conflict as a way of facilitating the construction of a new Temple. Interestingly, the newest *Mission: Impossible* movie (*Fallout*) depicts a renegade arms dealer named John Lark who works with a global gang of thugs called "The Apostles" who possess three containers of plutonium, which they plan to use to fulfill the very scenario first outlined in my best-selling books *Petrus Romans* and *The Final Roman Emperor* by bombing the Vatican, the Temple Mount in Jerusalem, and Mecca. In a recent *Jerusalem Post* article, Palestinian President Mahmoud Abbas charged that Israel is secretly planning to make that happen "to destroy the Al-Aqsa Mosque in order to rebuild the Third Temple."[12]

And then there is a third possibility involving how the Third Temple could be built. On June 18, 2009, it was announced in Jerusalem as a result of theological research that "a prophetic rabbi" could allow for an extension of the Temple Mount to be made, on which the third Jewish Temple could be constructed. In an article called "A New Vision for God's Holy Mountain," Ohr Margalit, rabbinical studies professor at Bar-Ilan University in Israel, wrote that "the scenario of a holy revelation given to an authentic prophet that the temple be rebuilt on the current or an extended Temple Mount in peaceful proximity to the Dome, Al Aqsa Mosque, and nearby Christian shrines" is all it would take to approve such a plan.

> According to Jewish law...such a prophetic mandate would then be binding. It would also be in keeping with the words of the twelfth-century Jewish sage Maimonides that Christianity and Islam are part of God's ultimate plan "to direct the entire world to worship God together." Interestingly, Theodore Herzl, the preeminent secular Zionist, detailed the same vision for a rebuilt temple in peaceful proximity to Islamic and Christian shrines on what he called "the holy region of mankind."[13]

As alluded in the bullet points earlier, due to the occult value or sacredness of the numerous elements surrounding Freemason versions of Solomon's Temple (on which all Masonic lodges and ceremonial rituals are based), there has been an idea for some time that groups from among the Freemasons and illuminated fraternities intend to rebuild or to participate in the rebuilding of a glorious new Temple in Jerusalem fashioned after the one built by Solomon. Disclosure of this has occasionally reached the public's ear. The *Illustrated London News*, August 28, 1909, ran a spectacular supplement detailing this goal. The article was titled, "The Freemason's Plan to Rebuild Solomon's Temple at Jerusalem." Three years later, September 22, 1912, the *New York Times* published an outline by Freemasons to rebuild the Temple under the title, "Solomon's Temple: Scheme of Freemasons and Opinions of Jews on Rebuilding." By 1914, some publishers had begun adding unprecedented details, including a report that the land on which the Dome of the Rock now stands was secretly purchased and plans were already under design for the construction of the third and final Temple. Researchers since have produced intelligence that a hushed collaboration is firmly in place, held back only against the right time, opportunity, and circumstances when exalted Freemasons and their associates will move with haste to reconstruct a new Temple, and then their messiah will pass through the golden Masonic portals of the Temple, announcing to the world that the universal savior of mankind has come (Apollo incarnate, Antichrist).

In addition to occultists, groups including the Temple Mount Faithful and the Temple Institute in Jerusalem are busy restoring and constructing the sacred vessels and vestments that will be used for service in the new Temple at the arrival of their "Messiah" (see http://www.templeinstitute.org). Students of Bible prophecy recognize the importance of such plans as signaling the coming of Antichrist. Old and New Testament Scriptures explain that a false Jewish messiah will appear, enthroning himself as God in the Temple in Jerusalem, but afterward, he will defile the holy place by setting up a sacrilegious object—perhaps an

Image of the *Illustrated London News*, August 28, 1909, The Freemasons' Plan to Rebuild Solomon's Temple at Jerusalem

image of himself—in the Temple and ordering the sacrifices and offerings to cease (see Daniel 9:27; 2 Thessalonians 2:3–4). For any of this to
occur, it is necessary for the Temple to be rebuilt, thus making claims by
Freemasons or other groups interested in fulfilling this monumental task
highly suspect with regard to unfolding end-times events.

Whether or not circumstances will be sufficient to build the new
Temple before America elects (or re-elects) its next president in 2020,
what the rabbis in Israel believe Donald Trump started in 2016 may well
have laid the foundation upon which this Man of Sin shall reign.

This raises a few serious questions.

Did God, who works all things together for good (see Romans 8:28),
ordain the election of Donald Trump for a specific purpose and mission
related to the Third Temple?

If so, did the year of his election—2016—hold specific prophetic
significance? Did something start in 2016 like a clock winding down to
this momentous event(s)?

"Those members of the clergy that laid hands on Trump and prayed
at the New Spirit Revival Center in Cleveland Heights, September 21,
2016 must have thought so," I wrote in my book *Saboteurs*, "as did other
prominent Christian leaders during the campaign and most of the clergy
that offered invocations at his unforgettable inauguration. Some of these
Christians trust in Trump's statement of faith, while others simply see
him as imperfect but chosen by God."

I then connected the dots in *Saboteurs* between the year 2016 specifically and what prophets and seers down through time foresaw as related
to that date in particular:

> For instance, Dr. Lance Wallnau refers to Trump as God's
> "chaos" president, a line he borrowed from Jeb Bush who had
> coined the phrase in describing Trump during the final Republi-
> can debate. Wallnau draws analogies between Trump and Cyrus
> "the Great," the pagan Persian king that Isaiah prophesied by
> name 200-years in advance (Is. 44:28), saying he would con-

quer Babylon (happened in 539 BC), the waters of the Euphrates would "dry up" to make way for the army, the city's gates would "not be shut," and thereby the Jews would be liberated and return to Jerusalem where they would rebuild the temple, all of which happened just as the prophet foresaw many years in advance. According to Wallnau, Trump was chosen by God to similarly rescue America from its catastrophic alternative (Hillary) [and to initiate the building of the Third Temple]....

Curiously, Cyrus isn't the only example of a pagan leader used by God to providentially influence the ancient Jewish nation. Nebuchadnezzar was also called "the Servant of the Most High God" and I understand why many modern believers prefer not to think about that example. Unlike Cyrus the deliverer, Nebuchadnezzar was the instrument of God's chastisement against Judah, resulting in most of the people (approximately seventy thousand) being brought into captivity with desolation upon their land. This was the providence of God too, because they would not listen to His words (Jeremiah 25:8ff). The prophet Habakkuk bemoaned God using such a heathen to spank his own children, but God told him it was necessary and that Nebuchadnezzar would be dealt with later (Habakkuk 1:5-11; cf. Jeremiah 25:12ff).

Assyria and Babylon are two more examples of pagan entities used by God to correct His people after they had fallen into apostasy. The Assyrians went to war against Israel under Tiglath-pileser (2 Kings 15:29, 16:7–9), and again under Shalmaneser and Sargon all because they would not obey "the voice of Jehovah their God" (2 Kings 18:9–12).

These contrasting illustrations raise a serious question. If God did, through providence, choose Trump to become America's president, is he our Cyrus (deliverer) or Nebuchadnezzar (agent of judgment)? I want to believe Trump was God's way of putting His foot down on the socialist-globalist runaway agenda to allow a respite and opportunity for spiritual awakening in this country. But what if I'm wrong?

Speaking of Nebuchadnezzar, his example also illustrates how in times past God sometimes used pagans to utter divine insights. An amazing case in point is when God chose to reveal a prophecy spanning from 605 BC through the Second Coming of Christ to the arrogant, narcissistic, idol-worshipping Nebuchadnezzar. Of course, it required God's holy servant, Daniel, to interpret the dream. Similarly, God used Balaam, a sorcerer hired by Balak, a Moabite king, who was exceedingly fearful of the encroaching multitude of Israelites. Accordingly, the king sent for Balaam, a darkened wizard who now lives in prophetic infamy (2 Peter 2:15; Jude 11; Revelation 2:14). Despite Balaam's incorrigible status, God used him to prophesy, "I shall see him, but not now: I shall behold him, but not nigh: there shall come a Star out of Jacob, and a Sceptre shall rise out of Israel" (Numbers 24:17). Ronald Allen, professor of Hebrew Scripture at Western Baptist Seminary, writes, "In agreement with many in the early church and in early Judaism, we believe this text speaks unmistakably of the coming of the Messiah. That this prophecy should come from one who was unworthy makes it all the more dramatic and startling." Thus, we see that God uses the most unlikely characters and situations to get His message across and work done. This Pethorian prophecy was well over one thousand years before the birth of Christ and from a hostile source, yet it is probably what led the magi to Bethlehem.

Another interesting thing about Trump and unlikely agents who lead wise men to Bethlehem is the mysterious and metaphysical logic some currently share involving God's possible providence in the arrival of Trump as a "savior" figure. Nowhere is this language more pronounced than in the Holy Land itself where several respected rabbis and kabbalists have insinuated that America's new president is a forerunner of Messiah and the final redemption.

"Donald Trump (424) is the Gematria of 'Messiah for the House of David' (דוד בן חישמ)," wrote Adam Eliyahu Berkowitz for *Breaking Israel News* on May 16, 2016. "That is not to say that Donald Trump is the Messiah, but that his presidency will usher in the Messianic era."[14]

Others, including Rabbi Matityahu Glazerson, who accurately predicted the Trump victory before the election using Bible codes,[15] have chimed in. Glazerson found various connections between Trump and *moshiach* ("messiah") in the codes, which in Hebrew means "anointed," and led Glazerson to conclude that his election is connected to the coming of Messiah.

Rabbi Hillel Weiss is a Trump-Messiah-connection believer, too, and he also sees in the president the agent of God's favor for building the Third Temple, another Cyrus linking.[16]

Then there is the Sanhedrin in Israel, the nascent tribunal that has styled itself after the Second Temple-era Jewish court, which has sent letters to Donald Trump and Russian President Vladimir Putin asking them to join forces to build the Third Temple for Messiah.

Professor Weiss is a spokesman for the Sanhedrin and notes how Donald Trump made support for Israel and recognition of Jerusalem as their capital part of public discourse during 2016. Combining that with Putin's expressed opinion that the Third Temple ought to be built now caused him to say that both men should do what King Cyrus did 2,500 years ago and build the religious complex for the benefit of all Jews and the world. "We are poised to rebuild the Temple," Weiss said, and "the leaders of Russia and America can lead the nations of the world to global peace through building the Temple, the source of peace."[17]

Rabbi Yosef Berger, who oversees King David's tomb in Jerusalem, takes it a step farther. He believes Trump actually won the election through "the power of Moshiach [Messiah], which gave him the boost he needed" and is "connected to the Messianic process which is happening right now."[18,19]

More recently, the Sanhedrin authorized the minting of two coins—the "Half Shekel Cyrus Trump Temple Coin," and shortly thereafter, the "70 Years Israel Redemption Temple Coin," both of which depict Donald Trump and the ancient Persian King Cyrus (who empowered the building of the Second Temple) on the front side with the Third Temple on the back.

In an article for *Breaking Israel News*, the reasons for the commemorative coins were tied specifically to the Trump administration as the catalyst for building the Third Temple. In fact, rabbis associated with the effort go so far as to say the success of Trump's presidency *depends* on his efforts to initiate the building of the new Solomon-like house of worship.

"In gratitude to US President Donald Trump for recognizing Jerusalem as the capital of Jerusalem, the nascent Sanhedrin and the Mikdash (Temple) Educational Center are minting a replica of the silver half-shekel Biblically mandated to be donated by every Jewish male to the Temple," the report stated, before adding, "Rabbi Weiss stressed that Trump's [US administration] goals will come to fruition *only if they are geared towards rebuilding the Jewish Temple*" (emphasis added).

"Cyrus and Balfour, non-Jews who played an enormously important role in Jewish history fell short and their political success suffered as a result," Rabbi Weiss said.

"Trump's political agenda can only succeed if it is focused on building the Third Temple on the place that God chose: the Temple Mount. He must not advance any two-state solution or this will lead to his downfall."[20]

To further stipulate the role that the rabbis see Trump divinely appointed to perform, the following amazing statement is published inside the official Sanhedrin sanctioned "70 Years Israel" Redemption Coin brochure:

> President Trump is advancing a **prophetic** process that will usher in—when the time comes—**the rebuilding of the Third Temple**. It is as if he is following in the footsteps of King Cyrus who pronounced, after 70 years of Jewish exile, that: Hashem, the Lord of the World, charged me to build him a house in Jerusalem. (bold added)

All of this brings me to another important point involving messianic prophecies, political players, providence, the exact year of Trump's election (2016), and the prophetic ramifications of where we may be headed.

Was Zenith 2016 Just Fulfilled?

In 2009 I released the book, *Apollyon Rising*, that was later updated and re-released as *Zenith 2016* due to important information I came across after the initial publishing of the first version, which many consider my seminal work and *magnum opus*. I hope with the release of this book to find similar accolades, as I truly believe this to be the most important and timely research I've released since.

Besides having a full year in 2009 to travel, interview, and research related topics as well as taking the sabbatical I needed for the actual writing, what made *Zenith* unusual was the big question about why so many ancients—some from hundreds of years ago and some from much further back—foresaw the year 2016 specifically as the date when the Messiah, or, alternatively, the Antichrist, would manifest on earth, with most believing "his" presence would become known to a select few in 2016 but remain unrecognized by wider populations until slowly "he" is revealed for who and what he actually is at the appropriate time in the immediate years following. Even a major Sunni website set these dates years before Trump's election after studying the ancient Quran and Hadith, saying: "Based on our numerical analysis…the official beginning of the End of Time and the coming of the Imam Mahdi [their messiah, but for others like Joel Richardson, the antichrist] will most likely be in…2016 and Jesus Christ will come down from Heaven to Earth in 2022."[21]

Of all the most ancient prognosticators that intrigued me in *Zenith* for whom the year 2016 and the coming Third Temple appeared prophetically significant were as follows:

Prophecy from the Zohar on Messiah's Arrival

Widely considered the most important work of Jewish Kabbalah, the *Zohar* is a collection of books written in medieval Aramaic over seven hundred years ago containing mystical commentary on the Pentateuch (five books of Moses, the Torah). In addition to interpreting Scripture, the Vaera section (volume 3, section 34) includes, "The signs heralding Mashiach," or, "The coming of the Messiah." The fascinating date for "his" secret presentation to the rabbis in Israel was set in the *Zohar* for 2012–2013 (given the rejection of Jesus by Orthodox Jews as Messiah, evangelicals would say this seven-hundred-year-old prediction indicates the Antichrist could have arrived circa 2012–2013).

And, sure enough, on the heels of that date some of Israel's foremost rabbis began behaving as if they know something the rest of the world does not involving the arrival of "Messiah." In addition to the ones I quoted earlier in this chapter who believe the Messianic era has started, Chaim Kanievsky, one of Israel's most prominent rabbis and a leader of the Haredi branch of Judaism and a recognized authority on Jewish law, has recently been warning his students not to leave the Holy Land, because, "The Messiah is already here. He will reveal himself very soon.… Don't travel."[22]

These same rabbis starting in 2016 using "messianic" and "Third Temple" language around the election of Donald Trump.

The Eight-Hundred-Year-Old Prophecy of Rabbi Judah Ben Samuel

Will the years immediately following 2016 be prophetically important for Israel and the world? According to an eight-hundred-year-old prophecy, it certainly could. Before he died of cancer, J. R. Church analyzed the ancient predictions of Rabbi Judah Ben Samuel and noted:

> Ludwig Schneider, writing for *Israel Today* (March 2008), said, "Some 800 years ago in Germany, Rabbi Judah Ben Samuel was a top Talmudic scholar with an inclination for the mystical. Before he died in the year 1217, he prophesied that the Ottoman Turks would conquer Jerusalem and rule the Holy City for 'eight Jubilee Years.'" A biblical Jubilee year consists of 50 years. Fifty multiplied by eight equals 400 years.

> Afterwards, according to Ben Samuel, the Ottomans would be driven out of Jerusalem, which would remain a no-man's land for one Jubilee year. In the tenth Jubilee year [2017]...the Messianic end times would begin....
>
> Looking back at Ben Samuel's prediction, we should note that the Ottoman Empire did conquer Jerusalem in 1517, exactly 300 years after the rabbi's death, and was defeated 400 years later in 1917.
>
> In *Israel Today*, Ludwig Schneider continues, "This came to pass 300 years after Ben Samuel's death. He could not have based this prophecy on events that could be foreseen, but only on the results of his study of the Bible.
>
> "According to Leviticus 25, the nation is reunited with its

land in the year of Jubilee. Therefore, the Jubilee year plays an important role in Israel's history. In this case, the Jubilee began with the defeat and conquest of the Mamelukes in Jerusalem by the Ottoman Kingdom in 1517. The Turks reigned over Jerusalem until the British General Edmund Allenby defeated them exactly eight Jubilees later in 1917.

"Ben Samuel's prophecy was fulfilled precisely because 1517 to 1917 is exactly 400 years. Afterward, Jerusalem was a no-man's land for 50 years during the time of the British Mandate (1917–1967) and the time of Jordanian rule (1947–1967), another Jubilee year. During the Six Day War in 1967, Israel captured Jerusalem from Jordan and the city returned to the Jewish people after nearly two millennia of exile. After that, the countdown for the Messianic age began."

Schneider assumes that since Rabbi Judah Ben Samuel's prediction appears to be fulfilled to date, then 2017 should launch the beginning of the Messianic era.[23]

Protestant Reformers and What They Believed Would Start In 2016

Among the turn-of-the-century Protestant reformers, an astonishing number of theologians believed that the False Prophet and Antichrist would assume places of authority in 2016 and shortly thereafter ascend the world stage. The famous preacher Jonathan Edwards was convinced of this possibility and held a postmillennial view based on the 1,260 days the woman is in the wilderness in Revelation 12:6. He interpreted those days as the years that the true Church was to be oppressed by the papists. Clarence Goen writes of this, "Edwards considered that the most likely time for the…reign of Antichrist was 1260 years after AD 756 (the acceding of temporal power to the Pope),"[24] which would place the (beginning) of Antichrist's power squarely in 2016. When we were doing research for the book, *Petrus Romanus: The Final Pope Is Here*, we learned of this belief by Edwards and sought to verify it by examining a collection of his personal voluminous writings. We found confirmation within a series of his sermons, preached at Northampton, Massachusetts, in 1739, on how history and prophecy coincide.

As we endeavored to demonstrate in *Petrus Romanus*, the pope's rise to temporal power began when Pope Stephen began courting Pepin around 751 and then became a reality in 756 with the expulsion of the Lombards. We wrote how 756 placed the target sometime in 2016. Around that same time during our investigation, we became aware of a sermon collection from the 1800s, titled, "Lectures on the Revelation," by the Reverend William J. Reid, pastor of First United Presbyterian Church in Pittsburgh, Pennsylvania, which were given over a period ending in March of 1876. Like Jonathan Edwards had over a hundred years earlier, Reid deduced that the False Prophet and Antichrist would arrive sometime around 2016. Soon we uncovered numerous other ancient examples in which the year 2016 was specifically foreseen as when the False Prophet and the Antichrist would be on earth, followed by the destruction of Rome. These included:

- The *Theological Dictionary of Princeton University* (1830)
- *Critical Commentary and Paraphrase on the Old and New Testament* by Lowth and Lowman (1822)
- The *American Biblical Repository* (1840)
- *Notes on the Revelation of St. John* by Lowman (1773)
- The *Christian Spectator*, "The Monthly" (1885)
- *Abridgement of Ecclesiastical History* (1776)
- The *Works of the Rev. P. Doddridge, DD* (1804)
- The *International Sunday School Lessons Pub* (1878)
- *Character and Prospects on the Church of Rome in Two Discourses* by the Rev. William Mackray (1829)
- The *Panoplist and Missionary Magazine* (1809)
- *Lectures on Romanism* by Joseph F. Berg (1840)

- The *Congregational Magazine for the Year* (1834)
- The *Presbyterian Magazine* (1858)

The complete list of ancients who believed 2016 pointed to the year when Antichrist would begin making himself known on the global scene and initiate a process ultimately leading to construction of the Third Temple as well as the Great Tribulation period can be found in the book *Zenith 2016.*

Whether this will turn out to be connected to Donald Trump and the rabbis' view of him as a modern Cyrus whose arrival heralds the Messianic era during which the Temple will be built is increasingly convincing, as the following chapters hopefully convey.

two

Behind the Scenes: Players and a Plan

IN A FANTASTICALLY liberal feature by Kerry Bolton for *Foreign Policy Journal* titled "US Recognition of Jerusalem as Israel's Capital: A Travesty of History," the president's son-in-law Jared Kushner is depicted as an arch-Zionist Jew that, along with Donald Trump and his evangelical advisors, views the USA and Israel as synonymous in terms of policy objectives and prophetic destiny.[25]

Bolton's increasingly familiar animosity toward evangelicals and their biblical mandate to be a blessing to Israel results in his lament that "the Zionist dream for Palestine is based on three primary aims that are of messianic intent: (1) Greater Israel from the Nile to the Euphrates rivers, (2) Rebuilding of the Temple of Solomon on the site of the present al-Aqsa mosque, (3) Jerusalem not only as the capital of Israel, but as the central seat of universal law."[26] He then quotes the Temple Mount Faithful's website, which confirms:

> Consecrating the Temple Mount to the Name of G-d so that it can become the moral and spiritual center of Israel, of the Jewish people, and of the entire world according to the words of all the

29

Hebrew prophets. It is envisioned that the consecration of the Temple Mount and the Temple itself will focus Israel on:

(a) fulfilling the vision and mission given at Mt. Sinai for Israel to be a chosen people separate unto G-d, a holy nation, and a nation of priests (Exodus 19:6), and

(b) becoming a light unto all the nations (Isaiah 42:6) so that the Name of G-d may be revered by all nations and the biblical way of life may be propagated throughout the world.[27]

Bolton concludes: "Regardless of what any Israeli government states, these are the ultimate objectives which messianic Zionists believe are ordained by their God. They will never be relinquished." For example, the first prime minister of Israel, David Ben Gurion, a "moderate" and a socialist, asked by Look to describe his vision of the future, alluded to this:

In Jerusalem, the United Nations (a truly United Nations) will build a shrine of the prophets to serve the federated union of all continents; this will be the seat of the Supreme Court of Mankind, to settle all controversies among the federated continents, as prophesied by Isaiah.[28]

Other secular writers appear similarly suspicious that Trump recognizing Jerusalem as the capital of Israel and moving the US embassy there extends end-times "messaging" to his conservative Christian base, which has not gone unnoticed by the appropriate members of his audience. Enlisting the well-known craft of "actions in place of words," the president is viewed as encouraging his compatriots in Armageddon-planning to probe beneath the surface of his exploits where, *sotto voce* ("under voice"), he is telling them he understands and sympathizes with their eschatological worldview and that, when the time is right, he will offer full-throated voice in support of the Third Temple.

Nancy LeTourneau for the *Washington Monthly* suspects as much too, writing: "The most obvious gesture he's made towards Israel since he became president was to move the U.S. embassy to Jerusalem. That was targeted at his base of support among white evangelicals, and it isn't because they have so much affection for Jews." LeTourneau cited what Diana Butler Bass, a theologian, wrote:

> For decades, conservative evangelicals have been longing for this recognition. They believe it is necessary in order to regain control of the Temple mount. That is important because rebuilding the Temple is the event that will spark the events of the Book of Revelation and the End Times.... They've been waiting for this, praying for this. They want war in the Middle East. The Battle of Armageddon, at which time Jesus Christ will return to the Earth and vanquish all God's enemies. For certain evangelicals, this is the climax of history. And Trump is taking them there. To the promised judgment, to their sure victory. The righteous will be ushered to heaven; the reprobate will be banished to hellfire.[29]

Let me take a moment to make issue with LeTourneau and Bass, as I've been at the center of mainstream evangelical Christianity for five decades and have been blessed to personally know many leading prophecy scholars and theologians, and have yet to meet a single one who wants "war in the Middle East. The Battle of Armageddon, at which time Jesus Christ will return to the Earth and vanquish all God's enemies." We simply believe what Jesus taught, that "when these things begin to come to pass, then look up, and lift up your heads; for your redemption draweth nigh" (Luke 21:28). Movement toward the construction of a Third Temple could signal the imminent return of our Lord and Savior, Jesus Christ, and that is what we "want." While the objectives listed by the antagonists above do reflect some of the accomplishments many Jews and Christians anticipate, it is not for the reasons they insinuate, as they obviously don't seem to comprehend the "blessed hope" Christians have for the Second Coming of Jesus, which a Third

Temple could signal, or that which Jews have for their final redemption and Messianic era.

Having said that, any successful attempt at garnering support for a reconstructed Temple in Jerusalem will indeed require enough multi-cultural and international support. Thus, prejudices by Bolton and the other writers quoted above aside, their feelings about behind-the-scenes discussions and deals that could witness the materialization of a Third Temple is warranted, and, in this writers' opinion, they certainly should be suspicious that a plan is under consideration wherein international players are quietly moving chess pieces clandestinely toward a sooner-than-later realization of a rebuilt Temple.

In the parlance of Sherlock Holmes, *the game is afoot!*

Who might some of these powerful players be? My investigation leads to include:

- Trump, of course, and his Jewish son-in-law Jared Kushner, who have been working behind the scenes on aspects of a Middle East peace deal.
- Influential rabbis in Israel, some of whom have already recognized Trump as a source of inspiration for the Third Temple.
- And then there are right-wing Knesset members, the Yeraeh organization, Temple Mount loyalists, and other advocacy groups.
- Shockingly, even some Muslim scholars believe the Third Temple can now become a collaborative effort between them and the Jews. This include Zia H Shah MD, chief editor of the *Muslim Times*.[30] Yehuda Glick, a prominent Jewish advocate for the Third Temple, is even actively nurturing such interfaith dialogue, and recent reports claim progress to this end has been made with Muslim authorities.
- Some believe Brazil's recent election of Jair Bolsonaro—who unabashedly embraces Christianity and supports Israel—could

mark the beginning of the Third Temple, "which some believe will be initiated in South America in a process that has already begun."[31] Evangelicals wielding voting power across Brazil and Latin America are not hiding the fact that they believe "Jews should rebuild their biblical temple in Jerusalem, which is a key step in a series of events that will lead to a second coming of Jesus Christ on Earth."[32]

- The powerful Jewish Sanhedrin also recently showed their hand, advising Jerusalem mayoral candidates "to include in their plans for this city the rebuilding of the third temple."[33]

The list above could go on and on, but our probe into the issue suggests that things go much deeper than these headlines suggest and are in fact far more intriguing, including actual espionage and subterfuge by two of the very entities that could actually make a rebuilt Temple happen: 1) the United States, with back-channel negotiations between the Trump administration and Saudi Arabia that could result in Riyadh replacing the Jordanian Waqf's management of the Temple Mount; and 2) the Vatican. The Islamic Waqf is the religious trust that controls and manages the current Islamic edifices on and around the Temple Mount, including the Al-Aqsa Mosque and the Dome of the Rock. The king of Jordan supplies funding needed for operations by the Waqf, and in one form or another, they have governed access to the sites since the Muslim reconquest of the kingdom of Jerusalem in 1187.[34] Tensions between Jews and Muslims involving access to the mount where Israel's Temple once stood continually flow over often because, as stated earlier, Jewish prayer on the Temple Mount is completely forbidden. "Jews may enter only to visit the place, and only at limited times. Muslims are free to pray on Temple Mount, however, Christians and Jews may only visit the site as tourists. They are forbidden from singing, praying, or making any kind of religious display."[35] Why does such overbearing oversight of the Temple Mount exist? Why such restrictions on Jews and Christians? After spending several chapters in his books *The Great Inception* and

The Last Clash of the Titans outlining why the Temple Mount is biblical Zion and the very place where Armageddon will be initiated, Derek
Gilbert explains what's really behind the ancient—and future—struggle
over this sacred plot of land. *This is* where the capital of God's kingdom
on Earth will exist—Jerusalem and the Temple Mount—and thus why
the energies of evil are focused on it! As Derek notes:

> The faith of Abraham, the dynasty of David, and the divinity
> of Jesus were established there. At the heart of this plateau is
> the hill on which Yahweh, the Creator of the universe, estab-
> lished His "mount of assembly." The temples of Solomon and
> Zerubbabel were built there, and a prophesied Third Temple
> will someday occupy that place.[36] The long war by the Fallen
> against their Creator is ultimately for control of God's mount of
> assembly, Zion. That's His prize jewel, and that's why the enemy
> wants it: "For the LORD has chosen Zion; he has desired it for
> his dwelling place: 'This is my resting place forever; here I will
> dwell, for I have desired it'" (Psalm 132:13–14, ESV). Plenty of
> other verses support this idea, but you get the point. God's holy
> mountain, His mount of assembly, is Zion—the Temple Mount
> in Jerusalem.[37]

These implications and anxieties surrounding the building of a
Third Temple at Zion are not lost on ardent students of prophecy. They
know the contest over this consecrated plot of land reflects profounder
malaise that cannot be superficially perceived. Principalities and powers manipulate earthly governments, and the forthcoming construction
project sits in the navel of an end-times clock that, once initiated, will
quickly count down to the arrival of Antichrist, Armageddon, and the
Second Coming of Jesus Christ. That's the real reason secret meetings
over control of the Temple Mount are proceeding outside the public's
view. Yet for the perceptive—those "with eyes to see and ears to hear," as
the Bible puts it—we clearly understand what is behind Palestinian and

Muslim news agencies worried over the fact that "'Saudi Arabia is currently investing a great deal of behind-the-scenes effort into taking away from Jordan its guardianship of the holy sites of Jerusalem,' a senior official in the Palestinian Authority (PA) told *Al-Monitor* on condition of anonymity. The pressure seems linked to the Saudis' friendly relations with the United States, and with President Donald Trump's desire to win Arab support for his Middle East peace plan, which Jordan has not backed."[38]

Until the murder of journalist Jamal Khashoggi—who publicly opposed the policies of Saudi Arabia's new heir, Crown Prince Mohamed Bin Salman—the Saudi prince had been assiduously cultivating a relationship with Donald Trump and his son-in-law Jared Kushner (who has spent dozens of hours in phone calls and private meetings with the crown prince cementing a personal relationship with him[39]) to guard the pursuits of his administration and Arabian interests in the US Congress and around the world. In trade for—or as part of—this diplomacy, the prince has spoken publicly in support of Israel having a right to their own land,[40] and he even met in 2018 with American evangelical Christians "as the ultra-conservative Muslim kingdom seeks to open up more to the world and repair an image of religious intolerance."[41] Now that the CIA believes the Saudi prince may have played a role in the murder of Khashoggi, it is unclear what effect this may have on US relations.

Regardless, I am told and do believe that placing management of the Temple Mount into the hands of Saudis and progressive or "secular" Muslims and the US administration would be, by design, intentionally inching the world toward one aspect of Donald Trump's "Deal of the Century" for Middle East peace (though the Third Temple negotiation could be part of a separate agreement) that cannot yet be uttered involving compromises that could ultimately allow for construction of the Third Temple. Even the secretary-general of the Muslim World League recently took "the unprecedented and potentially controversial step of urging Muslims to form a delegation alongside Christians and Jewish religious leaders to visit Jerusalem as a step toward peace."[42]

Besides Muslim authorities, the United States, and Saudis, another powerful player that has shown interest in controlling the Temple Mount will assuredly play a role in the eschatology surrounding it. Let's consider this force from Rome.

The Vatican, the Third Temple, and the Burdensome Stone

> And in that day will I make Jerusalem a burdensome stone for all people: all that burden themselves with it shall be cut in pieces, though all the people of the earth be gathered together against it. (Zechariah 12:3)

As investigated by myself and Cris Putnam in our bestselling book *Petrus Romanus*, there is ample evidence to suggest that the Vatican has had a long-running interest in controlling Jerusalem and, by extension, the Temple Mount—with possibly the objective of a Third Temple.

Over the last ten years alone, surreptitious negotiations have included Netanyahu seeking to give David's Tomb to the Vatican,[43] claims that the Vatican is hoarding Second Temple treasures until geopolitics allow for a rebuilt Temple under their control,[44] and even efforts by the United States via Secretary of State John Kerry involving plans "for eastern Jerusalem that calls for an international administrative mandate to control holy sites in the area" including the Temple Mount. Kerry's plan recommended a coalition under Vatican oversight with Muslim countries such as Turkey and Saudi Arabia.[45]

The possible Vatican connection to a rebuilt Temple is intriguing when one considers Peter Goodgame's convincing argument that the Roman prince seen in Daniel 9:27 who sets up the Abomination of Desolation is the False Prophet rather than the Antichrist.[46] He cites Revelation 13:14, in which the False Prophet "deceiveth them that dwell on the earth by *the means of* those miracles which he had power to do in the sight of the beast; saying to them that dwell on the earth, that they should make an image to the beast, which had the wound by a sword, and did live" (emphasis added), and Daniel 11:31, which prophecies, "And **arms shall stand on his part**, and they shall pollute the sanctuary of strength, and shall take away the daily *sacrifice*, and they shall place the abomination that maketh desolate" (boldface added; italics added). These passages clearly show it is the confederates of the Antichrist who set up the desolating image connected to a rebuilt Temple. Goodgame also argues that because Daniel refers to the Antichrist as a king (Hebrew *melek*) in 7:24, 8:23, and 11:21–35, it seems unlikely that he would call him a prince (Hebrew *nagiyd*) in 9:26–27. We can safely assume that he is Roman by the phrase, "And **the people of the prince** who is to come, shall destroy the city and the sanctuary" (v. 26; boldface added), which necessarily refers to the Roman sacking of Jerusalem in AD 70. Goodgame's exegesis and reasoning are sound and compelling.

In line with Daniel 9:27's prediction of a covenant for one week, Goodgame argues that this infers that a pope will broker an agreement over Jerusalem.

This final seven-year period will begin when the future Roman prince "confirms a covenant" that will involve the nation of Israel and the city of Jerusalem, which many evangelical scholars connect to a "deal" resulting in the building of the Third Temple. This has led to the belief that this future Roman prince will be the False Prophet of Bible prophecy, and that he may indeed be a leader of the Roman Catholic Church. It is clear from Scripture that the False Prophet will be a powerful and well-respected global spiritual leader, and there is none more powerful or more respected in religious matters than the Roman Catholic Pope.[47]

Even some Catholic scholars have connected the current Pope Francis with the rise of the False Prophet and Antichrist.[48]

To some, this may seem like a scenario lifted right out of the *Left Behind* novels, but it coheres nicely with Malachi Martin's finishing assertions about the role the Vatican will play in assisting Antichrist. As far as Jerusalem and the coming Third Temple, formally classified US State Department memos have been obtained that suggest "religious figures, non-governmental people" should be put in charge of the Holy City.[49]

On December 15, 2011, this story ran on the *Israeli Arutz Sheva 7* website:

Exposé: The Vatican Wants to Lay Its Hands on Jerusalem

"Peace negotiations in the Middle East must tackle the issue of the status of the holy sites of Jerusalem," Cardinal Jean-Louis Tauran, head of the Vatican's Council for Interreligious Dialogue, declared several days ago in Rome.

The Vatican's former foreign minister asked to place some Israeli holy places under Vatican authority, alluding to the Cenacle on Mount Zion and the garden of Gethsemane at the foot of the Mount of Olives in Jerusalem.

The first site also houses what is referred to as King David's tomb.[50]

As stated earlier, if you take the Bible seriously, Jerusalem has a prophesied future as the spiritual capital of the world, and for this reason, there are natural and supernatural interests in who controls its axis. The Hebrew prophets all spoke of a golden age, a righteous reign of the Messiah, and their oracles often included references to Jerusalem (Isaiah 44:26–28, 52:1–10; Joel 2:28–3:21). Of course, before that happens, we expect a usurper to sit in a rebuilt Third Temple declaring that he is God. As we will examine, there seems to be evidence that the Vatican wants to participate in building that Temple. We now come full-circle to the bombshell 2008 leaked classified US State Department memo that recorded this exchange between Secretary of State Condoleezza Rice (CR) and Dr. Saeb Erekat (SE), a Palestinian representative:

CR: I understand that there is no agreement without Jerusalem. 1967 as a baseline. But if we wait until you decide sovereignty over the Haram or the Temple Mount…your children's children will not have an agreement! Sometimes in international politics you need to have a device to solve the problem later. When it comes to holy sites, no one will argue the sovereignty of the other—leave it unresolved [i.e. both Palestine and Israel could simultaneously claim sovereignty over the Haram].

SE: And actually in life?

CR: There are two other issues—who will administer? Make sure that the sewer system, the municipal issues are resolved [notes that this was a problem in Berlin], safe access to all the holy sites for all. I understand that this worked well before 2000. Some kind of custodians appointed by the world, possibly religious figures, non-governmental people…. One problem is that under the Dome is crumbling. Every time Israel tries to fix it, you call it excavations![51] (brackets in original; the formatting *but no content* was altered)

While Condoleezza Rice's relationship with the Vatican was murky, her suggestion that "religious figures" become custodians of the Old City of Jerusalem is in line with the exposés by Israeli journalists. In August of 2007, Rice met with Cardinal Tarcisio Pierto Bertone (a leading candidate for Petrus Romanus at the time), who said of the American Secretary, "If the angels did not accompany her, then she would not be able to knit back together all of these relationships that have been so fragile."[52] Could this strange coalescence of diplomacy and prophecy be leading toward the final manifestation of apostate ecumenical faith predicted in Revelation 17 to be headquartered in Jerusalem? We think there is compelling evidence suggesting just that.

Prophecy scholars have long suspected that the Antichrist will seemingly resolve the Middle East conflict, which will drive his meteoric rise to fame and adoration. This idea is drawn from Daniel's seventy-weeks prophecy, which predicts that in the final week, "he shall confirm the covenant with many for one week: and in the midst of the week he shall cause the sacrifice and the oblation to cease, and for the overspreading of abominations he shall make it desolate, even until the consummation, and that determined shall be poured upon the desolate" (Daniel 9:27). We think this interpretation must be correct, because the "consummation" is rendered from the Hebrew term *kālâ,* which carried the basic idea of "to bring a process to completion." The beginning of the seventy-weeks prophecy listed things like "to bring in everlasting righteousness" (9:24b), which simply has not yet occurred. Furthermore, the same term is used in Daniel 12:7, rendered as "end," unambiguously referencing the Day of the Lord. This firmly places the initial covenant at the beginning of the final seven years prior to Armageddon and Jesus' return. Another problem with interpretations that place this final week in the past is that Jesus spoke of the "abomination of desolation" as a future event occurring just prior to His return: "When ye therefore shall see the abomination of desolation, spoken of by Daniel the prophet, stand in the holy place, (whoso readeth, let him understand)" (Matthew 24:15). The seventieth week includes "the overspreading of abominations he shall make it desolate," and Jesus mentions Daniel explicitly so one cannot take Him seriously while arguing that the events of the seventieth week are previous history. Furthermore, the population forming the context of this prophecy was Daniel's people, the Jews, and the covenant violation is interference in the Temple sacrifice. Accordingly, we believe that the "covenant with many" speaks to the two-state solution for the Israel/Palestinian issue and forecasts the Tribulation Temple being built in Jerusalem.

It is also reiterated in the new documentary *Belly of the Beast* that the design of Washington DC in the likeness of Vatican City, with its proportionate Dome and Obelisk, was no accident, but rather the product of an arcane science ostensibly related to apotheosis. These parallel apotheotic sites seem poised to spawn the beast from the bottomless pit (Revelation 11:7) and the beast from the earth (Revelation 13:11).

While it is speculative, this could suggest coordination between the two locations—the Vatican as the spiritual influence (False Prophet) and Washington as the political (Antichrist). From Washington, a figurehead could initiate the covenant spoken of in Daniel 9 (Donald Trump's peace plan and/or work by his Orthodox Jewish son-in law, Jared Kushner?). While the Washington figure could be a Jew, that is not really necessary. The late Messianic Christian author Zola Levitt wrote, "It is an outsider that has to sign a legal covenant with the Jewish people, not one of their own.… They wouldn't need a special covenant drawn up between them and one of their own citizens."[53] In fact, while it is possible, there is no direct evidence that the Antichrist will be accepted as the Jewish Messiah. Rather, he could simply be the one who facilities the building of the Tribulation Temple like the Persian King Cyrus (to whom Trump has been widely compared), who was designated a *mashiyach* ("anointed one") for freeing the Jews to build the Second Temple (Isaiah 45:1).

In fact, Orthodox Jews are not likely to be fooled by the Antichrist. Midrash tradition, including works like *Sefer Zerubbavel*, contains warnings about a character named Armilus, who will deceive the whole world into false idolatrous worship. He is said to come to power when ten kings fight over Jerusalem, and after emerging victorious, he rules the entire world for a brief time before Messiah comes. According to Randall Price, "Other sources describe Armilus as rising from the Roman empire, having miraculous powers, and being born to a stone statue of a virgin."[54] This sounds remarkably congruent with Roman Catholic Mariolatry, wherein stone statues feature prominently. Other traditions say he is the offspring of Satan and a virgin, which sounds eerily similar to the pedophilic rite described by Malachi Martin that occurred on June 29, 1963, at the parallel enthronement site in Charleston, South Carolina, and that was connected to the enthronement of Lucifer at the Vatican. Furthermore, this stone statue aspect of the Jewish tradition could find some sort of bizarre realization in the image of the beast, which seemingly comes to life (Revelation 13:4, 15). While a minority of religious Jews are aware of these traditions, the secular Jews probably are not. Still, with the centuries of papists corralling Jews into ghettos and mandating yellow badges, one wonders how they could be persuaded by a future pope leading an ecumenical religion in Jerusalem. Time will tell, but one thing is certain. Not in our lifetime has more interest been raised in building the Third Temple, around which and in which religious and political figures will soon rise in a theater of fantastic finality.

three

God's Second Hand

ANALOGY HAS BEEN made to God's prophetic clock and His chosen nation, Israel. Israel, in this analogy, is the hour hand. The attempted peace process between Israel and its enemy neighbors is the minute hand. The desired Third Temple construction is the second hand.

We will look at all three elements here, with emphasis on the building of the Third Temple—the matter that can indeed move the end-time clock swiftly toward the consummation of this dispensation.

The Hour Hand: Israel

No issue on the geopolitical landscape holds the potential for planet-rending devastation as that of war and peace involving Israel. Daniel the prophet gave the following about God's chosen people—the Jews—in scriptural passages familiar to all students of Bible prophecy.

> And he shall confirm the covenant with many for one week: and in the midst of the week he shall cause the sacrifice and the

oblation to cease, and for the overspreading of abominations he shall make it desolate, even until the consummation, and that determined shall be poured upon the desolate. (Daniel 9:27)

The old prophet was told to proclaim that Jerusalem and Israel will be at the center of the most horrific conflict ever perpetrated upon mankind, and that the conflict will culminate in the catastrophic consummation of human history at the time of Christ's Second Advent.

This prophecy, of course, could not be in view for the present generation, if Israel weren't back in the land as a nation. We know from our daily news—no, now it is our *hourly news*—that not only is Israel again a nation, but that it is constantly in the spotlight of world news reporting.

Israel is the most hated nation on earth, as manifest by the overwhelming, anti-Semitic balloting of most nations within the United Nations every time a vote is taken involving the Jewish state. Jerusalem has become the "cup of trembling" and "burdensome stone" prophesied by Zechariah (Zechariah 12:1–3).

The Balfour Declaration of 1917 began the process of prophetic fulfillment at the time World War I was in full rage. The "war to end all wars," as WWI was called, began in 1914 between Great Britain and its allies and Germany, Austria, Hungary, and, later that year, the Ottoman Empire.

The Islamist Ottoman Empire, which controlled the area constituting what became known as the Holy Land, was on the losing side of the great first worldwide conflict. The Balfour Declaration finally incorporated into the Sèvres peace treaty the terms that would begin bringing God's chosen people back into the land as a nation.

The document was signed by the British Foreign Secretary Arthur James Balfour on November 2, 1917. It was issued to Baron Walter Rothschild, a leader of the British Jewish community. The letter was for Rothschild to transmit to the Zionist Confederation of Great Britain and Ireland.

The gist of the notice was as follows: His Majesty's government would view with favor the establishment in Palestine of a national home for the Jewish people, and will use its best endeavors to achieve this, it being clearly understood that nothing would be done that might prejudice the civil and religious rights of existing non-Jewish communities in Palestine or the rights and political status enjoyed by Jews in any other country.

This all appeared well and good. However, many treacheries developed as the Jews began to re-enter their God-promised homeland. The British reneged on their promises in ways that caused the struggle to become one of survival for the Jewish people as they sought to reclaim the hostile, swampy land. All of Islam eventually swarmed against the effort to reestablish a Jewish state.

However, God, unlike human governments, never reneges on His promises, and we know the rest of the story to this point. All other nations of the world might fall, but, one thing is sure: Israel is now a nation and a people forever.

> Yet for all that, when they are in the land of their enemies, I will not cast them away, neither will I abhor them, to destroy them utterly, and to break my covenant with them; for I am the LORD their God.
>
> But I will remember for them the covenant with their ancestors, whom I brought out of the land of Egypt in the sight of the nations, that I might be their God. I am the Lord. (Leviticus 26: 44–45)

> And I will bring again the captivity of My people of Israel, and they shall build the waste cities, and inhabit them; and they shall plant vineyards, and drink their wine; they shall also make gardens, and eat the fruit of them.
>
> And I will plant them upon their land, and they shall no more be pulled up out of their land which I have given them, saith the LORD, thy God. (Amos 9:14–15)

The hour hand of God's prophetic clock, Israel, is nearing midnight. The second hand *is* the peace process being forced upon that nation. The diplomatic world, in total disregard of biblical truth, willfully, if unknowingly, long ago set the timer of the Armageddon timebomb.

The Minute Hand: The Peace Process

Since the 1967 war, when the Israelis struck preemptively to head off the Arab coalition preparing to attack, there have been many attempts at peace-making. Some of these efforts are listed here:

- **UN Security Council Resolution 242, 1967**—Resolution 242 was passed on November 22, 1967, and embodies the principle that has guided most of the subsequent peace plans—the exchange of land for peace.
- **Camp David Accords, 1978**—US President Jimmy Carter capitalized on the new mood and invited President Sadat and the Israeli Prime Minister, Menachem Begin, for talks at the presidential retreat at Camp David near Washington. The talks lasted for twelve days and resulted in two agreements.
- **The Madrid Conference, 1991**—This conference, co-sponsored by the US and the Soviet Union, was designed to follow up the Egypt-Israel treaty by encouraging other Arab countries to sign their own agreements with Israel.
- **Oslo Agreement, 1993**—The Oslo negotiations tried to tackle the missing element of all previous talks—a direct agreement between Israelis and Palestinians, represented by the PLO. Its importance was that there was finally mutual recognition between Israel and the PLO.
- **Taba, 2001**—Although he was about to leave office, Bill Clinton refused to give up and presented a "bridging proposal"

that set up further talks in Washington and Cairo, and then Taba in Egypt.

- **Arab Peace Initiative, 2002**—Under the plan called the Arab Peace Initiative, Israel would withdraw to the lines of June 1967, a Palestinian state would be set up in the West Bank and Gaza, and there would be a "just solution" of the refugee issue. In return, Arab countries would recognize Israel.

- **Roadmap, 2003**—The roadmap is a plan drawn up by the "Quartet"—the United States, Russia, the European Union, and the United Nations. It does not lay down the details of a final settlement, but suggests how a settlement might be approached. It followed efforts made by US Senator George Mitchell to get the peace process back on track in 2001.

- **Geneva Accord, 2003**—The Geneva Accord reverses the concept of the Roadmap, in which the growth of security and confidence precede a political agreement and puts the agreement first, which is then designed to produce security and peace.

- **Annapolis, 2007**—Late in his second presidential term, US President George W. Bush hosted a conference at the US Naval Academy at Annapolis, Maryland, aimed at relaunching the peace process.

- **Washington, 2010**—After taking office, US President Barack Obama was quick to try to restart the peace process. Contact between Israel and the Palestinians resumed in May 2009, after a hiatus of nineteen months, in the form of indirect "proximity talks" through US Middle East envoy George Mitchell.[55]

President Donald J. Trump, elected in 2016, has been a friend to Israel and is embraced by Israeli Prime Minister Benjamin Netanyahu. The president championed moving the American Embassy from Tel Aviv to Jerusalem and is a staunch supporter of the Jewish state, while the world of UN diplomats views Israel as the holdup to peace.

Yet, even this president is caught up in the drive toward forcing peace in the land God has declared He has given to the Jews.

A news story reported that President Donald Trump said as part of an interview that he was "not necessarily sure" Israel was seeking to reach a peace agreement with the Palestinians. The American president once before denounced the Palestinians for what he views as their refusing to negotiate. At the same time, he, in general, hasn't been critical of Israel in the matter of negotiations that haven't come to fruition.

The president said to *Freesheet Daily's* Israel Hayom that even though relations between the U.S. and Israel were "great," things would be made "a lot better" if peace with the Palestinians was achieved.

"Right now, I would say the Palestinians are not looking to make peace. They are not looking to make peace," Trump repeated in the interview.

He concluded, "And I am not necessarily sure that Israel is looking to make peace. So we are just going to have to see what happens."

Trump, although his administration has been less critical of Israel's settlements than was the Obama administration, expressed concerns about Israeli settlement building.

David Friedman, ambassador to Israel for the Trump government, has supported Israeli-occupied West Bank settlements in the past.

He issued caution in present efforts to make peace: "The settlements are something that very much complicates and always have complicated making peace, so I think Israel has to be very careful with the settlements."

Trump previously has stated he intends to get the Israelis and Palestinians together in the "ultimate deal"—thus to work toward resolving the seemingly never-ending conflict. However, he wondered whether negotiations would be possible at present.

"I don't know frankly if we are going to even have talks," Trump said. "We will see what happens, but I think it is very foolish for the Palestinians and I also think it would be very foolish for the Israelis if they don't make a deal. It's our only opportunity and it will never happen after this."

Trump's decision to move the American Embassy from Tel Aviv and to strongly recognize Jerusalem as the Jewish state's capital has put a great strain on the relationship between the United States and the Palestinians.

Palestinian leaders are adamant that there will be no talks with the American administration until there is reversal on Jerusalem, which they see as their capital. Add in to the pressures to bring Palestinians to the negotiating table, President Trump is withholding many millions of dollars from UNRWA, the UN agency for Palestinian refugees.

The man-made peace process, in every case, involves the requirement that Israel give up land that is theirs according to God's covenant promises. The following Scriptures involve those promises. These are key to understanding the unalterable truth wrapped up in God's prophetic Word. These land promises will be reemphasized in a later chapter of this book.

1) **God's first promise to Abraham about a nation:**
   - Genesis 12:7a: "The Lord appeared to Abram and said, 'To your descendants I will give this land.'"
   - Genesis 17:7–8: "And I will establish My covenant between Me and you and your descendants after you throughout their generations for an everlasting covenant, to be God to you and to your descendants after you. And I will give to you and to your descendants after you, the land of your sojourning, all the land of Canaan, for an everlasting possession; and I will be their God."

2) **Words to those who say God's covenant with Israel concerning the nation/land is conditional:**
   - Psalm 89:30–37: "If his sons forsake My law, and do not walk in My judgments, if they violate My statues, and

do not keep My commandments, then I will visit their
transgression with the rod, and their iniquity with stripes.
But I will not break off My loving kindness from him,
nor deal falsely in My faithfulness. My covenant I will not
violate, nor will I alter the utterance of My lips. Once I
have sworn by My holiness; I will not lie to David. His
descendants shall endure forever like the moon, and the
witness in the sky is faithful."

- Jeremiah 31:35–36: "This is what the Lord says, 'He who
  appoints the sun to shine by day, Who decrees the moon
  and stars to shine by night, Who stirs up the sea so that its
  waves roar—the Lord Almighty is His Name; Only if these
  ordinances vanish from My sight,' declares the Lord, 'will the
  descendants of Israel ever cease to be a nation before Me.'"
- Genesis 12:1–3: "The Lord has said to Abram, 'Leave your
  country, your people and your father's household and go to
  the land I will show you. I will make you into a great nation
  and I will bless you; I will make your name great, and
  you will be a blessing. I will bless those who bless you and
  whoever curses you I will curse; and all the peoples on earth
  will be blessed through you.'"

3) Abraham's idea for Ishmael versus God's plan:
- Genesis 17:18: "Oh that Ishmael might live before Thee."
- Genesis 17:19: "God answered Abraham, 'No, but Sarah
  your wife shall bear you a son, and you shall call his name
  Isaac; and I will establish My covenant with him for an
  everlasting covenant for his descendants after him.'"

4) Isaac's words giving God's blessings to Jacob:
- Genesis 28:4: "May He [God] also give you the blessing of
  Abraham, to you and to your descendants with you: that

you may possess the land of your sojourning, which God gave to Abraham."

5) God's revelation of His plan for the land/nation to Jacob:

- Genesis 28:13–15: "I am the Lord, the God of your father Abraham and the God of Isaac; the land on which you lie, I will give it to you and to your descendants. Your descendants shall also be like the dust of the earth, and you shall spread out to the west and to the east and to the north and to the south; and in you and in your descendants shall all the families of the earth be blessed. And behold, I am with you, and will keep you wherever you go, and will bring you back to this land; for I will not leave you until I have done what I have promised you."

6) God's words to Moses:

- Deuteronomy 1:8: "See, I have placed the land before you; go in and possess the land which the Lord swore to give to your fathers, to Abraham, to Isaac, and to Jacob, to them and their descendants after them."

7) God's words to Joshua:

- Joshua 1:2–4, 6: "Moses My servant is dead. Now then, you and all these people, get ready to cross the Jordan river into the land I am about to give to them—to the Israelites. I will give you every place where you set your foot, as I promised Moses. Your territory will extend from the desert and from Lebanon to the great river, the Euphrates—all the Hittite country—and to the Great Sea on the west. Be strong and courageous, because you will lead these people to inherit the land I swore to their forefathers to give them."

8) God's promise to return Israel to the land:

- Leviticus 26: 44–45: "Yet in spite of this, when they are in the land of their enemies, I will not reject them, nor will I so abhor them as to destroy them, breaking My covenant with them; for I am the Lord their God. But I will remember for them the covenant with their ancestors, whom I brought out of the land of Egypt in the sight of the nations, that I might be their God. I am the Lord."

- Amos 9: 14–15: "'Also I will restore the captivity of My people Israel, and they will rebuild the ruined cities and live in them. They will also plant vineyards and drink their wine, and make gardens and eat their fruit. I will also plant them on their land, and they will not again be rooted out from their land which I have given them,' says the Lord your God."

9) God's warnings to the world's diplomatic enforcers who are determined to cause Israel to give up land for their specious peace promises:

- "For, behold, in those days, and in that time, when I shall bring again the captivity of Judah and Jerusalem, I will also gather all nations, and will bring them down into the valley of Jehoshaphat, and will plead with them there for my people and *for* my heritage Israel, whom they have scattered among the nations, and parted my land." (Joel 3:1–2)

The result of dividing God's land of promise will be the killing fields of Armageddon.

The Second Hand: The Third Temple

The peace process being foisted upon God's chosen people, then, is likened to the minute hand on God's prophetic timepiece. With that minute hand moving steadily toward merging at the 12 with Israel, the hour hand, it is appropriate to look carefully at the second hand, which is moving incrementally toward the final instant at the midnight hour of fulfillment of Bible prophecy.

To begin looking at developments moving toward the building of the Third Temple, consider the words of one of the foremost authorities on the subject. Dr. Randall Price, author, Bible scholar, university professor, and world-renowned biblical archaeologist, gives this brief introduction to matters involving efforts to rebuild the Temple on Moriah:

> The importance of rebuilding the Temple to Orthodox Judaism lies in its conception of the redemption of the world, which they believe can only take place once the Temple is rebuilt. Gershon Salomon, Director, Temple Mount Faithful, an organization that has been trying to prepare Israeli society to accept and promote the rebuilding of the Temple through demonstrations at the Temple site, the construction of a cornerstone for the Third Temple, and the making of various Temple-related utensils, has said: "[Building the Third Temple] is an act which must be done to complete the redemption of the people of the Bible in the Land of the Bible. I cannot imagine an Israeli State or Israeli life in this country without the Temple Mount in the center of this life."
>
> However, many religious Jews do not support this idea because they have adopted a Diaspora mentality and a spiritualized way of thinking, which sets aside hope in a literal fulfillment of the biblical prophecies regarding a future Temple. For them, the present political situation on the Temple Mount with Muslims controlling the site is acceptable. Jewish leaders in the Temple movement understand that the Jewish people are not living on the spiritual level God intended because of the absence of the Shekinah (Divine Presence) from the world. Rabbi Chaim Richman, Director of the Temple Institute which has produced

all the ritual vessels necessary for the function of the Temple and works to train priests for this future work, says there is a connection between the need for a new level of spiritual attainment and the rebuilding of the Temple: "The Shekinah is brought about only through the Temple....in terms of our mission as a people, we cannot in any way reach our spiritual status without the Temple." So, for Orthodox Judaism, the present problems of the world, and especially the Jewish People, can only be solved by the rebuilding of the Temple.

But, are we any closer to the rebuilding of the Temple today? The world is radically opposed to Israel's claims in Jerusalem, much less their contested ownership of the Temple Mount. On a practical level, Jews are banned by Israeli law from praying at the site, and those who visit are daily accosted by Muslims (such as the Women in Black who maintain a constant vigil on Jewish presence at the site). In addition, the Islamic authorities officially deny that a Temple ever existed at the site. Nevertheless, recent developments have taken place that contribute to the Temple Movement's goals and the realization of the rebuilding of the Temple in our lifetime.

Answering the charge of Temple denial, archaeologists discovered in decades old research, that the site of the Al-Aqsa mosque, believed by Muslims to have been built by Abraham, was once a place for Jewish ritual preparation for entering the Temple. The evidence for this came from a filed report by British archaeologist Robert Hamilton who had documented excavations of the mosque's foundations after it was destroyed in an earthquake in 1927. He discovered beneath the floor of the mosque the remains of a Jewish *miqveh* (ritual pool used for purification). It dated to the time of the Second Temple when Jews immersed at this site before entering the Temple precincts. These findings, hidden deep in the British Mandatory archives department because they embarrassed Muslim officials, now provide evidence that the ancient Temple stood on the modern Temple Mount and was a place of Jewish presence.

Concerning the preparations for the Temple service, the Sanhedrin has taken steps necessary to reinstating the future Temple service. One project Update on the Rebuilding of the Third Temple.[56]

David, king of Israel, wanted to build a house wherein God could reside. Jehovah, who called David "a man after my own heart," proposed the question of whether He could be contained in such a structure. The answer, of course, is *no.*

The Lord did appreciate the thought, though, obviously. He told David that he couldn't build a place where God could dwell among men in that fashion. David had too much blood on his hands from all the wars he had fought to defend Israel and acquire land God had given the chosen people. Instead, God told David that Solomon, David's son, would build God such a dwelling place. The Temple that Solomon built had at its heart the Holy of Holies, a fifteen-foot-cubed inner sanctum that housed the Ark of the Covenant, the elaborately prepared container wherein the shekinah glory, the very presence of God, would dwell.

That spot is still somewhere upon the Temple Mount—Mt. Moriah, most scholars believe. Religious Jews still are afraid to walk upon the Temple Mount grounds for fear of accidentally treading upon that one spot on earth where God chose to reside.

The Temple and the Holy of Holies constituted God's touchstone to humanity—and particularly to the Jews. It is where Abraham went to offer Isaac before God intervened with the ram caught by its horns in a thicket, thus providing the sacrifice Abraham made to the God of Heaven.

Not far from the spot of the Holy of Holies is Golgotha, where Jesus Christ hung on the cross. When Christ died, the veil in the Temple's Holy of Holies tore from top to bottom, giving man direct access to God the Father through that sin sacrifice, God's only begotten Son.

Solomon's Temple, then, was the First Temple. It was so glorious that it stunned even the queen of Sheba when her eyes fell upon its splendor.

Nebuchadnezzar destroyed it in 587 BC, and a Second Temple was completed in 516 BC, following Israel's Babylonian captivity. This structure became known as Herod's Temple, because it was commissioned by the king to be greatly expanded and beautified to the extent that it was considered magnificent by those who looked upon it.

This Temple was destroyed by the Roman military in AD 70, when Roman Emperor Vespasian sent his son, General Titus, to put down insurrection in Jerusalem. This fulfilled Daniel's prophecy (see Daniel 9:26–27) and Jesus' foretelling (as recorded in Matthew 24:1–2).

The Third Temple is foretold to be in place during the last seven years of human history prior to Christ's return. Daniel prophesied about Antichrist: "In the midst of the week he shall cause the sacrifice and the oblation to cease" (Daniel 9:27b). This last, vicious tyrant will enter the Third Temple and desecrate it.

Paul the apostle says of that future Temple and Antichrist: "Who opposeth and exalteth himself above all that is called God, or that is worshipped; so that he as God sitteth in the temple of God, shewing himself that he is God" (2 Thessalonians 2:4).

We will take an in-depth look at things involving these prophesied matters later.

The Third Temple is mentioned in the last book of the Bible. In Revelation 11:1–2, John is told to "measure" the Temple. This, apparently, is a symbolic way to assess its spiritual status.

Exactly *when* the Third Temple will be built is unknown. We know only that it will exist during the Tribulation—specifically, at the three and a half-year mark of that seven-year span.

Many who study the Third Temple believe its planning and construction must be begun well in advance of the Tribulation era. Its completion, they believe, will take quite some time. Others hold that the Jews are even now considering building a tent-like structure similar to Moses' Tabernacle. They believe that worship, with sacrifices reinstituted, could be going on in such a place while the more grandiose Temple is constructed around the temporary structure.

There are, of course, problems working against beginning the construction of the Third Temple.

Dr. David Reagan has weighed in on some details:

Currently there are two major obstacles to the reconstruction of The Third Temple. One pertains to its location. The next temple can only be built where the two previous temples stood because the Holy of Holies must be on the exact same spot. But no one knows for sure where the previous temples were located on the Temple Mount. Most scholars believe that they stood where the Dome of the Rock currently stands. That conclusion may be wrong, but there is no way to prove the exact location without conducting archeological excavations on the Temple Mount, something which is currently prohibited by the Muslims. If the Third Temple is to be built where the Dome of the Rock now stands, then that Muslim structure must first of all be removed either by Man or God. It could, of course be burned to the ground by a saboteur, or it could be destroyed by an earthquake.

The second obstacle is the attitude of the Jewish people and their leaders. Currently, there is no desire among [most of] them to build a third temple. The average Israeli is very secular. He knows that any attempt to build a third temple would result in immediate war with the Muslims. Only a handful of ultra-Orthodox Jews have a passion for The Third Temple. They are the ones who have made all the preparations. But they have no popular support. Something will have to happen to create a surge of nationalistic pride that will demand a new temple. This catalytic event could be the discovery of the Ark of the Covenant.[57]

Reagan's comments about "a surge of nationalistic pride" and "the discovery of the Ark of the Covenant" are intriguing, because the original

Temple built by King Solomon was to be God's dwelling place on earth and the repository of the Ark of the Covenant. Such a discovery (or unveiling, if the Ark has already been recovered and is in safekeeping) in modern times would ignite international support for a new Holy of Holies—and thus a Third Temple—to house the gold-covered, sacred wooden chest of the ancient Hebrews.

Some argue that the Ark rests beneath the Temple Mount directly below the Dome of the Rock, where the original Holy of Holies existed. When the Babylonians destroyed the first Temple, they hauled away many of the sacred vessels. But the location of the Ark of the Covenant was unknown, reportedly because King Josiah hid it from the Babylonians who sacked the Temple. Some say this secret location remains below the original resting place of the Ark in the Temple of Solomon.

Maimonides—the medieval Sephardic Jewish philosopher who is considered one of the most prolific and influential Torah scholars of the Middle Ages—recounted from the ancient sages:

> When Solomon built the Temple, he was aware that it would ultimately be destroyed. [Therefore,] he constructed a chamber, in which the ark could be entombed below [the Temple building] in deep, maze-like vaults.
>
> King Josiah commanded that [the Ark] be entombed in the chamber built by Solomon, as it is said (II Chronicles 35:3): "And he said to the Levites who would teach wisdom to all of Israel: 'Place the Holy Ark in the chamber built by Solomon, the son of David, King of Israel. You will no [longer] carry it on your shoulders. Now, serve the Lord, your God'"
>
> When it was entombed, Aaron's staff, the vial of manna, and the oil used for anointing were entombed with it. All these [sacred articles] did not return in the Second Temple.[58]

Whether that location beneath the Temple Mount will produce the Ark of the Covenant, the ancient Jewish midrash promises, "When the

Jewish people are gathered in from the exiles from the four corners of the world [officially began in 1948], they will suddenly find the holy vessels of the Temple."[59]

Ark Hidden at Mount Nebo in Jordan?

The late Christian genius (and my personal friend) David Flynn made an alternative argument for exactly where the Ark of the Covenant may be discovered. In chapter 8 of his masterpiece, *Temple at the Center of Time*, he speculated:

> Most researchers consider the Ark lost from view after the narra-
> tive of Solomon's temple in the Bible, and various theories have
> been proposed as to the Ark's fate through history. Many histo-
> rians speculate that because Babylon destroyed the Temple of
> Solomon, it also removed the Ark to Babylon. There it is said the
> Ark was eventually destroyed along with the other artifacts from
> the temple, the gold melted down and set into coins for their
> treasury. It is difficult to imagine that the Babylonians would
> have destroyed it however, if they'd even captured it at all.
>
> The Book of Daniel makes specific mention of the golden
> menorah from the temple of Jerusalem in the palace of Belshaz-
> zar. The Babylonian king had preserved it, a major artifact from
> the Jewish temple, in an attempt to demonstrate the superiority
> of Babylonia's gods to the God of the Hebrews. That the meno-
> rah was set on display in this manner underscores how unlikely
> the Babylonians would have been to destroy the Ark, the greatest
> symbol of the God of the Hebrews. It would have been consid-
> ered an ultimate statement of the superiority of the Babylonians
> if it had been obtained. The Bible documents the menorah hav-
> ing remained intact until the last night of Babylonian rule. Its
> light illuminated the scene of the writing on the wall in the book

of Daniel. After the fall of Babylon, the Medes and Persians were friendly to the Jews and allowed them to rebuild the temple. It is most likely that the menorah was returned along with the other furnishings and vessels that had been captured by Nebuchadnezzar. However, the Ark was mentioned as *not* existing in the second temple of Zerubbabel, the raised foundation stone was the only feature inside the Holy of Holies.[60]

Certain tracts of the Midot in the Jewish Talmud dealing with temple laws, practices and rituals allude to the creation of more than one Ark, the second made as a decoy to protect the original. It claims that certain articles of the temple furnishing including the true Ark remain in a secret vault underneath the temple mount in Jerusalem.[61] However, it seems highly unlikely that the Ark would have been left to fate under the temple mount, open to any treasure hunter with the motivation to merely dig. It is difficult to explain how the location could remain secret, as Jerusalem remained open for excavation and plundering for hundreds of years after its fall to the Romans in AD 70. Motivated treasure seekers over the ensuing centuries have had ample time to excavate the area underneath the temple.

The recovery of the Temple treasure of Solomon was the highest goal of the Knights Templar that established their center on the Temple Mount during the crusades. The fact was documented in 1884, when the British conducted an ordinance survey of the Jerusalem and discovered Templar artifacts, left in extensive tunneling beneath the temple mount.[62] As to the extent of the underground features, a later publication of the British survey explained:

> Jerusalem, as is well known, is honeycombed with excavated caves, natural caverns, cisterns cut in the rock, subterranean passages and aqueducts…. In its underground chambers and catacombs it is richer than any known city.[63]

Various Judaic sects of Ethiopia believe that the Ark has been guarded and kept in the city of Axum in their country for thousands of years.[64] The legend claims that it was brought to Axum by the son of King Solomon and the Queen of Sheba, Prince Menelik I. It has been said that Menelik removed the Ark from the Temple at the behest of his father in order that it be kept safe after the division of his kingdom (into Judah and Israel), because Solomon knew that the dissolution of his kingdom was inevitable after his death. First Kings 11:9–12 says that the Lord Himself told Solomon that...

> ...the LORD was angry with Solomon, because his heart was turned from the LORD God of Israel, which had appeared unto him twice....Wherefore the LORD said unto Solomon, Forasmuch as this is done of thee, and thou hast not kept my covenant and my statutes, which I have commanded thee, I will surely rend the kingdom from thee, and will give it to thy servant. Notwithstanding in thy days I will not do it for David thy father's sake: [but] I will rend it out of the hand of thy son.[65]

Though intriguing, the legend of Menelik I is not consistent with the biblical record, as will be shown in this chapter. If the Ark was not moved to Ethiopia, it is speculated that after the division of the Kingdom of Solomon, Rehoboam, King of Judah, gave the Ark to the Egyptian Pharaoh Shisak (Sheshonk I, ca. 929 or 924 BC) to avoid the destruction of Jerusalem by his armies, ca. 940 BC.

> So Shishak King of Egypt came up against Jerusalem, and took away the treasures of the house of the LORD, and the treasures of the king's house; he took all.[66]

Some historians believe that the Egyptians took the Ark and hid it underground in the city of Tanis, Egypt, the seat of Shishak's dynasty. The location was lost over the course of history.[67] Because it was written that Shishak "took all" the articles of the Temple, many researchers conclude that the Ark was among the spoils taken to Egypt. However, after Judah's conflict with Shishak, the Temple was ransacked again seventy years later by Jehoash, king of Israel. At that time, the Temple treasures were removed to Samaria.[68] In this instance, as with the encounter with Shishak, the Bible again uses the phrase, "All the temple treasures were removed." Despite these two accounts, the Ark appears again in the biblical narrative when King Josiah ordered the return of the Ark of the Covenant to the Temple.[69] This occurred more than two hundred years after the pillage of the Temple by Jehoash, and three hundred years after the pillage of Shishak.

> And [Josiah] said unto the Levites that taught all Israel, which were holy unto the LORD, Put the holy ark in the house which Solomon the son of David king of Israel did build; [it shall] not [be] a burden upon [your] shoulders.[70]

This one biblical passage renders the legends of the Ark's present location in Axum, Ethiopia, or in Tanis, Egypt, completely impossible, as both theories place the hiding of the Ark several hundred years before the reign of King Josiah. It was a central feature of the Temple of Jerusalem and reinstitution of worship during the reign of Josiah.

It is noteworthy, also, that the Bible is extremely detailed concerning the only account of the Ark's capture by the foremost enemy of Israel, the Philistines. After the vessel had been captured by the Philistines, their entire country was afflicted by God. The judgment was so great that the people begged their lords to find a respectful way to transport the Ark back to its rightful place, and it was returned. It is illogical that the same judgments would not have befallen any other country that removed the Ark from the Israelites. Although God allowed its capture by the Philistines due to the idolatry of Israel, the pagan Philistines were certainly not able to abide its presence. For that matter, either Babylon—the epitome of world idolatry—or Egypt would survive the Ark's presence. Certainly, if one of these countries had captured it, the account would be as notable as the removal by the Philistines. Yet, no scriptural record of such an event exists.

Robert Jamieson's biblical commentary explains the Ark's location before its return to the Temple in the reign of Josiah, king of Judah:

> Some think that it had been ignominiously put away from the sanctuary by order of some idolatrous king, probably Manasseh, who set a carved image in the house of God (2 Chronicles 33:7), or Amon; while others are of opinion that it had been temporarily removed by Josiah himself into some adjoining chamber, during the repairs on the temple. In replacing it, the Levites had evidently carried it upon their shoulders, deeming that still to be the duty, which the law imposed on them. But Josiah reminded them of the change of circumstances. As the service of God was now performed in a fixed and permanent temple, they were not required to be bearers of the ark any longer; and, being released from the service, they should address themselves with the greater alacrity to the discharge of other functions.[71]

An amazing story follows the reinstitution of the Ark to the Temple of God in the account of Josiah's death:

> After all this, when Josiah had prepared the temple, Necho king of Egypt came up to fight against Carchemish by Euphrates: and Josiah went out against him. But he sent ambassadors to him, saying, what have I to do with thee, thou king of Judah? [I come] not against thee this day, but against the house wherewith I have war: for God commanded me to make haste: forbear thee from [meddling with] God, who [is] with me, that he destroy thee not. Nevertheless Josiah would not turn his face from him, but disguised himself, that he might fight with him, and hearkened not unto the words of Necho from the mouth of God, and came to fight in the valley of Megiddo. [72]

This supports Vilikovski's claim that the Egyptian pharaohs revered the God of Abraham in the time of the kings of Israel and Judah. Although King Josiah and the people of Judah had a strong bias for alliance with Egypt, during the reign of Manasseh, the country had become a vassal of Assyria. Josiah thought himself bound to support the interests of Assyria. Therefore, when "Necho King of Egypt" came up to fight Carchemish, Josiah went out against him. Bible commentators are not agreed whether Necho had been given a divine commission by the God of Israel, or whether he merely used the name of God as an authority that Josiah would not refuse to obey. [73] However, it appears likely that God *was* a benefactor to the pharaoh, as the Bible records Josiah's death by Necho's archers. [74]

Jeremiah the prophet lamented the death of Josiah when his body returned after the battle. In 2 Chronicles 35:25, Jeremiah had been a major force in Josiah's restitution of the Ark to the

Temple of Solomon. He was also the main player in the most well documented *and biblical* account of the fate of the Ark and theory of its present location.

The Mountain of the Ark

The book of 2 Maccabees 2:4 explains that before the destruction of Solomon's Temple by the Babylonians in 587 BC, the Ark was hidden by the prophet Jeremiah in a cave at the base of Mount Nebo in the Pisgah range of Jordan. Second Maccabees, as well as other apocryphal works, are retained in modern Catholic Bibles as well as the Septuagint and Vulgate.[75] It is found in the records…

> …that Jeremy the prophet, being warned of God, commanded the tabernacle and the ark to go with him, as he went forth into the mountain, where Moses climbed up, and saw the heritage of God. And when Jeremy came thither, he found an hollow cave, wherein he laid the tabernacle, and the ark, and the altar of incense, and so stopped the door.
>
> And some of those that followed him came to mark the way, but they could not find it. Which when Jeremy perceived, he blamed them, saying, As for that place, it shall be unknown until the time that God gather his people again together, and receive them unto mercy. Then shall the Lord show them these things, and the glory of the Lord shall appear, and the cloud also, as it was showed under Moses, and as when Solomon desired that the place might be honourably sanctified.[76]

This account of the Ark from 2 Maccabees is also mentioned in the Jewish Talmud, in Huriot 12A and Tractate Yoma

72a. These texts explain that the Ark's location would not be recovered until the Jews were brought back to Israel following the Diaspora, an event that miraculously *did* occur in 1948. The pseudepigraphic book, 2 Baruch, written near the first century, repeats the prophetic age in which the Ark would be recovered:

> Oh earth…guard them [the Temple vessels and the Ark] until the last times, So that, when thou art ordered, thou mayst restore them, So that strangers may not get possession of them. For the time comes when Jerusalem also will be delivered for a time, until it is said, that it is again restored for ever.[77]

According to prophecy, the Jews of the end time would return to Israel from all the nations of the Earth. Isaiah 11:11–12 explains that Israel would be populated by exiles that formerly lived in every part of the world. This has been the situation since 1948, and is not related to the first return of Jews to Israel after the Babylonian exile:

> And it shall come to pass in that day, that the LORD shall set his hand again the second time to recover the remnant of his people…. And he shall set up an ensign for the nations, and shall assemble the outcasts of Israel, and gather together the dispersed of Judah from the four corners of the earth.

Amos 9:14–15 declares that after the second return of the exiles, they would never again go into dispersion: "And I will plant them upon their land, and they shall no more be pulled up out of their land which I have given them, saith the LORD thy God."

The legendary accounts of Jeremiah and the Ark provide a

hidden clue to its location at Mount Nebo. This is a symbolic link that exists between the names of the Babylonian king who threatened to destroy the Ark and the mountain where it was hidden by Jeremiah. Both "Nebuchadnezzar" and "Nebo" stem from the Semitic root *nebu*, meaning the god "Mercury." This was also intimated in the prophecies of Ezekiel condemning Jerusalem (chapter 2). The name "Nebuchadnezzar" means "the prince of the god Merucury."[78] The Hebrew word *nebo* is from the root *neba* ("to prophesy" and also "a prophet").[79] In the same role as the prophets of the God of Israel, Nebo was worshiped as the celestial scribe of the Assyrians, the "interpreter of the gods, and declarer of their will."[80]

According to the Bible, the greatest prophet of all time was Moses: "And there arose not a prophet [*neba*] since in Israel like unto Moses, whom the LORD knew face to face."[81] Ironically, Mount Nebo was the site of the death of Moses:

> And Moses went up from the plains of Moab unto the mountain of Nebo, to the top of Pisgah, that [is] over against Jericho. And the LORD shewed him all the land of Gilead, unto Dan…. And the LORD said unto him, This [is] the land which I sware unto Abraham, unto Isaac, and unto Jacob, saying, I will give it unto thy seed: I have caused thee to see [it] with thine eyes, but thou shalt not go over thither. So Moses the servant of the LORD died there in the land of Moab, according to the word of the LORD.[82]

The Hebrew words *nobe*, meaning "high place," and *nabab*, meaning "to hollow out," "gate," or "pupil of the eye," also correlate with the location for the resting place of the Ark in a "hollow cave" on Mount Nebo, described in 2 Maccabees.[83]

The Talmud explains that the tower of Babel was dedicated

to Nebo, son of Marduk (Greek Jupiter) and that its destruction coincided with the confusion of languages and forgetfulness of knowledge.[84] The emblem of Mercury, a snake entwined on a pole, was first recorded in Exodus, which was the brazen serpent on a pole lifted by Moses to cure the rebellious Israelites of a plague of snakes (Numbers 21:9).[85]

The serpent on the pole was used as a Messianic symbol, and was illustrated by Christ Himself, as told in John 3:14: "And as Moses lifted up the serpent in the wilderness, even so must the Son of man be lifted up." However, this object was preserved and later worshiped as Mercury—Nebo by the Israelites—until being destroyed by King Hezekiah ca. 725 BC, when "he broke into pieces the bronze serpent that Moses had made, for until those days the people of Israel had burned incense to it; it was called Nehushtan."[86]

It is fitting with the cryptic name of Mount Nebo that a modern sculpture in metal of a serpent on a pole stands at its summit near the Church of Moses.[87] If the Ark was hidden in Mount Nebo, it was to remain forgotten until the end of days. This prophecy has remarkable similarities to the theme of Mercury as god of knowledge and forgetfulness. Its recovery sometime before the return of Christ fits the prophetic scheme of Sir Isaac Newton wherein a rebuilt temple, the Ark, and a world rule by "Babylon the Great" predominate.

Although Babylon's power over Israel resulted in the loss of the Ark and the destruction of the Temple, the resurgence of Babylon as a spiritual force that governs the world at the end of days will accompany the rebuilding of the structure and the discovery of the Ark.

As Moses viewed the Land of Promise from Mount Nebo, but was prevented from entering, the Ark's location upon Mount Nebo is seen, but not yet been obtained. However, according to prophecy, Moses will walk in Jerusalem in the end times, having finally gained access to the land viewed from atop Mount Nebo. As he waits for his designated time to enter the Promised Land, the Ark waits until the hour chosen by God.

The Bible records that the "glory of the Lord" moved into the Holy of Holies at the first installation of the Ark in Solomon's Temple.[88] Ezekiel, the prophet who warned of the destruction of Solomon's Temple while exiled in Nippur, Babylonia, had witnessed the glory of the Lord move away from the Temple to the east, directly in line with Mount Nebo. This was in reference to God abandoning the Temple to its enemies, and is stated in Ezekiel 11:23: "And the glory of the LORD went up from the midst of the city, and stood upon the mountain which [is] on the east side of the city."[89] Later, Ezekiel was shown the vision of the restored Temple of the future in which the glory of the Lord *returned* from the east, stated in Ezekiel 43:4: "And the glory of the LORD came into the Temple by the way of the gate whose prospect [is] toward the east."[90]

The "glory of the Lord" was a distinct feature of the Ark between the cherubim. Translated, "glory" is *shekinah* in Hebrew, meaning "presence." This presence of God was in form of a pillar of fire by night and a pillar of smoke by day during the travel of the Israelites in the desert. Whenever the glory of the Lord moved from the Tabernacle in the wilderness, the people followed. As the pillar of fire or smoke stood above the Ark, the Israelites stopped and set up camp. The glory of the Lord stood in a vertical column extending from Heaven to the surface of the Ark. The book of Exodus records that the Holy of Holies in the Tabernacle had no lamps, largely because none were needed due to the intense glow of the Ark itself. In fact, when Moses went into the Holy of Holies to speak to God at the mercy seat, his face glowed so intensely that the Israelites were afraid to come near him unless he wore a veil[91] (Exodus. 34:35). These descriptions associate the Ark with the glory of the Lord. When the Philistines captured the Ark and removed it from Israel, the daughter-in-law of Eli, the high priest, referred to the Ark as the glory of the Lord itself, saying, "The glory is departed from Israel: for the ark of God is taken."[92]

The Apocalypse of 2 Baruch provides the direction in which the Ark may rest in relation to the Temple. While the Babylonians began their siege of Jerusalem in 587 BC, Jeremiah the prophet threw the keys of the Temple and its sanctuary towards the sun:

> But taking the keys of the temple, Jeremiah went outside the city and threw them away in the presence of the sun, saying: I say to you, Sun, take the keys of the temple of God and guard them until the day in which the Lord asks you for them. For we have not been found worthy to keep them, for we have become unfaithful guardians.[93]

This legend is found with variations in the Jewish Talmud and pertains to the destruction of the First and Second Temples.[94] As the sun rises in the east, throwing the keys of the Temple to the sun implies this direction. It is remarkable that the story of the keys and the hiding of the Ark are both connected to Jeremiah. This story is also significant metaphorically. The "keys" of the Temple represent both the stewardship of the priests of God and the sacred knowledge embodied by the Temple and its rituals. In the Talmud versions, the Levites or the high priest climbed to the structure's roof and threw the keys into Heaven, from whence a divine hand caught them and disappeared into a cloud.[95]

Jewish mystics believe that this act represented the loss of the correct pronunciation of the name of God, or the knowledge of Solomon. When viewed from this perspective, the "lost key" story represents the *priscia theologia* of the Temple of God as a divine receptacle of pure knowledge. It is a line of reasoning that Newton certainly had perused.

The Ark, representing the whole of the Law, was a designed using the Sacred Cubit. Because the 25.20-inch Sacred Cubit is a ratio of the Earth, being a fractal of 2,520 (and 2,520 x *pi* is earth's diameter), the Ark reflects this *geo-metry* (literally, "earth-measure"). The solution for determining its present location might be found in the very word used for the divinely chosen resting place of the Ark, the *naus* or *navis*, the origin of the word "navigation," which is the skill of measuring the Earth. As an expert in the Law, Jeremiah may have reasoned that if the Ark could not dwell in the Temple that was designed as its permanent resting place, it might at least remain in alignment with it, which suggests a specific navigational process for locating the Ark.

A measuring line extended *directly towards the east* from the foundation stone of the Temple Mount must remain on the latitude of the foundation stone where the Ark rested in the Holy of Holies, which is north 31 degrees, 46 minutes, and 43 seconds. Its length must also be related to the Sacred Cubit, which is exactly 25.20 nautical miles. The result at the end of the measuring line touches the north slope of Mount Nebo less than a mile from its summit.

Image by author

That 2,520 is a constant is incredible. The terminus of this measuring line touches a point on the north slope of Mount Nebo 1,260 feet above sea level, which is half of 2,520, and the Temple Mount in Jerusalem rests on a hill 2,520 feet above sea level.[96] In fitting with the altitude of the location of the Ark on Mount Nebo, the letters of the name of Solomon in Greek equal 1,260; it is revealed that *it was* he who built the First Temple and established the Ark in the Holy of Holies.

These values are consistent with Newton's scheme of the Temple's *prisca theologia*, based on 25.20 of the Sacred Cubit and 2,520 of time recorded in the book of Daniel and Revelation. This numeric signature of prophecy and law is redundantly apparent in the proposed location of the Ark, situated in an area corresponding to the *only* description found in the biblical texts of its hiding place. Current satellite maps of the area reveal no modern settlements or excavations. In addition, the geology of the area is similar to the Qumran region of the Dead Sea, in which many caves exist. It would have been an extremely favorable location to deposit the Ark and furnishings of the Temple of Solomon.

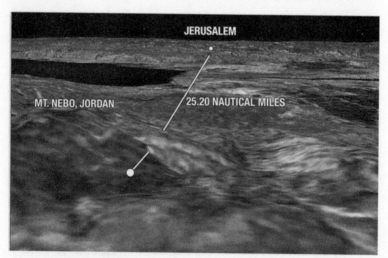

Courtesy of NASA World Wind

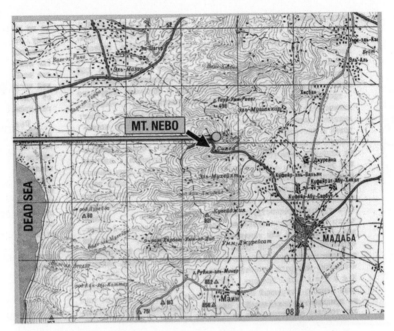

Geographic location of the ark on the north slope of Mt. Nebo, Jordan. Map, Soviet general staff sheet H36VI, 1985

There are questions that arise concerning the exposure of the location of the Ark, if this calculation is accurate. Is it wise to uncover it? Will it fall into the wrong hands? Will the Ark be present in the rebuilt Temple of the end times?

It is reasonable that God would not provide information to find the Ark unless it was part of His divine plan. Although the acacia wood comprising it may have disintegrated, the gold overlaid around it, as well the solid gold of the mercy seat and cherubim, would have certainly withstood the effects of time. Its recovery would follow the precise design of God from the beginning. If the Ark's location has been revealed, then it is God's intention that it be discovered in this age. One specific detail must be worked out, however. The site of Ark of the Covenant on Mount Nebo is dependent on the exact location of the foundation stone on the Temple Mount. There are several theories concerning this question, the most promising is, significantly, linked to the Eastern Gate of the Temple.[97]

David Flynn's reasoning is spectacular to be sure, but one thing is certain: If the Bible is to be accepted as God's Word on the matter, the Third Temple will be built and the revealing of the Ark of the Covenant and other Second Temple Treasures could—any day now—ignite global impetus for its construction.

In the fascinating article, "Oklahoma Noahide on the Trail of Temple Gold" by Adam Eliyahu Berkowitz for *Breaking Israel News*, we learn exactly where the Temple treasures may be hidden. The report is based on the Copper Scroll Project work by SkyWatch TV friend Shelley Neese, and Adam gave me permission to include his report here:

> After nearly a decade of writing, the remarkable story of one man's quest to decipher the ancient map leading to the gold and silver Temple vessels is being published.
>
> Shelley Neese, vice president of the Jerusalem Connection, became involved in the story over a decade ago and has spent nearly eight years writing the Copper Scroll Project, the story of an unlikely hero who may have unraveled one of history's most enduring mysteries.
>
> In 2007, Neese was the editor for *Jerusalem Connection Magazine* and she met Barfield at a Christian conference in Texas.
>
> "I was unfamiliar with the Copper Scrolls, and at first I didn't believe his story about treasure maps, gold, and the Jewish Temple," Neese, told *Breaking Israel News*. "All the alarm bells in my head went off. But after I looked it up, I realized that he hadn't embellished it at all."
>
> Discovered in 1952 near Qumran on the shores of the Dead Sea, the Copper Scroll is unlike the other Dead Sea Scrolls which are mostly religious manuscripts written on parchment. The Copper Scroll, as its name suggests, is engraved on a thin

sheet of copper. And, in contrast to the others, the Copper Scroll is a list of gold and silver items and the 64 locations where they can be found.

Many archaeologists believe the Copper Scroll is an inventory from the Second Temple. In addition to gold and silver, Temple vessels and priestly vestments are listed. No archaeologist has ever succeeded in deciphering the directions contained in the Copper Scroll and finding the treasure.

The book follows the efforts of Jim Barfield, a man who, at first glance, seems entirely unsuited to search for the Temple artifacts, but whose unique skills may have solved one of history's most enduring mysteries. Barfield, a Noahide who speaks no Hebrew, also has no background in archaeology. A retired criminal investigator for the Oklahoma Fire Department, Barfield was used to patiently sifting through the ashes to find the truth.

In 2006, Barfield was interested in the Dead Sea Scrolls and their relevance to Bible study. At first, he was uninterested in the Copper Scroll which had no theological significance. Barfield's fascination turned into a burning desire after he met Vendyl Jones. Jones, a Texas preacher turned Biblical archaeologist, believed Qumran to be the hiding place for the Temple vessels and spent 30 years searching for them using the Copper Scroll as a guide. Jones discovered a small vial of persimmon oil used to anoint kings and high priests, and a large quantity of what he believed was Temple incense. Barfield met with Jones, now deceased, and Jones suggested he revisit the Copper Scroll.

"Vendyl told Jim the Copper Scroll had more prophecy in it than any of the other Dead Sea Scrolls," Neese said.

Barfield's curiosity turned into passion and he returned to deciphering the Copper Scroll. He searched maps for the "ruins of the Valley of Achor" mentioned in the scroll. The valley is believed to be near Jericho but the precise location is unknown. As a young man, he had piloted helicopters for the U.S. Army.

Using his map-reading skills to triangulate, he was able to pin-point locations on an aerial map of Qumran. Very quickly, pieces of the puzzle began falling into place.

"It's really not revolutionary what he did," Neese said. "He figured it out using available sources in his office in Oklahoma, relying on his skills as an arson investigator."

In one case, the scroll described steps, 40 cubits long, heading east. Barfield did indeed find stairs. The archaeologist reported the stairs to be 60 feet, or precisely 40 cubits. He also discovered the remains of a pool, precisely 40 cubits long, exactly where the scroll said it would be. He believed he had found many of the locations listed on the scroll but to verify his theories, he needed to visit the site.

In 2007, Barfield travelled to Israel to do exactly that, but to pursue his investigation, he needed the approval of the Israel Antiquities Authority to search Qumran. Barfield met with Israel Antiquities Authority (IAA) director Shuka Dorfman. Dorfman was unreceptive at first, but as Barfield laid out his proofs, explaining the signposts described in the Copper Scroll, Dorfman became enthusiastic and arranged a meeting with vet-eran archaeologist and Qumran expert, Yuval Peleg.

Peleg agreed to dig some exploratory holes at the site with Barfield. Less than an hour after beginning shallow test pits, Peleg received a phone call and without any explanation, Peleg shut down the dig.

This was the beginning of many bureaucratic stone walls preventing Barfield from verifying his theory. He purchased a sophisticated metal detector that could penetrate 50 feet while differentiating between ferrous and non-ferrous metal, i.e. gold and silver. Barfield applied to the IAA, asking to run a non-intrusive scan of a few spots in Qumran. His request was denied.

In 2013, Barfield was in New York where he was intro-duced to Moshe Feiglin who, at the time, was a Likud Member of Knesset. Feiglin was a strong advocate for the Temple and became enthused when he heard Barfield's story, even offering to accompany him on a tour of the site. A few weeks later, the two were wandering around the tourist site, a large duffel bag in tow. They visited five spots that Barfield felt were most likely repositories for Temple treasure.

One hour later, Barfield ran the data from the metal detector through his computer. Every spot was a hit and one locus especially so.

"It showed up on the metal detector like Fort Knox," Neese said.

The Israeli government is still not permitting Barfield to investigate and there has been a moratorium on archaeological digging at Qumran.

"It is in area C and different laws apply to the archaeology than in other parts of Israel," Neese said. "It is disputed territory and anything that comes out of the ground can be disputed. It is possible that the Israeli government is concerned that if they dig up this massive treasure, Jordan or the Palestinian Authority will sue for it. Even if it comes from the Jewish Temple."

In fact, the Copper Scroll, an ancient artifact inscribed in Hebrew, is currently in a museum in Amman, Jordan.

In an interview with *Breaking Israel News* last year, Barfield stated his motives.

"I am a Noahide," he explained to *Breaking Israel News*. "I want to return the Temple artifacts to the Jewish People. It's time."

If Barfield is successful, it will bring the Third Temple much closer.

Not only does Neese chronicle this amazing story, but she was an integral player in much of it. A native of Louisiana, she first came to Israel in 2000 with her husband, a U.S. Air Force physician. With no knowledge of Israel, she became intensely curious about the country and received her M.A in Middle Eastern Studies from Ben Gurion University. She spent the months leading up to the Gaza disengagement in 2005 in Israel, working with a team of negotiators. When she went back to the U.S., she became the assistant to the Consul General at the Consulate of Israel to New England.[98]

Though translations differ, the Copper Scroll does not directly reference the holiest Temple furniture, says Neese: the menorah, table of showbread, or altar for incense. Nevertheless, the Copper Scroll's language points to other sacred furniture, including a possible cryptic reference to the Ark of the Covenant that may coincide with David Flynn's research cited earlier in this chapter. Neese notes in her research:

Wolters reads the final hiding place, In the cavern of the Presence [Shekinah] on the north of Kokhlit—its opening is north and tombs are at its mouth. Shekinah, when used in the Bible, designates the divine radiance as it dwells in the Holy of Holies, both in the Tabernacle and the Temple in Jerusalem. The Shekinah is the spirit or presence of God. At least to me, the cavern of the Presence sounds like a cleverly worded reference to *a cave hiding the Ark.* (emphasis added)[99]

Of course, as stated earlier, there are those who believe the Ark of the Covenant is buried under the Temple Mount, perhaps directly beneath where the Holy of Holies once stood (would make sense), and goals by such organizations as the Mitzvah Project see building the Third Temple a realizable objective once the Ark materializes. They are raising funds now with a plan to "search the tunnels under the Temple Mount in order to find the Golden Ark and other important artifacts."[100]

four

Temple Location Controversy

DR. RANDALL PRICE'S words frame the controversy that constitutes today's debate involving the place the Third Temple is prophetically scheduled to stand.

> The current controversy, in case you haven't heard, is that the so-called Temple Mount universally recognized and revered by the Jewish People is not the original site of the two Temples in history, but only a "traditional" view based on a misinterpretation that arose hundreds of years after the Jews had forgotten where their Temple(s) had stood. One of the writers who holds this view (hereafter "the proponents") makes the claim: "The results certify the correct interpretation of Christ's prophecy that not one stone of the temple would be standing upon another, a stark contrast to the myth claiming the 10,000 Herodian stones, now called the Jerusalem temple mount."
>
> The original site has now been claimed to have been identified and recovered by several Christian academics, popular authors and documentary filmmakers as half a mile away

from the "traditional" site in the City of David. The remains of structures on and around the "traditional Temple Mount," they claim are of the Herodian Fortress Antonio, which they believe occupied the entire 35-acre platform. As the originator of this view states. They contend their new "discovery" needs to be recognized by the world and Israel's history revised: "Now is the time to remove this profound ignorance and forgetfulness.... What we now know from these new archaeological and biblical discoveries is this: Though the whole world over the past generations has forgotten where the original Temple of Solomon was constructed, we are now assured that the Temples of Solomon, Zerubbabel and Herod were built just above the once fresh and pure waters of the Gihon Spring located on the southeast of Jerusalem."[101]

The Jewish archeological community has for the most part dismissed the claims that the previous Temples existed in places other than upon Moriah. Thus, the whole debate might be considered as merely academic differences, with each side content to hold its own view as the one with the facts. But charges have been leveled that there is a cover-up of sorts regarding the historical site.

Proponents of the Temple site being other than Moriah go so far as to call Mount Moriah being named the Temple Mount the "hoax of the Millennium." The proponents go on to say they have, through research, proved their findings that the City of David site, *not* Mount Moriah, is the location. They state their findings constitute a "game changer." By this, they mean that the entire world of Temple history is dramatically altered. If their "findings" can be proven true, it will upset the world. Not only the Jews, but the entire geopolitical and Muslim worlds will be profoundly upset in ways yet unimagined. The proposition of the Temple site being other than Mount Moriah, the proponents claim, affect the rollout of biblical prophecy.

Some among the proponents believe that the Temple's rebuilding being held up because of religious and political conflict is thereby delaying the return of Christ. By bypassing the problems associated with the Muslim Dome of the Rock, which prevents a Temple from being constructed on the traditional site on Moriah, and accepting the City of David as the *real* site of the first two Temples, the Second Advent can occur sooner rather than later—i.e., the Third Temple can be built without the problem of first getting rid of the Dome of the Rock and fighting a war with all of Islam.

Excerpts from an article by one of the chief proponents of a Temple site other than Mount Moriah gives some insight into that side of the Temple location controversy.

> There is no place that is considered a more significant as well as volatile, piece of real estate than the Temple Mount. Some say that World War III will erupt there. More blood has been shed over disputes of ownership and control of the traditional temple platform than any other location on earth. But some now believe the temple of Solomon was never even there at all, and that the legend of it being at that spot has gone unchallenged for so long now that tradition seems to have sealed reality into a long forgotten tomb.
>
> Like so many, I thought that the location for the temple of Solomon had been proven to be on the traditional Temple Mount in Jerusalem. But, I became suspicious after reading the work of the late archaeologist and author, Dr. Ernest L. Martin. My research efforts would not have been possible without his ground-breaking insights....
>
> David took control of what the Bible calls the Stronghold of Zion (Metsudat Tsion), that is, the City of David. These last two locales (Stronghold of Zion and the City of David) are the huge keys to solving the riddle as to where the true temple is located....
>
> The City of David was rediscovered in the later 1800s and its

walls begin at about 600 feet south of today's traditional Temple Mount/Dome of the Rock. I found that the Bible further states, "So shall you know that I am the Lord your God, dwelling in Zion My holy mountain" (Joel 3:17). This is reflective of the verse which reads, "My holy mountain Jerusalem as the children of Israel bring an offering in a clean vessel into the house of the Lord" (Isaiah 66:20).

These verses indicate that "My holy mountain" is the same as "the House of the Lord," which is synonymous with the temple. Since the threshing floor is the site of the temple, which is in the City of David, as well as the true place of Zion, it seems all three converge and solidify in logical summation, as well as logical submission, that the true location of the temple needs to shift to its proper and original site south of the traditional Temple Mount. Micah 4:2–13 gives a further prophetic picture of the temple being located on the threshing floor in the City of David. From the Oxford Study Bible (OSB), let me seam several verses together to make that point: In the days to come, The mountain of the Lord's house Will be established higher than all other mountains; The Lord will bring their King on Mount Zion They do not know the Lord's thoughts or understand His purpose; For He has gathered them like sheaves to the threshing floor; Start your threshing you people of Zion.

The Lord's house (as referenced above) is the temple itself. So we have another non-retractable connector with the temple, Zion, and the threshing floor. Once again, the threshing floor (see 2 Chronicles 3:1) is all important in identifying the temple location. Its connection to Zion, in the City of David, adds to the corroborative evidence of the true temple location.

Many ancient historians site a spring at the true temple location. The Roman historian Tacitus recorded that the temple at Jerusalem had a natural spring of water that welled from its interior. Again, these references could only be describing the Gihon

Spring. It is located close to what is referred to as the Ophel, which is a bulge of the earth abutting the City of David (Zion) laying just to the south, and roughly about 1,000 feet, from the Temple Mount. There are no springs, however, on top of the Temple Mount. A spring is crucial for the true temple locale. "A fountain shall flow from the house of the Lord" (Joel 3:18)....

According to the Bible (as referenced previously in 2 Chronicles 3:1), the threshing floor is, in effect, the anchor point for the temple. It was in the area of the Gihon Spring. It also seems to be close to where the angel of the Lord stepped in to abort Abraham's attempt to sacrifice his son. A future judgment will occur on this ancient, missing threshing floor where a new temple will be built.[102]

Counter Argument

Dr. David Reagan counters the City of David argument:

> Cornuke's only basis for this assertion [that the threshing floor David purchased for the location of the Temple was situated within the City of David (2 Samuel 24:18–25)] is that since the Temple was located in Zion, the threshing floor had to be in the City of David. But the Bible says otherwise in 2 Chronicles 3:1—

>> Then Solomon began to build the house of the LORD in Jerusalem on Mount Moriah, where the LORD had appeared to his father David, at the place that David had prepared on the threshing floor of Ornan the Jebusite.

>> This verse makes it very clear that the threshing floor on which the Temple was built was located on Mount Moriah, and

not in the City of David. Furthermore, threshing floors in biblical times were never located inside cities. Instead, they were
located on high places in agricultural areas where the wind could
catch the chaff.

Cornuke makes the bizarre claim that the threshing floor
that David purchased was actually located over the Gihon
Spring in the City of David. But as one of his critics has put it:[10]

The reason the Temple was not built on top of the Gihon
Spring is the same reason people do not put a toilet in the middle
of the kitchen table where food is eaten. The temple was built on
a threshing floor. Threshing floors are dirty and were never built
near springs. The particles would contaminate the water as the
chaff from the wheat was blown away from the husk.

All these factors make it clear that a threshing floor inside
the tiny City of David is just not a possibility.

The Water

Cornuke's third major argument relates to the Jewish Temple's
need for abundant water in order to wash away the blood of animal sacrifices. He asserts that because of this need, the Temple
had to be situated in the City of David over the Gihon Spring.
He cites two biblical passages—Joel 3:18 and Ezekiel 47:1–7—
to prove that the Gihon Spring was under the Temple.

The passage in Joel says, "…and in that day the mountains
will drip with sweet wine, and the hills will flow with milk, and
all the brooks of Judah will flow with water; and a spring will go
out from the house of the LORD to water the valley of Shittim."
Similarly, the passage in Ezekiel says that water will flow from
under the threshold of the Temple. The water will form a river
that will flow to the Dead Sea, and when it reaches that point,
it will refresh the sea and bring it alive with "living creatures."

The problem with these passages is that they are both presented in a Millennial context, and therefore they have nothing to do with the biblical temples. The verses are talking about the Millennial Temple which will be built after Jesus returns. And keep in mind that the Bible says that when the Second Coming occurs, there will be the greatest earthquake in history—one that will impact the entire world (Revelation 6:12–17 and Revelation 16:18–20).

Every island will be moved. Mountains will be lowered, plains will be lifted, and the topography of Jerusalem will be drastically changed (Zechariah 14:10). So, there is no way that Cornuke can prove that these verses are talking about the Gihon Spring.

The fact that the topography of Jerusalem is going to be radically revised is attested to by the size of the Millennial Temple that is described in Ezekiel 40-48. Bible prophecy expert Dr. John C. Whitcomb describes it this way:[11]

> The area of the Temple courts (500 x 500 "reeds," or about one square mile) would be larger than the entire ancient walled city of Jerusalem, and the holy portion for priests and Levites (20,000 x 25,000 reeds, or about 40 x 50 miles) would cover an area six times the size of greater London today and could not possibly be placed within present-day Palestine, that is between the Jordan River and the Mediterranean Sea (Ezekiel 47:18), to say nothing of the *"portion of the prince"* on either side of this area (Ezekiel 45:7, 47:21). The Millennial Jerusalem would be about 40 miles in circumference and thus ten times the circumference of the ancient city. Furthermore, it would be somewhat north of the present site of the city, and the Temple area would be about ten miles north of that, on the way to Samaria![103]

Part of the argument for the Temple being anywhere other than on Mount Moriah, the traditionally accepted site, is that memory of the exact location has been lost over the millennia. It simply appeared to be the place where such an important edifice would have been placed. Thus, the Mount Moriah advocates for the traditional location have been mistaken over the centuries.

Instead, some proponents of the City of David as the Temple site hold that the top of Mount Moriah was where the Antonia Fortress that housed Roman troops were garrisoned. More than six thousand Roman soldiers, they say, would need such a platform for accommodating their numbers.

Regarding the debate point that memory of the Temple Mount site has been lost to Jewish antiquity, Dr. Randall Price writes the following:

The location of the historic Temple(s) were never lost to Judaism. An unbroken chain of Jewish testimony has uniformly maintained that the site of the Temple(s) is to be located only on the historic Temple Mount.

F. M. Loewenberg, Professor Emeritus at Bar-Ilan University In his Middle East Quarterly journal article "Did Jews Abandon the Temple Mount," traces the Jewish connection with the Temple Mount through time, revealing that not only has the Jewish Community maintained an unbroken 2,000 year-long connection with the Temple Mount, but from time to time, as foreign rulers permitted access, the Jewish communities in Israel, joined by others from the Diaspora, attempted to rebuild the Temple on its site or to establish regular services there.[104]

Price writes that Professor Loewenberg observed further that for the past two thousand years, there has always been a Jewish community in Jerusalem. Despite terrible persecutions as the city and country were under foreign rulers, Orthodox Jews never left the site because of their fidelity to the words of Psalm 137:5–6:

If I will forget thee O Jerusalem, let my right hand forget her skill. Let my tongue cleave to the roof of my mouth, if I remember thee not; if I set not Jerusalem above my chiefest joy.

It seems that because of the Jewish people's concentration on rebuilding the Temple, the location's place of previous construction could not have been forgotten. The spot where the Holy of Holies sat has been debated, but never has any rabbi, historian, or archaeologist argued against the Temples being located on the Temple Mount. After twenty-five years of intensive research on the Temple, based upon original, historical and religious sources, the Temple Movement determined that the only place the Temple can be built is upon Mount Moriah. They believe this is in continuity with the Bible, Jewish history and oral tradition.

Price further reminds that the place of Jewish Temples is remembered.

The location of the historic Temple(s) was never lost to Islam. Early Muslim scholars, as well as modern Muslim scholars, stated that the Jewish Temple(s) were located only on the historic Temple Mount.

Soon after Muslim presence was established on the Temple Mount the Caliph Umar permitted Jews access to pray on the Temple Mount and at the Western Wall. The successor of Umar, Caliph Abd al-Malik, made ten Jewish families guardians of the Holy Temple Mount in the name of the Jewish people. Sometime afterward, the situation changed, and geographer and historian Sebeos wrote in A.D. 660: "I will relate a little more about the intentions of the rebellious Jews, who having earlier received help from the leaders of the children of Hagar, conceived a plan to rebuild the Temple of Solomon. Having discovered the place which is called the Holy of Holies, they then built on its foundations, a place of prayer for themselves. However, the Ishmaelites, jealous of them, drove them from this place and called it their house of prayer." From this early account we can see that both the Jews and the Muslims recognized the historic Temple Mount as the site of the former Temple(s). It would seem that Abd al-Malik's allowance of the renewal of Jewish worship at the site (if this was in fact permitted), led to his erection of the Dome of the Rock as a shrine (commemorating the site of the Jewish Temple) as a theological statement of Islamic supercession.

This understanding of the site was held by Islamic clerics until recent times. The Supreme Muslim Council, the body entrusted with the jurisdiction of the modern Temple Mount, publishes a guidebook in English for tourists to the site. Since 1966 this guide has made no reference to the Temple, but from 1935 into the 1950's, the guidebook made this statement in its opening pages: "This site is one of the oldest in the world. Its sanctity dates from the earliest times. Its identity with the Temple of Solomon is beyond dispute." Even though officially the Palestinian Authority denies the Temple ever existed on the modern Temple Mount, Palestinian academics know better. A case in point is Sari Nusseibeh, President of Al-Quds University in Jerusalem, who confessed, "If you went back a couple of hundred years, before the advent of the political form of Zionism, I think you will find that many Muslims would not have disputed the connection that Jews have toward the Temple Mount.

The problem began arising with the advent of Zionism, when people started connecting a kind of feeling that Jews have toward the area with the political project of Zionism."[105]

The Stones Argument

Another assertion by those who hold that Mount Moriah isn't the site of the Jewish Temples is that evidence presented by the locations of the many large stones surrounding Moriah bolsters their case. The following excerpt presents the argument.

Jesus warned His disciples of the coming destruction of the temple and that not one stone of the temple would be left on top of another. Matthew 24:1–2 says, "Then Jesus went out and departed from the temple, and His disciples came up to show Him the buildings of the temple. And Jesus said to them, 'Do you not see all these things? Assuredly, I say to you, not one stone shall be left here upon another, that shall not be thrown down.'" Christ's words clearly state that the entire temple, each and every stone, would be dug up, dislodged, and tossed away. It is interesting to note that there are massive stone blocks by the thousands set in the wall supporting the Temple Mount platform. Was Jesus wrong in His prophesying that not one stone would remain standing?

Historian Flavius Josephus wrote that the entirety of the temple was indeed in total ruin and destruction after 70 AD. He went on to say that if he had not personally been in Jerusalem during the war and witnessed the demolition by Titus of the temple that took place there, he wouldn't have believed it ever existed. Josephus (*Jewish Wars*, VII, 1.1) speaks of widespread destruction in all Jerusalem as well.

So, if the Temple was completely destroyed to the last stone being toppled over, what is, and was, the huge stone fortress we see today rising over Jerusalem? I believe, as do others, that it once was the Roman fort occupied by the mighty Tenth Legion (Legio X Fretensis). I also believe that the true site of Solomon's temple is about a thousand feet south of the temple mount in the City of David. This would mean that Jesus was correct in His prophetic words and that each and every stone, to the last one, was thrown down.

Where Was the Temple?

The garrison of Fort Antonia in Jerusalem was as big as several cities, according to Josephus, housing approximately 6,000 men

plus the needed support staff. All told, as many as 10,000 per-
sonnel served there. But this huge fort has never been found in
Jerusalem by archaeologists. I feel that the reason archaeologists
have not found the mighty Roman fort is because the tradition
of the Temple Mount complex being the temple site has blinded
them.[106]

Confuting the Stones Argument

Dr. David Reagan again weighs in on the Mount Moriah vs City of
David Temple issue:

One of Cornuke's cornerstone arguments that he emphasizes
repeatedly is that Jesus prophesied that the entire Temple complex would be destroyed to the point that "not one stone will
be left upon another" (Matthew 24:2). He then points out that
the retaining walls of the Temple Mount remain standing to this
day. Therefore, he concludes that the Temple could not have
been located on the Temple Mount. In contrast, he points out
that nothing is left of the Temple in the City of David.

This argument is nothing but hot air. Jesus did not prophesy
the destruction of the Temple complex, and the reason there is
nothing left of the Temple in the City of David is because it was
never there.

You can find Jesus' prophecy in three places: Matthew
24:1–2, Mark 13:1–2 and Luke 21:5–6. In all three places it
is very clear that His prophecy relates only to the buildings on
the Temple Mount and not to the retaining walls around the
Mount. Consider Matthew 24:1–2 —

1) Jesus came out from the temple and was going away when
His disciples came up to point out the temple buildings to Him.

2) And He said to them, "Do you not see all these things?

Truly I say to you, not one stone here will be left upon another, which will not be torn down."

As you can clearly see in this passage, the prophecy relates to the Temple *buildings*, and not the retaining walls.

The Coin

Cornuke makes a big deal out of a coin that archaeologists found at the base of the southwest corner of the Temple Mount retaining wall. He says the coin was dated 20 AD and it proves that the walls were not completed by that date. He concludes that the western wall was not built by Herod, and therefore Herod's Temple could not have been located on the Temple Mount.

The fact of the matter is that the construction of the Temple complex continued long after King Herod's death. John 2:20 says that the building of the Temple complex took 46 years— until about 27 or 28 AD. And recent archaeological excavations have revealed that although the Western Wall, where Jews pray today, was built in Herod's lifetime, the southwest corner of the Temple Mount where the coin was found, was not completed until around 30 AD. In fact, Josephus reports that the Temple complex was still receiving further embellishments and repairs right up to the time that the First Jewish Revolt broke out in 66 AD.

The Debris

One important point that Cornuke overlooks is that there is tons of debris on the east and west sides of the Temple Mount. This rubble was piled up when the Roman soldiers pushed the stones of the Temple buildings off the top of the Temple Mount.

This debris is so deep that when people stand at the Western Wall (or "Wailing Wall") today, they are actually standing 50 feet above the base of the wall where a street was located in the time of Jesus. On the eastern side of the Temple Mount, the debris is so deep that it covers the top of the ancient Eastern Gate which exists directly below the present gate.

This leads to a crucial question: If the Temple Mount was the location of the Roman fortress, why did the Roman soldiers tear down their own fortress and then go to the enormous trouble of pushing the remains over the top of the Temple Mount? It just makes no sense...

In the midst of the rubble that has been left at the southwest corner of the Temple Mount is a stone that is inscribed with the words, "To the place of trumpeting." It marks the spot at the top of the Temple Mount where the priestly trumpeter would have stood to sound the trumpet signaling the beginning and end of Sabbath days and festivals. This stone clearly indicates that the Temple Mount was a Jewish sacred place, and not the site of a Roman fortress.[107]

Further Proof

Dr. Randall Price writes the following regarding further evidence of Mount Moriah's validation as location of Jewish Temples:

Israeli archaeologist Ronny Reich who with Eli Shukron excavated the destruction layer beneath the southwestern wall of the Temple Mount in the late 1990's said "The stones being revealed are the remains of the Temple Mount. The Temple stood in the center, of which nothing survived, but the Temple Mount and the big Herodian enclosure—this is what you see there fallen and destroyed. This is important. You can see it only there." This underscores the point that we have made that there were remains of the Temple and that these identify the site as the Jewish Temple, not a Roman fortress.[108]

More evidence has emerged from digs around the Temple Mount, according to Price. A small stone seal with an Aramaic inscription reading Daka Le'Ya ("Pure for God") was found at the northwest corner of the Temple Mount. This seal was placed on objects devoted to Temple worship practices. It designated these objects as ceremonially pure.

This, according to Dr. Price, is the first written evidence confirming Temple ritual practice on the Temple Mount. A related artifact was found inside the Old City walls a short distance from the modern site of the Temple Mount. It was a tiny gold bell, and Exodus 39:25 mentions "bells of pure gold around the hem of the priest's robe between the pomegranates."

Dr. Price says that further evidence has come forth of construction activity by the Muslim authorities. They have inadvertently uncovered a possible Temple-related structure. While digging a trench for electric cabling on the Temple Mount in 2006, a layer of apparently undisturbed material from the First Temple period was discovered. In this trench was a large section of a First Temple period wall, and near the wall were pottery remains dating from the Iron Age II (the seventh and eighth centuries BC), most likely from the reign of King Hezekiah. The remains included fragments of bowl rims, bases, and body shards, the base of a juglet used for ladling oil, the handle of a small juglet, the rim of a storage jar, fragments of ceramic table wares and animal bones. Based on the location of the wall and the type of vessels found, archaeological architect Dr. Leen Ritmeyer proposed that it formed part of the House of Oil in the First Temple.

Price's documentation of the Jewish Temples' location is overwhelming. The Temple platform's size and the intricacies of its various expansion aspects from the time of Solomon to the Herodian era have produced no other evidence-based deduction. The physical features themselves are so conclusive that we wish we could devote the required space in this volume to go in-depth in that regard.

Price concludes that in English law, a court will not be deterred from a conclusion because of regret at its consequences; a court must arrive at such conclusion as is directed by the weight and preponderance of the evidence. In weighing the evidence from the archaeological excavations at the modern Temple Mount, the preponderance of evidence shows that it was the site of the historic Temple(s).

five

Building toward Tribulation

ZECHARIAH, THE SIXTH-CENTURY B.C. prophet, spoke words that pierce today's ears in thunderous decibels:

> Behold, I will make Jerusalem a cup of trembling unto all the peoples round about....
>
> And in that day will I make Jerusalem a burdensome stone for all peoples; all that burden themselves with it shall be cut in pieces, though...gathered together against it. (Zechariah 12:2–3)

Jerusalem is a city as ancient as any still in existence, yet it is as contemporary as today's front-page headlines. It is destined to become the center of the world's most volatile geopolitical conflict ever and, ultimately, the precise spot on the planet where God's own foot will touch down to put an end to man's genocidal madness.

The beginning of the end of human history is traceable to a general geographical area of the Earth, portions of which the world, in 1991, watched the United Nations Desert Storm coalition forces decimate with unprecedented military might. It has been termed "Mesopotamia" by the geographers and the "Cradle of Civilization" by historians and anthropologists.

According to the Bible, it is the region where the Garden of Eden was home for the first human beings. When Adam and Eve broke fellowship with the Creator by yielding to the serpent's temptation, the end-time clock began ticking for the present Earth.

The first murder followed, setting in motion the blood-drenched record upon which we now look back. Such dynamics will produce the indescribable carnage and gore that are prophesied to take place during the last seven years of this dying, decaying age.

What Are the Signs?

Apocalypse and Armageddon loom just ahead. But, can we know if those long-talked-about, worried-over events will even come to pass—much less whether they will occur within our own lifetime? Haven't doomsday prophets for centuries been predicting such things? Most have been saying that those end-time events would occur during their lifetimes. What makes predictors and predictions today any different from then?

Perhaps to begin answering such questions—good ones, at that—inquiries of another kind are in order. Why are you reading this treatment of the subject of the biblically prophesied Apocalypse and all it will entail of the matter of the building of the Third Temple, in particular? Something has piqued your ears, your eyes, your attention.

Why the suddenly increased fascination with things to come—with that once-hazy matter called Armageddon? Something has happened. Something drastic, almost irresistible, calls people to begin looking more seriously at what the immediate future holds for the world.

Jesus found Himself surrounded by a group of people who asked what the signs of His return to Earth and of the end of the world would be. As He always did, Jesus spoke to the heart of the subject with precision and truth, outlining the major signs that would immediately precede the Second Advent.

His followers asked in Matthew 24:3, "What shall be the sign of thy coming, and the end of the world?" Jesus gave them more than they asked for as He answered:

Take heed that no man deceive you.

For many shall come in my name, saying, I am Christ; and shall deceive many.

And ye shall hear of wars and rumors of wars; see that ye be not troubled, for all these things must come to pass, but the end is not yet.

For nation shall rise against nation, and kingdom against kingdom; and there shall be famines, and pestilences, and earthquakes, in various places.

All these things are the beginning of sorrows.

Then shall they deliver you up to be afflicted, and shall kill you; and ye shall be hated of all nations for my name's sake.

And then shall many be offended, and shall betray one another, and shall hate one another.

And many false prophets shall rise, and shall deceive many.

And because iniquity shall abound, the love of many shall grow cold.

But he that shall endure unto the end, the same shall be saved.

And this gospel of the kingdom shall be preached in all the world for a witness unto all nations; and then shall the end come. (Matthew 24:4–14)

In these few passages, Jesus swept the entire panorama of world history from His time on Earth forward, using specific word pictures of things in the future. These signs are recorded in God's Holy Word to be understood by each person of each generation that the prophecies involve. God's Word has many levels of meaning. However, one must seek to know what is given. We do not simply absorb these truths as a sponge absorbs liquid, nor can we through osmosis assimilate God's holy ways as a plant draws nutrients.

If we want to know God's instructions, information, and truth, we must "know" the Bible for ourselves. This "knowing" begins with the heart of the gospel, John 3:16. To know God is to know Jesus Christ.

The Beginning of the End

Each of the signs Jesus expounded upon in the foregoing passages of Scripture are, of course, quite important. However, one sign is crucial to understanding where this generation stands on God's prophetic timeline. We have been living a part of that sign since 1948, when the nation of Israel was born in a single day—May 14.

Of that time of Israel's rebirth, Jesus—speaking in parabolic language to His disciples—said:

> Now learn a parable of the fig tree; When his branch is yet tender, and putteth forth leaves, ye know that summer is nigh:
> So likewise ye, when ye shall see all these things, know that it is near, even at the doors. Verily I say unto you, This generation shall not pass, till all these things be fulfilled. (Matthew 24:32–34)

Jesus was looking through the eras of future man; He spoke to future disciples, the generation that would be alive at the time of His Second Advent. The nation Israel, in symbolic language sometimes used in God's Word, is likened at times to a fig tree, in that God intended the children of Israel to be fruitful and a blessing to all the world. (See Judges 9:10–11, Joel 1:7–12, and Habakkuk 3:16–17, for example.)

Jesus clearly used the fig tree parable to tell the last generation of believers that the re-establishment of the nation Israel would be a key sign of His nearing Second Advent as well as a sign of the end of the world system. All other signs given by Jesus would accompany this major sign as the end of the age approached. Since Jesus had told of the destruction of Jerusalem and implied the dispersion of the Jewish people just prior to giving the parable of the fig tree, He spoke most pointedly of the time when Israel would be regathered and begin to "shoot forth" its leaves. The golden summer of His millennial reign would be near when this came to pass. His return would be imminent.

First, however, the black winter clouds of Apocalypse would have to storm upon a world gathering to commit collective suicide.

Possessing the Land

The prophet Ezekiel spoke of the Diaspora and rebirth of God's chosen nation—the same nation that made the world tremble nervously in anticipation of its reaction to Saddam Hussein's Scud missile attacks during the first Persian Gulf War.

> And I scattered them among the heathen, and they were dispersed through the countries: according to their way and according to their doings I judged them....
>
> For I will take you from among the heathen, and gather you out of all countries, and will bring you into your own land. (Ezekiel 36:19, 24)

God's promises to this beleaguered, precariously perched nation, the nation most prominent in the process of pursuing world peace, are numerous throughout the Scriptures.

Consider the profound assurances given through Moses:

That then the Lord thy God will turn thy captivity, and have compassion upon thee, and will return and will gather thee from all the nations, whither the Lord thy God hath scattered thee....

And the Lord thy God will bring thee into the land which thy fathers possessed, and thou shalt possess it. (Deuteronomy 30:3, 5)

And:

Shall the earth be made to bring forth in one day? or shall a nation be born at once? for as soon as Zion travailed, she bought forth her children.

Shall I bring to the birth, and not cause to bring forth? saith the Lord. (Isaiah 66:8–9)

The Exodus of Jews from the Soviet Union, since the supposed benevolent institution of *glasnost* and *perestroika*, has been staggering. The dissolution of much of Eastern Europe's communist superstructure has freed many more to migrate to Israel. They have streamed from Ethiopia and from around the globe to the Land of Promise. We are witnesses to God's promises to Israel in ways unthinkable a few years ago. God is indeed making manifest, through the Jews, His great prophetic truth in this generation!

Dry Bones, Live!

Put yourself in the prophet Ezekiel's place for a moment. While you do so, consider the things you know about the Jews in the day in which we now live.

Think for a moment on the blowing sands of the Palestinian region and of the empty, desolate places, void of human life for the most part.

Now, remember the stark, black-and-white images of starving, dying people you've seen on documentary footage of the death camps called Auschwitz, Buchenwald, Dachau, Mauthasen, Sachsenhausen, and Treblinka. Remember the trenches, the bulldozers, the skeletal forms beneath loose, pasty-white skin. See again the corpses intermingling and meshing together, rolling over each other as the bulldozers pushed the bodies into the ditch-like common graves.

Recall the scenes of the Allied commander, Dwight D. Eisenhower, as he and his staff walked among the pathetic, stick-like, human figures following the liberation of the concentration camps. See again the German people—robust and well fed, even though bone weary of war. Picture them in your mind's eye as they held handkerchiefs to their noses, some of them weeping, others retching, and still others trying to leave the lines in which they were forced to walk while viewing the rotting bodies of the dead Jews.

Remember all this as you put yourself, for one moment, in the place of God's prophet, Ezekiel:

> The hand of the LORD was upon me, and carried me out in the spirit of the LORD, and set me down in the midst of the valley which was full of bones,
>
> And caused me to pass by them round about: and, behold, there were very many in the open valley; and, lo, they were very dry.
>
> And he said unto me, Son of mart, can these bones live? And I answered, O Lord God, thou knowest.
>
> Again he said unto me, Prophesy upon these bones, and say unto them, O ye dry bones, hear the word of the LORD.
>
> Thus saith the LORD GOD unto these bones; Behold, I will cause breath to enter into you, and ye shall live.
>
> And I will lay sinews upon you, and will bring up flesh upon

you, and cover you with skin, and put breath in you, and ye shall live; and ye shall know that I am the LORD.

So I prophesied as I was commanded: and as I prophesied, there was a noise, and behold a shaking, and the bones came together, bone to its bone.

And when I beheld, lo, the sinews and the flesh came up upon them, and the skin covered them above: but there was no breath in them.

Then said he unto me, Prophesy unto the wind, prophesy, son of man, and say to the wind, Thus saith the LORD GOD; Come from the four winds, 0 breath, and breathe upon these slain, that they may live.

So I prophesied as he commanded me, and the breath came into them, and they lived, and stood up upon their feet, an exceeding great army.

Then he said unto me, Son of man, these bones are the whole house of Israel: behold, they say, Our bones are dried, and our hope is lost: we are cut off for our parts.

Therefore prophesy and say unto them, Thus saith the LORD GOD; Behold, O my people, I will open your graves, and cause you to come up out of your graves, and bring you into the land of Israel. (Ezekiel 37:1–12)

The Nazis would have built their Reich atop ground filled with the dry bones of God's people of destiny. Adolf Hitler, Heinrich Himmler, Joseph Goebbels, Hermann Goering, Reinhard Heydrich, Martin Bormann, and the other elitist, Aryan monsters of the Third Reich fired the engines of satanic, ideological hatred with the skeletal remains of more than six million of the house of Israel. The Final Solution, once and for all, would have rid the world of the despised Jew. Instead, Hitler's ashes were scattered in the bloody soil of German shame. The bones of all the other Nazi diabolists are strewn in ignominy…who knows where. Yet, the Jew remains, thrives, and prospers in every facet of life from the arts to industry, medicine, science, and beyond.

"Never Again!"

God began His chosen nation's restoration to Palestine nearly a century before the Nazi beast began its genocidal work. Migration, though a trickle at first, began about 1838. The revival of national Jewish life in that land started in earnest in 1878.

Then came the event that distinguishes it as perhaps the most important signal that Apocalypse is near, that Armageddon approaches. Jerusalem was reclaimed for the Jew in precisely the manner the prophet Isaiah had foretold more than 2,700 years earlier: "As birds flying, so will the Lord of hosts defend Jerusalem; defending also he will deliver it; and passing over he will preserve it" (Isaiah 31:5).

In 1917, General Edmund Allenby, commander of occupied Palestine for the British Empire, was ordered to take Jerusalem for the Jews. He found the city in possession of the Turks. To take the city by force meant risking initiation of hostilities that might so inflame the region as to cause a massive conflict to result. Bloodshed could have raised the indignation of the whole world.

Allenby, seeking advice from his government, was told to use his own judgment. He again contacted his superiors, who told him to pray, offering no further counsel in the matter. Allenby then ordered the commander of a fleet of airplanes to fly over Jerusalem. This action so terrified the Turks, who had never seen aircraft, that they surrendered the city without a shot being fired.

Isaiah's prophecy was thus fulfilled: "As birds flying," God "delivered" Jerusalem; the city was "'defended" while aircraft "passed over."

As a result of this action, the Balfour Declaration was signed on November 2, 1917, recognizing Palestine as the rightful homeland for the Jew. The regathering began to take on new dimensions. So, too, did the ugliness of anti-Semitism.

Hatred for the Jew seemed driven by dynamics that transcended reason, reaching fever pitch in Germany on the evenings of November 9 and 10, 1938. During these "Crystal Nights," as they have become known, Jewish homes and businesses were ravaged and destroyed, and many Jewish people were brutally assaulted.

Nazi inner-circle members haughtily termed it the "Week of Broken Glass." Hitler's plan, taken from the pages of his prison-dictated writings, *Mein Kampf,* had taken root. The persecution had become full blown.

From the valley of dry bones—the crematorium/gas-chamber hells of Nazi Europe—arose a God-breathed spirit that screamed then and screams still, "Never again!" The crucible of Holocaust tempered a people for the rebirth prophesied almost three millennia earlier.

Modern Israel was born on May 14,1948. The Jews have miraculously prospered. From a people near extinction in 1945, they are today the focal nation of the world. Surely, Israel is the primary sign that God's prophetic clock approaches the midnight hour.

The Time of Jacob's Trouble

Saddam Hussein's demented obsession to become a twentieth-century Nebuchadnezzar, through the elimination of Israel, was short-circuited by unseen forces greater than those of the United Nation coalition, valiant though those men and women were. Israel in the twenty-first is being compressed and funneled into an unalterable course. It will be a forced march that, for the last few years of human history, will cause Jewish people to wish they could trade their plight for even that suffered by their ancestors during the Holocaust of the Nazi death-camp years.

> Alas! for that day is great, so that none is like it: it is even the time of Jacob's trouble. (Jeremiah 30:7)

For then shall be great tribulation, such as was not since the beginning of the world to this time, no, nor ever shall be. (Matthew 24:21)

What will set in motion for the world in general and Israel in particular a time described by Jesus Himself as the worst mankind has ever known? There is an event that brings forth Apocalypse from the self-assured smugness of man's effort to at last establish world peace and safety.

For when they shall say, Peace and safety; then sudden destruction cometh upon them, as travail upon a woman with child; and they shall not escape. (1 Thessalonans 5:3)

Prophetic Peace Process

In Daniel 9:27, the prophet Daniel speaks of the event and the time that will begin human history's final seven years, called the time of Jacob's trouble by Jeremiah:

And he shall confirm the covenant with many for one week: and in the midst of the week he shall cause the sacrifice and the oblation to cease, and for the overspreading of abominations he shall make it desolate, even until the consummation, and that determined shall be poured upon the desolate.

To see the awesome import of this prophecy, one must understand that it relates directly to what Jesus Christ said in expounding on that most terrible time. The abomination of desolation is a future dictator whose record of atrocity will make Hitler, Stalin, Mao, and all other preceding tyrants seem hardly worthy of mention.

Jesus' words on this dictator are recorded in Matthew 24:15–16.

Confirming the words of Jeremiah and Daniel, He is speaking to the
Jews of Palestine at the end of the age:

> When ye therefore shall see the abomination of desolation, spo-
> ken of by Daniel the prophet, stand in the holy place, (whoso
> readeth, let him understand:)
>   Then let them which be in Judea flee into the mountains.

These words foretell the Temple that must stand atop Moriah during the midpoint of the seven years of Tribulation. The "holy place" the
Antichrist will desecrate, according to Jesus, must be constructed directly
upon the place atop the Temple Mount where the Holy of Holies was
located. This is the exact, fifteen-foot-cubed spot where the Ark of the
Covenant once rested within Solomon's Temple.

Notice that immediately before the time of unprecedented terror, a
"covenant with many" is negotiated. The "many" in this passage are the
Jews—the nation Israel—who returned after their dispersion. It is the
Israel born in a single day, May 14, 1948.

Do we see any evidence today of a peace process in which Israel is
involved in a major way?

Saddam Hussein, before the Persian Gulf crisis was enjoined by the
United Nation coalition forces, reported a dream in which he said the
prophet Mohammed appeared to him and told him that in the event of
war, he—Saddam—had his Scud missiles pointed in the wrong direction. "Oh, great prophet," Saddam asked the figure in his dream, "which
way should they be pointed?"

The prophet answered, "You know which direction to point them."
Israel was Saddam Hussein's real target all those years ago and it remains
the target of every anti-Israeli nation and organization in the world
today. Jerusalem and that tiny nation are the thorns in the side of the
chaotic, incendiary, militant, Arab conglomerate. Even so, the Palestinian homeland issue is merely a rifle scope through which to focus the
hostility.

Center of the Storm

What is the true source of the world's rage against Israel?

> And there appeared a great wonder in heaven—a woman....
>
> And she, being with child, cried, travailing in birth, and pained to be delivered.
>
> And there appeared another wonder in heaven; and behold a great red dragon....
>
> and the dragon stood before the woman who was ready to be delivered, for to devour her child as soon as it was born.
>
> And she brought forth a male child, who was to rule all nations...and her child was caught up unto God, and to his throne. (Revelation 12:1–5)

Here is the nucleus of the geopolitical storm gathering in the Middle East. More than a mortal storm, it is a cosmic, universal maelstrom of eternal consequence. Lucifer stirs the black, brewing tempest that will soon unleash his fury into man's final war. His hatred for the people through whom God chose to give fallen man His supreme love gift, His only begotten Son, Jesus Christ, in order that people can be reconciled to the Creator, grows more intense and more manifest by the hour.

The Jews and the nation Israel are the centerpiece of the Mideast turmoil. Why? Because they are at the center of the struggle over which man and his intellect have philosophized since antiquity but have never comprehended. The conflict is between good and evil. Many governments have tried to deal with the trouble in this region. Some seemed for a time to succeed. But, the ancient conflict goes on, and more and more often, it inflames to the point of eruption.

The wars are legendary. Modern Israel, though surrounded on three fronts by forces thirty times greater and backed against the Mediterranean Sea, has not only survived major assaults in 1956, 1967, and 1973—in fact, it was born in the midst of battle in 1948—but it has miraculously and completely routed the enemies each time while gaining additional territory. Now, Israel faces a subtle aggression, but one much more virulent and dangerous. Diplomatic cries for peace and safety through a negotiated solution to the problem of a homeland for the Palestinian refugees are becoming demands. The "Palestinian problem," the diplomats say almost without exception, "is the key to war and peace."

The Conquering Leader

Out of all these peace-making efforts, a leader from a reunited Europe is coming who will go "forth conquering, and to conquer" (Revelation 6:2). "There was given unto him a mouth speaking great things" (Revelation 13:5). This person will come riding a white horse as peacemaker and will confirm the "covenant with many" for one week. Translation: This leader from a Europe united in a configuration equivalent to the Europe of the Roman Empire days—a revived Roman Empire, a neo-Roman order, of sorts—will make a covenant treaty Israel will sign.

The pact will be for seven years, with one year equaling one day of the seven-day week indicated in the Scriptures. The "conquering" the leader will do at this point no doubt will be in the realm of diplomacy. Undoubtedly, he will offer brilliant initiatives, magnified by his charismatic, personal charm that convinces Jews and Arabs alike to trust him as a friend of all. As the guarantor of the peace not just for that region, but for a global peace upon which can be built a New World order and a new age of prosperity, he will succeed where others have failed. His promises will be sweet to the ears of a world ravenous for such lies.

And lies they will be.

Globe-trotting exploits by would-be peacemakers have met with fates ranging from abject failure to moderate, though temporary, success. Recall documentary films of the well-intentioned but fuzzy-thinking

Neville Chamberlain holding up the piece of paper Hitler duped him into believing was the megalomaniac's true desire for "peace for our time." Henry Kissinger impressed us mightily many years ago with his seeming inexhaustible energy while pursuing an honorable peace in Vietnam. Even his brilliant efforts ultimately faded and failed. Secretary of State James A. Baker III of the Bush administration eclipsed even Kissinger's air mileage as he jetted in and out of the capitals of the world in search of a formula that might defuse the Middle East time bomb. He, too, failed to secure the lasting peace the world hungers for.

Groundwork is being laid for peace. But it will be a peace that will "destroy many," according to Daniel. It will be a false peace foisted on the world by the greatest deceiver in human history.

America's well-meaning diplomacy, demanding that Israel give up its God-promised land for a peace agreement, might be the effort that clears the pathway for the Final Führer to perform his diabolical work when his time comes to step onto the world stage. But Christians are not looking for the Antichrist. Rather, they are looking for Jesus Christ, who will "descend from heaven."

> Then we which are alive and remain [until His secret coming in the clouds above the earth] shall be caught up together with them [those who have died during the age since Christ's redemptive work on the cross] in the clouds, to meet the Lord in the air: and so shall we ever be with the Lord. (1 Thessalonians 4:17)

Israel is beset on all sides with demands that they submit to a peace process that will prevent their own expansion while giving the Palestinians a homeland and the world relief from the constant tensions in the region. This is the clear signal that the end has already begun!

Allowing building the Third Temple will most likely be a major part of establishing the false covenant of peace that the man of sin will confirm.

SIX

America's Astonishing Appointment

IN THINKING ON the building of the Third Temple, we must examine America's juxtaposition to Israel's rebirth May 14, 1948. The hand of God has been so obviously on the situation as to designate it accurately as a miracle.

The Jewish state has returned after dispersion in AD 135. Its coming back into nationhood is a supernatural orchestration by the master director in Heaven. To begin comprehending the scope of the miraculous return and America's part in the nation being back in its ancient land, we need to understand the prophetic implications.

Many who look at world conditions and examine the issues and events of our time believe they are witnessing Bible prophecy being fulfilled. Things seem aligned geopolitically, socioeconomically, religiously, and in most any other category of end-times signals one might care to examine.

It is relatively easy to make the case that Bible prophecy is being fulfilled today. As previously indicated, Jesus' Olivet Discourse seems to outline almost without exception each of the many things leaping from today's news headlines. For example, He gave end-times prophecies in answer to His disciples' questioning:

> And as he sat upon the mount of Olives, the disciples came unto him privately, saying, Tell us, when shall these things be? and what shall be the sign of thy coming, and of the end of the world?
>
> And Jesus answered and said unto them, Take heed that no man deceive you.
>
> For many shall come in my name, saying, I am Christ; and shall deceive many.
>
> And ye shall hear of wars and rumours of wars: see that ye be not troubled: for all these things must come to pass, but the end is not yet.
>
> For nation shall rise against nation, and kingdom against kingdom: and there shall be famines, and pestilences, and earthquakes, in divers places.
>
> All these are the beginning of sorrows. (Matthew 24:3–8)

Fulfilled Prophecies?

Jesus answered some of His closest disciples' questions by foretelling the signals that would immediately precede His Kingdom coming into its full authority and power. He said:

1) People would come in His name, claiming He is Christ, but they would be deceivers.
2) There would be unusually widespread wars.
3) There would be rumors of even greater wars.
4) Nations would rise in conflict against other nations.
5) Kingdoms would be in conflict with other kingdoms.
6) There would be famines.

7) There would be diseases and other natural disorders.

8) There would be earthquakes occurring in many places.

Jesus called these events the "time of sorrows" in language comparing the prophetic signals to the labor of a woman who is about to deliver her baby.

A Closer Examination

1. *False prophets and false teachers*—Jesus foretold that many people would come saying, "I am Christ." The meaning of this is twofold. First, people will come declaring that they are speaking in Christ's name. They will say that Christ is Lord. Second, people will come on the scene claiming to be Christ, or to have the "Christ spirit." But, these will be deceivers.

Certainly, many today claim they come in the name of Jesus Christ, but they deny that He is the only way to redemption (see John 14:6). The New Age movement and some religions that don't fit the biblical prescription for true Christianity—for example, Scientology—are prominent in the news, with celebrities like Tom Cruise and John Travolta leading the way. These don't hold Jesus Christ forth as the only way to salvation. Rather, they simply invoke His holy name, then preach human-centered ways to redemption.

Other false prophets and teachers say that they themselves are the Christ. One such well-known guru during recent decades has been the one called Lord Matreya, with his John the Baptist-type false prophet, Benjamin Creme, pointing to him as the Christ.

2. *Widespread wars*—Jesus said that just before He comes again, war will be rampant upon the earth. His words indicate unprecedented bloodshed. World Wars I and II were the most horrific ever, with WW II concluding only after hundreds of thousands of Japanese civilians were killed by atomic bombs dropped by American planes on Hiroshima and Nagasaki. Adolf Hitler's rage against the Jews ended with as many as six

million of God's chosen people murdered in the Holocaust. The twenti-eth century saw violence through war as no other era in human history.

3. *Rumors of war*—Following WWII, fear of nuclear war became part of the psyche of America and the world. The Bikini Island H-bomb tests—as well as archived films of the explosions over Alamagordo, New Mexico, then upon Japan—combined with knowledge that the inter-continental ballistic missiles (ICBMs) could carry thermonuclear pay-loads to get across the point that death from the sky could be upon everyone in a matter of minutes.

The worry of such horrific devastation being less than a half hour away made every rumor of potential conflict a matter of personal con-cern. We live under an even greater cloud of uncertainty at this hour, with rumors of terrorists possessing weapons of mass destruction.

4. *Nations rising against nations*—This is one of the more profound indicators of Bible prophecy juxtaposed against the realities of our times. The word used for "nation" in Jesus' Olivet Discourse is from the Greek word *ethnos,* which translates to "ethnic" in English. Jesus was saying that ethnic group rising against ethnic group would mark the time just before He returns to Planet Earth.

No matter which way we turn to observe what is happening in the socioeconomic and geopolitical arenas in today's world, the central aspect of conflict between peoples involves race, just as Jesus predicted.

We think on the ethnic elements of recent wars and know the pro-found truth of Jesus' words of prophecy. The Serbs/Croatians, Turks/Armenians, Arabs/Jews, and many other ethnic disputes ring the globe. In America, the senseless violence among rival youth gangs is steeped in ethnic differences. America, land of the free, increasingly suffers from ethnic rages that rob people of liberty and even of life through drive-by shootings and bloody battles just for the sake of racial pride.

Armageddon will have racial hatreds at its core. The Oriental world will invade the Occidental when the two-hundred-million-man force from east of the Euphrates invades the Middle East.

5. *Kingdoms rising against kingdoms*—This has been a human history-long problem for mankind: nationalism, steeped in lust for what other nations possess; dictator-spawned hatreds and greed. These and other fallen humanistic evils make this prophecy one that was in process even as Jesus gave it. The Lord, of course, was foretelling a greater conflict between kingdoms than those in which even the Romans had engaged in order to build the world-dominating empire it enjoyed during Christ's time.

6. *Famines*—There have been many great famines since Jesus foretold this horror as marking the very end of the age. Two world wars caused massive starvation and suffering, but dictatorships of more recent vintage, combined with the natural harshness of arid lands like that of Ethiopia, the Sudan, etc., have caused starvation that can only be described as apocalyptic. Jesus indicates a time of famine that even makes those just described seem relatively mild by comparison.

7. *Pestilence*—Planet Earth has seen humanity-staggering pestilence. The Bubonic Plague that caused the Black Death during the Middle Ages, outbreaks of cholera and other diseases that have killed millions—these are pestilences we've all heard about, but haven't experienced so much in this generation. AIDS is a plague/pestilence we think about today. This disease threatens to wipe out entire nations in Africa. Yet, the Lord foretold a time when the thing called "pestilence" will become much worse, and we can hardly imagine the role that modern bioweapons in the hands of terrorist laboratories or rogue nations could play (at any moment) to spawn these end-times plagues.

8. *Earthquakes*—Much controversy rumbles throughout the prophecy-watching community today about this indicator. Earthquakes are being reported from most every point on the globe. It seems the whole planet is quaking to one degree or another. Some say the greater profusion is due to better detection and reporting in these technological times. Others believe the planet is convulsing in testimony to Christ's soon return.

The magnitude of the tremblors experienced just in the twentieth and twenty-first centuries have indeed been impressive. The 1964 9.2 Alaska quake and the 2004 9-plus shaking in the Indian Ocean that spawned the tsunami that killed more than a quarter of a million people mark this as the most pronounced era of reported earthquakes, to be sure.

The Sure Indicator

An increasing number of people who consider themselves students of Bible prophecy are putting forth that the signals, as enumerated and explored above, signify that those prophecies given by Jesus are occurring today, as reported in daily news accounts. Prophecy IS being fulfilled in our time, is their declaration.

Although the issues and events inundating our daily lives look quite like the prophecies Jesus foretold, some, including this author, don't believe the things we are seeing now are the exact matters about which the Lord spoke. This opinion is based upon many factors that would involve an extensive body of scriptural explanation. Space limitations require stating only that rather than seeing actual Tribulation or apocalyptic events happening right now, this generation is witnessing the *stage being set* for what Jesus foretold.

The Great Storm of Apocalypse

The best way to describe where we are as an end-of-days generation is to liken our perspective to looking out across a great plain, such as that found in Oklahoma. We can see all the way across the flat distance to the horizon.

Boiling on that vast horizon are ominous, black clouds. The closer the storm gets, the more we can see the wicked, jagged flickering of lightning. We sense the audible distant rumbles, and soon our ears are assaulted by thunderous crashes of violence rushing our way.

These represent the many prophetic signals Jesus foretold. We are not yet inside that great apocalyptic tempest, but we certainly recognize that it will soon overtake our still relatively tranquil surroundings.

The world stage is setting up for the era about which Jesus said: "For then shall be great tribulation, such as was not since the beginning of the world to this time, no, nor ever shall be" (Matthew 24:21).

The Exception?

There is an exception to every rule, so the saying goes. Even God's Word sometimes has exceptions to the rules it contains. But this never happens in the case of unalterable truth, such as the following: "Neither is there salvation in any other: for there is none other name under heaven given among men, whereby we must be saved" (Acts 12:4).

The exception to the rule in the case of end-times prophecies not being fulfilled during the current dispensation (Church Age) might well be Israel once again being a nation.

Modern Israel's rebirth can be likened to Jesus being the only way to salvation. Israel being back in the Land of Promise, with Hebrew once again the national language, is the dramatic manifestation of God's inalterable truth. Israel will be His nation forever. Promises God made to Israel, highlighted in the list below, are key to understanding His never-failing truth about the security of Israel's future.

God's first promises to Abraham about a nation:

- "Unto thy seed will I give this land" (Genesis 12:7a).
- "I will establish my covenant between me and thee and thy seed after thee in their generations for an everlasting covenant,

to be a God unto thee, and to thy seed after thee. And I will give unto thee, and to thy seed after thee, the land wherein thou art a stranger, all the land of Canaan, for an everlasting possession; and I will be their God" (Genesis 17:7–8).

God's promises that His covenant with Israel is unconditional:

- "If his children forsake my law, and walk not in my judgments; If they break my statutes, and keep not my commandments; Then will I visit their transgression with the rod, and their iniquity with stripes. Nevertheless my lovingkindness will I not utterly take from him, nor suffer my faithfulness to fail. My covenant will I not break, nor alter the thing that is gone out of my lips. Once have I sworn by my holiness that I will not lie unto David. His seed shall endure for ever, and his throne as the sun before me. It shall be established for ever as the moon, and as a faithful witness in heaven. Selah" (Psalm 89:30–37).
- "Thus saith the LORD, which giveth the sun for a light by day, and the ordinances of the moon and of the stars for a light by night, which divideth the sea when the waves thereof roar; The LORD of hosts is his name: If those ordinances depart from before me, saith the LORD, then the seed of Israel also shall cease from being a nation before me for ever" (Jeremiah 31:35–36).
- "Now the LORD had said unto Abram, Get thee out of thy country, and from thy kindred, and from thy father's house, unto a land that I will shew thee: And I will make of thee a great nation, and I will bless thee, and make thy name great; and thou shalt be a blessing: And I will bless them that bless thee, and curse him that curseth thee: and in thee shall all families of the earth be blessed" (Genesis 12:1-3).

God's promises regarding Abraham's idea for Ishmael, versus God's plan:

- "And Abraham said unto God, O that Ishmael might live before thee!" (Genesis 17:18).
- "And God said, Sarah thy wife shall bear thee a son indeed; and thou shalt call his name Isaac: and I will establish my covenant with him for an everlasting covenant, and with his seed after him" (Genesis 17:19).

God's revelation of His plan for the land/nation to Jacob:

- "And, behold, the LORD stood above it, and said, I am the LORD God of Abraham thy father, and the God of Isaac: the land whereon thou liest, to thee will I give it, and to thy seed; And thy seed shall be as the dust of the earth, and thou shalt spread abroad to the west, and to the east, and to the north, and to the south: and in thee and in thy seed shall all the families of the earth be blessed. And, behold, I am with thee, and will keep thee in all places whither thou goest, and will bring thee again into this land; for I will not leave thee, until I have done that which I have spoken to thee of" (Genesis 28:13–15).

God's words to Moses:

- "Behold, I have set the land before you: go in and possess the land which the LORD sware unto your fathers, Abraham, Isaac, and Jacob, to give unto them and to their seed after them" (Deuteronomy 1:8).

God's words to Joshua:

- "Moses my servant is dead; now therefore arise, go over this Jordan, thou, and all this people, unto the land which I do give to them, even to the children of Israel. Every place that the sole of your foot shall tread upon, that have I given unto you, as I said unto Moses. From the wilderness and this Lebanon even unto the great river, the river Euphrates, all the land of the Hittites, and unto the great sea toward the going down of the sun, shall be your coast.... Be strong and of a good courage: for unto this people shalt thou divide for an inheritance the land, which I sware unto their fathers to give them" (Joshua 1:2–4, 6).

God's promise to return Israel to the land:

- "And yet for all that, when they be in the land of their enemies, I will not cast them away, neither will I abhor them, to destroy them utterly, and to break my covenant with them: for I am the LORD their God. But I will for their sakes remember the covenant of their ancestors, whom I brought forth out of the land of Egypt in the sight of the heathen, that I might be their God: I am the LORD" (Leviticus 26:44–45).
- "And I will bring again the captivity of my people of Israel, and they shall build the waste cities, and inhabit them; and they shall plant vineyards, and drink the wine thereof; they shall also make gardens, and eat the fruit of them. And I will plant them upon their land, and they shall no more be pulled up out of their land which I have given them, saith the LORD thy God" (Amos 9:14–15).

The Israel/America Miracle

The reestablishment of Israel in the land God promised His chosen people validates that God's promises never fail. This is the one element that can verify fulfillment of prophecy in our day. Israel's amazing relationship with America, likewise, gives the United States considerable credence as a nation of prophetic destiny.

Consider the profound assurances given Israel by God through Moses, in light of Israel being cut off as a nation occupying the land the Lord gave the Jews. Remember, this is a people who were scattered throughout the world and persecuted—without a country or a common language—for almost two millennia! "That then the Lord thy God will turn thy captivity, and have compassion upon thee....and will return and will gather thee from all the nations, whither the Lord thy God hath scattered thee. And the Lord thy God will bring thee into the land which thy fathers possessed, and thou shalt possess it" (Deuteronomy 30:3, 5).

A Stunning Fulfillment?

Isaiah the prophet was given view down the corridor of time to see God's people scattered, violently mistreated, and then brought back together as one. Ezekiel the prophet foresaw a similar thing in the prophecy about the valley of dry bones recorded in Ezekiel 37. Isaiah's is remarkably more dramatic than other prophecies—even than Ezekiel's vision—because of the stunning precision with which his prophecy was given, and, I believe, with which it came to pass.

As stated previously, Israel is the one sign Jesus gives that seems most directly to signal the beginning of the end. We have been living a part of that dramatic sign since May 14, 1948, when the nation of Israel was born in a single day.

The Center of the Storm

The true source of the world's rage against Israel is summed up in Revelation 12:1–5, as related earlier. This is the nucleus of the geopolitical storm presently gathering in the Middle East. More than a mortal storm, it is a cosmic, universal maelstrom of eternal consequence.

Lucifer stirs the black, brewing tempest that will soon unleash his fury into man's final war. His hatred for the people through whom God chose to give fallen man His supreme love gift, His only begotten Son, Jesus Christ, so they could be reconciled to the Creator, grows more intense and more manifest by the hour.

The Jews, the nation Israel, are the centerpiece of the Middle East turmoil. Why? Because they are at the center of that struggle over which man and his intellect have philosophized since antiquity but have never comprehended. The struggle is between good and evil. Many governments have tried to deal with the trouble in this region. Some seemed for a time to succeed in their efforts. But the ancient conflict goes on, and more and more often, it inflames to the point of eruption.

Israel, America's Saving Grace

This brings us to America's second-most important reason for existence—second only to this nation's destiny in broadcasting the gospel of Jesus Christ to the whole world. In my view, this secondary use of the phenomenally powerful American nation is among the most profound indicators we can find that America, indeed, is in Bible prophecy. God is using America to be midwife in Israel's modern birth into the land promised to Abraham, Isaac, and Jacob those thousands of years ago.

President Harry S. Truman insisted, despite many voices of opposition, that the embryo country still in the womb of the Holy Land, Israel, come to birth on May 14, 1948. America stood by Israel's struggle to get to its feet and its battles against its attacking, hatred-filled enemy neighbors.

God's hand was at work in unseen ways during the times leading up to Truman's presidency after Franklin D. Roosevelt died in 1945. Truman, who said he had read God's Word through a number of times, told those around him that the Jews had promises from God concerning the land. He apparently believed that America must bless, not curse, Israel. Historians would say that coincidentally, perhaps even ironically (yet certainly providentially), Truman had a Jewish friend—Edward Jacobson—with whom he had co-owned a haberdashery. His partner convinced Truman early on of that nation's prophetic destiny.

Although Israel now has its own nuclear arsenal, it is America—in human terms—that has provided the most military strength to discourage overwhelming assaults against the Jewish state. (Looking beyond the physical earthly protection for Israel, it is the Lord of Heaven who provides the ultimate hedge of protection.)

God has proved in war after war throughout Israel's earlier and latter incarnations that He keeps His promises to protect them from absolute destruction, despite their many diasporas and their tribulations as captives and/or outcasts. He uses human military to accomplish this promise that the Jew will always be His chosen people. But, many strange reports have come out of some of those battles proclaiming it was supernatural activity that turned the tide.

Reports of battles during Israel's rebirth as a nation in 1948, as an established nation in 1956, 1967, and 1973, brought such reports. And, at a spiritual warfare level in the sense of Ephesians 6:12, conflicts unseen by human eyes continue.

Christian Soldiers

Israel's nuclear capability and America's stupendous military and technological might are strong defensive ingredients for modern Israel's protection. But, while surrounded by forces of overwhelming numbers whose satanic rage cannot be stemmed, a most unconventional army is Israel's greatest ally.

This ally contingent holds the joint Israeli-American defensive coalition in place and in God's prophetic plan. It is a *spiritual force* that is Israel's closest friend. Christians, particularly those in America, make up the spiritual army that supports Israel's right to exist as does no other group on earth. This army doesn't bear physical arms or always fight literally on the bloody fields surrounding Israel. It fights with prayer for the peace of Jerusalem and does spiritual battle for Israel while that Jewish state moves in blind unrepentance toward its ultimate great destiny as the head of all nations during the Millennium, Christ's thousand-year reign on Planet Earth.

America Plunges While the Church Arises

America, the golden cup in the Lord's hand for more than two centuries—having disseminated the gospel to the world and having been the midwife of Israel's birth into modern times, then its protector—is not mentioned in Bible prophecy by name. However, supposedly lesser nations of history are mentioned, such as Persia (present-day Iran), Syria, and others. Many believe Russia fits into the region known in ancient times as the region called in Scripture "Rosh." But the once-shining city on the hill called America is nowhere to be found as the very end of days unfold.

So, what happens to the United States of America?

Not all born-again people believe Israel is God's chosen nation. Most Christians today don't even think in terms of Israel and its prophetic destiny one way or the other. This is because, in many cases, they aren't taught about these matters by their pastors and teachers. Also, they may not do enough study on their own so God the Holy Spirit can instruct them regarding Israel and prophecy.

So, it is a relatively small group that observes prophetic matters as outlined in God's Word. The others are ignorant of these things. Many are willfully ignorant.

No matter the tragic state of the spiritually weakened Church, God hasn't let slip from His mighty grasp upon the human condition the Israel/America miracle He began to form in history now long past. Be assured, those among the Heaven-bound, end-times Christians who do understand Israel's place in God's holy eyes are key to America's ultimate destiny.

Trump and Third Temple

The election of Donald J. Trump in 2016 has shaken up the geopolitical world as well as American politics and government. The most dramatic effects of the election, especially in prophetic terms, are those it has had upon Israel.

Soon after his election, Trump declared that the American Embassy would be moved from Tel Aviv to Jerusalem. It would be done on May 14, 2018, the seventieth anniversary of Israel becoming a nation again in 1948.

Since Trump's election, there has also been strange talk among Jewish religious authorities about exactly what role the new president might be assigned by the Higher Power in the matter of building of the Third Temple. The following news item is interesting in that regard:

> Our mouths shall be filled with laughter, our tongues, with songs of joy. Then shall they say among the nations, "Hashem has done great things for them!" Psalms 126:2 (*The Israel Bible*™)
>
> Rabbi Yosef Berger, the rabbi in charge of King David's Tomb on Mount Zion, revealed to *Breaking Israel News* a 600-year-old Jewish source stating that the Third Temple will be prepared by descendants of Edom as a "reparation" for destroying the Second Temple. Additional hints from esoteric sources indicate that US President Donald Trump has already begun this process.

"It sounds illogical that the Third Jewish Temple will be built by non-Jews," Rabbi Berger told *Breaking Israel News*. "But Rabbinic sources state explicitly that this is what they must do to fix the historic wrongs that were committed."

...Rabbi Berger also quoted Rabbi Bahya ben Asher ibn Halawa, a 13th century Spanish Biblical commentator also known as "Rabbeinu Behaye." The medieval scholar wrote that "the first and second Temples were built by the descendants of King David, but in the future, the Third Temple will be built by descendants of Edom.

Rabbi Berger emphasized that these sources state explicitly that the Third Temple will be built by the descendants of Rome, i.e. Christianity.

"Rabbeinu Behaye explained this is a *tikkun* (reparation). Rome destroyed the Second Temple so Rome's descendants, the Christians, are going to amend this by taking part in bringing the Third Temple."

Rabbi Berger's point of view includes that President Trump's election has started a Messianic process and notes that the *gematria* of Trump's name in Hebrew (טראמפ דונלד) equals 424—which is the value of the phrase, "*Moshiach* (Messiah) from the House of David (דוד בן משיח).

He also says, "Trump's connection to the Messiah is that he will play a role in one of the major functions of the Messiah. He will pave the way for building the Third Temple" and that Trump is the "representative of Edom that will perform that final historic reparation for his entire nation by building the Temple."

Rabbi Berger however, believes that despite strengthening the connection between the two countries and recognizing Jerusalem as Israel's capital, continuing the process will be more difficult but will yield much greater results.[109]

Another news item further clarifies the Jewish clerics' thoughts on Trump and the Third Temple:

President Donald Trump's epic proclamation…acknowledging Jerusalem as the eternal capital of the Jewish people was a major step towards establishing the Third Temple and bringing the Messianic era, said a number of Jewish activists working to rebuild the Holy Temple.… "There have been amazing advances towards bringing the Temple this year. It was clear that Trump was part of that process, guided by Hashem (God)," Fried declared.[110]

Yakov Hayman comments further on the Temple's rebuilding: "These processes are codependent. It depends on the Jews, our actions, but the non-Jews are an essential part of the process."

"Our task is to act as priests to make the whole world holy," Hayman said, citing Exodus, "You shall be to Me a kingdom of priests and a holy nation" (Exodus 19:6).

"That will only happen in a Temple in Jerusalem," he emphasized. "The next step, the most important step, must be taken by the Jews. We need to begin going up to the Temple Mount in massive numbers. Once we do that, the Temple is the next inevitable step."

He noted that Trump's personality is uniquely suited for the role of the non-Jewish leader who begins the Messianic process.

"There is something very special and holy in Trump," Hayman said. "Sometimes, he appears coarse and not connected to religion, but every time he addresses the nation he speaks about God. Last night, he said his motivation for recognizing Jerusalem was because it was the right thing to do. That is precisely how a leader guided by God should speak."

Rabbi Hillel Weiss, spokesman for the nascent Sanhedrin, was cautiously optimistic:

"One year ago, the Sanhedrin called on Trump to build the Temple as Cyrus did 2,000 years ago," Rabbi Weiss told *Breaking Israel News*. "He has clearly moved in this direction but there is still a long way to go and many pitfalls that could prevent that from happening."

"Trump is facing enormous political pressures," Rabbi Weiss noted. "The borders of Jerusalem are still open to negotiation. The Temple Mount is still not a settled issue and the United Nations is working hard at trying to convince the world the Jews have no place there. If Trump is to succeed, the Jews have to come together in unity in order for him to remain strong."[111]

seven

Globalists' Power Grab

GOD'S PROPHETIC WORD puts the finger of truth on the globalist ambition to establish rule apart from God.

> Why do the heathen rage, and the peoples imagine a vain thing?
> The kings of the earth set themselves, and the rulers take counsel together, against the LORD, and against his anointed, saying,
> Let us break their bands asunder, and cast away their cords from us. (Psalms 2:1–3)

One sure signal that God's Word is true is the nation Israel down through the ages. Even more specifically, the matter of building the Third Temple atop Mount Moriah—rather the resistance to building that structure—validates God's Word. As pointed out throughout this book, the Jewish people constitute the most hated, persecuted nation throughout history. Today, almost every country represented in the United Nations goes against the Jewish state in nearly every vote involving Israel's best interest.

Any talk of building a Jewish house of worship on the Temple Mount brings violence from Israel's enemies and touches off fears of Middle East—even worldwide—war. The Temple Mount is the one spot on the planet that, in the eyes of the world's diplomats, threatens to ignite nuclear conflict and World War III. It's as if Israel, Jerusalem, and the Temple Mount itself are the hold-up to world peace, safety, and unity.

The one-world anthems make the call to global unity sound so sensible, so inviting.

> Come, young citizens of the world, we are one, we are one
> Come, young citizens of the world, we are one, we are one
> We have one hope, we have one dream,
>   and with one voice we sing
> Peace, prosperity, and love for all mankind.

The lyrics to the above are set to an enchanting, rhythmic melody and are sung by a chorus of sweet-voiced children. Soon you are humming, then singing along. What could possibly be wrong with those sentiments so innocently expressed? Peace, prosperity, and love for all mankind—are these not among the most noble objectives?

Powerful humanistic allurements beckon seductively, promising a golden future if all of earth's people will come together as one. Such a glorious world order, long dreamed about and even fervently pursued, seems at last achievable. Those who hold the worldview that national boundaries must fall and sovereignties must diminish because we are all citizens of Planet Earth passionately embrace the earth-shrinking technologies such as the Internet that science continues to produce. Yes, the utopian dream at last seems achievable. However, while the sirens of globalism—like the twin sisters who lured unwary sailors to their deaths in Homer's *Odyssey*—sing their lovely, mesmerizing songs of New World Order, the words pronounced by the Ancient of Days reverberate through the corridors of antiquity and leap at this generation from the pages of God's Holy Word:

Behold, the people are one and they have all one language, and this they begin to do; and now nothing will be restrained from them which they have imagined to do. (Genesis 11:6)

The Creator of all things was not expressing His pride in His creation called man. God was concerned and saddened because all people of that time were united in their determination to build a world to their own specifications. And why was this very first globalist effort displeasing to the One who built into man the marvelous ability to do whatever he or she could imagine? Did not God Himself create us in His own image, infusing the creature with phenomenal creative drive?

The Cradle of Globalism

It seems at first glance a supreme paradox: The Creator made us in His own image, gifting us with powerful conceptual abilities, and thus with the ingenuity to build a tower that could ultimately reach into the heavens. Then, just as we began to fulfill our potential, the infallible Creator God manifested His displeasure in the people of that day as recorded here:

The whole earth was of one language and of one speech.

And it came to pass, as they journeyed from the east, that they found a plain in the land of Shinar, and they dwelt there.

And they said to one another, Come, let us make bricks and burn them thoroughly. And they had brick for stone, and slime had they for mortar.

And they said, Go to, let us build a city and a tower whose top may reach unto heaven; and let us make us a name, lest we be scattered abroad upon the face of the whole earth.

And the LORD came down to see the city and the tower, which the children of men built.

And the LORD said, Behold, the people are one and they have all one language, and this they begin to do; and now nothing will be restrained from them which they have imagined to do.

Come, let us go down and there confound their language, that they may not understand one another's speech.

So the LORD scattered them abroad from there upon the face of all the earth, and they left off building the city.

Therefore is the name of it called Babel, because the LORD did there confound the language of all the earth; and from there did the LORD scatter them abroad upon the face of all the earth. (Genesis 11:1–9)

When people used their God-given genius in this rebellious way, He confused that genius by disrupting their ability to communicate. Thereby He put an end to the globalist project. God's dealings with His creation seemed incongruous: Did He change His mind about having made people in His own image? Did He resent competition in matters involving the creativity this building project might have represented? Why did He break up the one-world building effort at Babel?

Image of God, Imagination of Man

God puts His mighty finger upon the answer to that question, piercing to the heart of the reason He had to destroy by Flood the entire antediluvian world except Noah, his family, and select animal life. The cause of why God scattered the Babel builders is found even farther back in human history than the era of the Flood:

The Lord smelled a sweet savor; and the Lord said in his heart, I will not again curse the ground anymore for man's sake; for the imagination of man's heart is evil from his youth; neither will I again smite anymore every thing living, as I have done. (Genesis 8:21)

The key thought from the mind of God for our purposes here is "the imagination of man's heart is evil from his youth." Let's examine this indictment in context.

God declared that He would never again curse the ground as He did after man's rebellion in the Garden of Eden. Neither, He said, would He ever again smite all living things as He did with the worldwide Flood of Noah's day. God placed between these two promises the statement of truth about the fallen state of man, a fact absolutely rejected by today's humanistic social architects. Their denial of this reality is at the core of globalism. So, too, is the demented assertion that man is evolving toward a higher order of being that will ultimately produce heaven on earth: peace, prosperity, and love for all mankind.

Adam and Eve's God-attuned senses must have changed from perfection to imperfection in one cataclysmic moment. What a heart-wrenching scene it must have been when they willfully disobeyed God, choosing instead to yield to the tempter, who told them they would be as God when they ate from the Tree of the Knowledge of Good and Evil. How devastating must have been that eternity-rending moment when those magnificently beautiful humans discarded the effulgence of God that had shrouded their nakedness. The image of God emanating from within their beings must have begun to change into frightening, darkened countenances. So, too, their minds no doubt convoluted within their sin-infected thought processes. Both image and imagination altered in that moment into a perpetual state of opposition to the Creator with whom they had previously walked in perfect trust and love along the Garden's lush pathways.

Mankind's course has been spiraling downward since that willful decision by the first man to do what was right in his own eyes rather than obey God. The Fall brought a curse upon Planet Earth and death to man. Every generation of people since Adam and Eve contributes ample proof that "the heart is deceitful above all things, and desperately wicked" (Jeremiah 17:9).

From the first murder, when Cain slew his brother Abel, to the slaughter during the more than fifteen thousand wars of recorded history, to the most recent terrorist atrocity or one-on-one killing, fallen humankind continues through vile actions to testify to the truth of God's indictment: "The imagination of man's heart is evil from his youth" (Genesis 8:21).

Babel Revisited

The mystery of the paradox is more understandable when we reconsider these fascinating facts. God, who is perfect in all His ways, created humankind perfectly, making us in His own image. Once again we realize that He gifted us with a powerful imagination so that whatever we could imagine, we could eventually do. However, when we began to use that imagination in building a tower that would reach into Heaven, God was displeased and stopped the project by confounding the language of the builders, then scattering them abroad. We again consider the question: If a perfect God created a perfect man, why did God act in such a seemingly harsh manner when the creature used God-given talent as recounted in the story of Babel?

The answer, of course, is that God also created us with free moral will. The creature was not made a robot, but was made with brilliant conceptual abilities, and was given freedom of choice—which includes discernment. But Adam chose to disobey God and so sin entered the world.

The human bloodstream became instantly contaminated by the infection. The minds of people, including their imaginations, became darkened in the mystery of iniquity that engulfed them.

The paradox understood, the question is now answerable: What is wrong with people coming together in a united effort to construct a one-

THE RABBIS, DONALD TRUMP, AND THE TOP-SECRET PLAN TO BUILD THE THIRD TEMPLE 135

world order with the objectives of achieving peace, prosperity, and love for all mankind? The answer is that we are spiritually separated from the Creator because of original sin. Our thinking is therefore fatally flawed. Nothing good can come from thinking and planning that excludes God.

Had God allowed the globalists of Nimrod's day to continue the tower project, He would have had to ultimately curse the Earth again as He did when Adam disobeyed, or He would have had to destroy all living things as He did because of the corruption that required cleansing by the great Flood of Noah's day. God was not acting harshly at Babel, nor was He acting contrary to His perfect character.

Rather, He was displaying unfathomable love by keeping His promises to the tiny fallen creatures who were deserving of judgment and for whom He would one day sacrifice His only begotten Son in order to redeem them.

The World Order Schemers

Children of the tower builders today carry on the globalist agenda despite the differences in language and geographical separation. They circumvent the barriers through technologies designed to serve their one-world purposes. The siren song grows louder: *We have one hope, we have one dream, and with one voice we sing., Peace, prosperity, and love for all mankind.*

The obsessive drive toward bringing all men, women, and children into one-world configuration arose shortly after the time Jesus Christ walked the earth. It is perhaps indicative of our sordid day that since that time, this era has been called "AD," for *anno domini*, which means "in the year of our Lord," but now we are to acknowledge that we live in the period of human history called the "common era," or "CE." The revisionists, you see, demand that all vestiges of Jesus Christ be erased from even our lexicon. There must be many ways for the people of the coming New World Order to come to God, if indeed there is one.

Jesus Christ, who said He is the Way, the Truth, and the Life, and that no one can come to the Father but by Him, simply does not fit the globalist mold. Thinkers who formed that mold wanted there to be no doubt that people, through our intellect, can do whatever we imagine. We can build a perfect world without input from any deity who might or might not be out there somewhere. This arrogant attitude of self-sufficiency is summed up in the document titled "The Declaration of Interdependence," released by the United Nations' World Affairs Council on January 30, 1976. It reads in part:

> Two centuries ago, our forefathers brought forth a new nation; now we must join with others to bring forth a new world order. To establish a new world order…it is essential that mankind free itself from limitations of national prejudice…. We affirm that the economy of all nations is a seamless web, and that no nation can any longer effectively maintain its processes for production and monetary systems without recognizing the necessity of collaborative regulation by international authorities. We call upon all nations to strengthen the United Nations and other institutions of world order.

The zeal for stampeding everyone into a totally controlled global village has not subsided. Elitist power brokers continue to fuel the humanist engine that drives the globalist machinery with grandiose declarations and promises of heaven on earth.

The Secretary General of Habitat II, the 1996 UN forum in Istanbul, Turkey, aimed at laying groundwork for the New World Order, predicted that there will be "a new beginning of the requests to implement the actions called for at this unprecedented continuum of global conferences that have marked the closing decade of this century." He then made this ominous statement: "A new global social contract for building sustainable human settlements must be forged for the new global urban world order." God's children through belief in His Son, Jesus

Christ, should not look with trepidation on these foreboding harbingers of the coming Tribulation period described by Jesus in the Olivet Discourse. However, it is abundantly obvious that developments we have seen in wave after wave of UN intrusions into the lives of Americans should make all of us know that real agendas and activities lie behind our concerns.

All the World as One

Neo-Babel builders construct even their music in a way that clearly demonstrates the luciferian desire to usurp God's throne. John Lennon's universally popular song could easily be mistaken as portraying the biblically prophesied millennial reign of Jesus Christ. But Lennon, like Lenin, preached man-made heaven on earth—an imitative mockery of the true Messiah's coming kingdom. The words and melody are infectious.

> Imagine there's no heaven
> It's easy if you try
> No hell below us/Above us only sky
> Imagine all the people/Living for today.
> Imagine there's no countries
> It isn't hard to do
> Nothing to kill or die for
> And no religion too
> Imagine all the people
> Living life in peace.
> You may say I'm a dreamer
> But I'm not the only one
> I hope someday you'll join us
> And the world will be as one.
> Imagine no possessions
> I wonder if you can

No need for greed or hunger
A brotherhood of man
Imagine all the people
Sharing all the world.
You may say I'm a dreamer
But I'm not the only one
I hope someday
you'll join us
And the world will live as one.

Globalism's siren song is a one-world anthem that the true child of God cannot follow to its murderous, destructive end. The Holy Spirit within us is the tether who binds us to the masthead of truth. With Jesus Christ as the Captain of our salvation, we navigate through the treacherous seas of our time.

Still, we must be alert and heed the wake-up call.

Globalist Storm Warning

The twenty-first century has brought great changes to American culture. It has been a spiraling out of control in most every facet of the nation's society. Movement away from God became so overt as to make the observant Christian question whether the Lord of Heaven had given up on the United States altogether.

Then, there seemed to come a calming, refreshing breeze that restored common sense in America with the election of November 8, 2016. The vicious, destructive winds of socialistic madness had begun to stir early in the twentieth century. They grew to full hurricane strength while being channeled through increasingly liberal legislative and judicial bodies, with powerful assistance from equally liberal media.

The storm raged throughout the nation's culture by the time the 1990s arrived. Occasional executive-branch resistance from 2001 to

2008 slowed it only momentarily while it roared against the country's rapidly weakening moral barriers.

Suddenly, just as the great storm seemed to reach its full fury, American voters arose in sufficient numbers, and the howling leftist assault was brought to a stunned calm for a time.

Many reasons have been suggested for the loud repudiation of liberal ideology and its influence upon America's governmental policies. Certainly, the electorate's majority voice unmistakably demanded that politicians begin serving the people in a way that benefits the nation rather than continue serving their own parochial interests at taxpayers' expense, as had been the case for decades.

But a sudden pulse of wind disrupted the calm only days after the people's actions in the voting booths brought the tempest to a standstill. The gust seemed to burst from out of nowhere.

A national dementia, manifested by a rage beyond anything that had been seen in the country, burst upon the scene with fury. Hatred of the newly elected president by the political left, enjoined by the mainstream media, both news and entertainment, brought charges against Donald J. Trump that have never been substantiated, even partially.

The rage remains as of this writing. It is satanic in its virulence. It threatens the very constitutional fabric of America as founded.

When the American voters swept the one-nation-under-godlessness liberal utopian schemers out the front door, the ejected ones quickly ran around the side of the house, where they joined with the globalist New World Order builders, who were being welcomed in the back door with eager smiles and open arms. I wrote an entire book on this phenomenon (which some believe to be my best, ever) titled *Saboteurs* (Defender Publishing, 2017).

These Deep State globalists, whose master is Lucifer the fallen one, enjoined the rage felt by the losers in the 2016 presidential race. Their plans for building their new world order had been slowed by an act of Heaven. The new president is an ardent anti-globalist who wants to "put America first," as his campaign slogan stated.

Under the guise of free trade, the one-world parasitic, global apparatus long ago began siphoning strength and resolve from this nation and others. The globalists elite now channel America's wealth, along with funds from other geopolitical and economic spheres, into Third-World countries at a rate greater than ever before. They constantly strive to solidify their one-world power base through material goods giveaways. They continue to create and consolidate an ever-increasing constituency dependent on the New World Order hierarchy for absolutely everything as those poorest of people move through their miserable lives from cradle to grave.

The one-world schemers would have us believe that all this *noblesse oblige* is being undertaken on behalf of humanity for humanity's own good: egalitarianism at its most glorious peak of achievement!

Mankind in general and Americans in particular fell prey to the sedative effects of globalism's siren song while the eye of the storm passed calmly overhead.

GATT (General Agreements on Tariffs and Trade) certainly was not perceived to be a storm warning by most; rather, it was proclaimed to be salvation for the economic stability of the world. God, however, is never fooled and cannot be sedated. He put out the storm warning long ago that just such a time in human history will arrive when an elitist ruling class will combine its power and authority to create a mechanism of control through which it will attempt to enslave every human being on the planet.

God's warning foretold that the world's authority and power will ultimately be given to one man, the world's last and most terrible despot (read Daniel 9:27, Revelation 13, and Revelation 17:12, 13).

What Is America's Role?

Those who analyze prophetic matters have long puzzled over why the United States of America is not mentioned specifically in God's prophetic Word. Certainly, there has never been a nation more blessed or more active in the spread of the gospel of Jesus Christ. Small and seemingly insignificant nations and regions like Libya and Ethiopia are recorded in passages of prophecy yet to be fulfilled, but not America.

A Reprieve for America?

To repeat the opening thought expressed at the beginning of this section: With the election of November 8, 2016, there seemed to come a calming, refreshing breeze that promised a return to government that serves the people rather than that seeks to rule with mastery over them. America seemed to have been given a reprieve from the death sentence the woolly-minded had pronounced upon religious and a growing number of other liberties. But how deep a commitment to return to those earlier, saner principles (and thus how realistic the reprieve) remains to be seen.

To those who have truly studied the Word of God, it is clear that man-made government that refuses to be guided by God's principles of morality will inevitably degenerate and fall to tyranny within its own borders or without. Political parties cannot muster the fortitude to either restrain or constrain the oppression and tyranny that incessantly seek to enslave. Government of, by, and for a moral people can ensure those inalienable rights which our forefathers fought, bled, and died to secure for us. It is we the people, under God, who must determine to govern wisely. President George Washington said in his farewell address, "Reason and experience both forbid us that national morality can prevail in exclusion of religious principle." John Adams, America's second president, said, "The United States Constitution was made only for a moral and religious people. It is wholly inadequate for the government of any other."

We must begin by governing our own lives in a way that is pleasing to the Creator. There is only one way to please Him, and that is to put ourselves under the lordship of His blessed Son, Jesus Christ, who shed His blood on the cross of Calvary for the remission of our sins. How wonderful it would be if not just the majority of American people but a majority of people throughout the entire world turned to Jesus Christ in humble repentance!

But, tragically, we can be certain that this will not happen prior to Christ's return. God in His omniscience tells us through His Holy Word that "in the last days perilous times shall come" and that "evil men and seducers will become worse and worse, deceiving and being deceived." The man who will be the world's last and most vicious tyrant is perhaps even now waiting in the shadows just beyond the spotlight's circle. He will take the crown given to him by his New World Order sycophants and use the platform of globalism they have erected to build a mono-lithic throne upon which he will ultimately sit, claiming to be deity while demanding worship.

Paving the Way for Antichrist

Today, movers and shakers in the world of global politics are paving the way for the world's last dictator, the Antichrist. They do so most likely oblivious to biblical prophecy. But whether wittingly or unwittingly, they rush headlong into that dark night of apocalypse.

Jerusalem, the Burdensome Stone

Globalism is the system of geopolitics, with the ideology at its center that desires exactly what God's declaration forbids. Today's so-called international community's rant against Israel, considering the Jewish state an *occupier* of the territory given by the Creator of all things to the Jewish people in perpetuity, is at the heart of the rebellious hatred that will eventuate in horrendous consequences. The utterance that frames the preciseness of this generation's position on God's prophetic timeline cannot be repeated too often:

> The burden of the word of the LORD for Israel, saith the LORD, which stretcheth forth the heavens, and layeth the foundation of the earth, and formeth the spirit of man within him.
>
> Behold, I will make Jerusalem a cup of trembling unto all the people round about, when they shall be in the siege both against Judah *and* against Jerusalem.
>
> And in that day will I make Jerusalem a burdensome stone for all people: all that burden themselves with it shall be cut in pieces, though all the people of the earth be gathered together against it. (Zechariah 12:1–3)

This is God's answer to the raging heathen who want Him off their backs:

> He that sitteth in the heavens shall laugh: the Lord shall have them in derision.
>
> Then shall he speak unto them in his wrath, and vex them in his sore displeasure.
>
> Yet have I set my king upon my holy hill of Zion.
>
> I will declare the decree: the LORD hath said unto me, Thou art my Son; this day have I begotten thee.
>
> Ask of me, and I shall give thee the heathen for thine inheritance, and the uttermost parts of the earth for thy possession.
>
> Thou shalt break them with a rod of iron; thou shalt dash them in pieces like a potter's vessel.
>
> Be wise now therefore, O ye kings: be instructed, ye judges of the earth.
>
> Serve the LORD with fear, and rejoice with trembling.

Kiss the Son, lest he be angry, and ye perish from the way, when his wrath is kindled but a little. Blessed are all they that put their trust in him. (Psalms 2:4–12)

The divine message is clear. The Lord Jesus Christ, not the rebellious world's choice as ruler, will ultimately sit on the throne established by the God of Heaven.

Third Temple Trickery

A careful study of what is coming, meantime, according to Bible prophecy, reveals that the Third Temple is destined to sit atop Mount Moriah. There's no getting around it.

Whether the Arabs, the Islamist world, the international community, or anyone else hates the very thought of a Temple of Jewish worship being built upon that promontory, it will be done. As a matter of fact, it will be the ultimately evolved globalist who, many prophecy students believe, will see to it that the Third Temple will be built.

Again, the primary Scriptures that many sense prove the point are the following.

And he shall confirm the covenant with many for one week: and in the midst of the week he shall cause the sacrifice and the oblation to cease, and for the overspreading of abominations he shall make it desolate, even until the consummation, and that determined shall be poured upon the desolate. (Daniel 9:27)

When ye therefore shall see the abomination of desolation, spoken of by Daniel the prophet, stand in the holy place, (whoso readeth, let him understand:) Then let them which be in Judaea flee into the mountains. (Matthew 24:15–16)

The Antichrist is referred to in the book of Daniel as "the prince that shall come" (Daniel 9:26). Daniel 9: 27 foretells that "he" will "confirm the covenant with many." The "he" is the "prince that shall come" of Daniel 9:27. Jesus calls this personage "the abomination of desolation" as recorded in Matthew 24:15. Therefore, it is reasonable to assume that the Antichrist will have something to do with the reconstruction of a Temple that he will enter and desolate.

Some claim the prophecy refers to the time of the initiation of the Maccabean Revolt in 168 BC when Antiochus IV Epiphanes entered the Second Temple and defiled it with swine blood and an idol. But, this occurred well before Jesus foretold that the "abomination of desolation" will stand in the "holy place"—the Third Temple—declaring himself to be God and demanding worship.

The conclusion to this volume deals much more in-depth with biblical proof texts of the Third Temple and its desecration.

The globalist drive to establish a new world order, likely unknown by most who are part of that drive, is a dark determination to establish Antichrist's reign on earth. The apex of that reign—obviously, in Satan's view—will be when his man of sin, the son of perdition, goes into the Third Temple and blasphemes God. Lucifer, since the rebellion in Heaven, has wanted to usurp the throne of God. This is as close as he will ever get. His chief desire is to rule over God's creation called *man* and, ultimately, destroy as many people as possible.

The insanity of the anti-Trump political ideology that has been witnessed since the 2016 presidential election is because the minions of Satan, both human and demonic, are enraged. The globalist drive has been slowed, their program for world domination temporarily neutered.

Thankfully, even though God's judgment upon sin is sure, He is also slow to anger and His mercy is great. It appears that we are currently in a lull that God has graciously granted just before the prophesied end-of-time storm that will devastate a wrath-deserving generation. Even so, a brisk wind is already snapping the flag of warning that apocalypse approaches.

God the Holy Spirit earnestly and tenderly beckons all who will heed His call to take shelter within the only harbor where protection from the deadly whirlwind to come can be found. That safe harbor is Jesus Christ. Those who refuse to accept the haven of safety offered by Christ will perish beneath the raging, crashing surge as surely as did the antediluvians during the judgment of Noah's day.

eight

Trump Transfers Embassy

BIBLE PROPHECY OBSERVERS of the Middle East and Israel view the move of the American Embassy from Tel Aviv to Jerusalem with great interest and, in some cases, much trepidation. The American government has for some time officially approved the transfer. However, nations have not recognized Jerusalem as Israel's capital, thus US presidents have routinely postponed the relocation.

A Brief History

America's involvement in dealing with Israel has displayed a degree of schizophrenia of sorts—a split personality. The US is responsible more than any other nation for bringing the Jewish state back into existence. At the same time, America has seemed to oppose the progress of Israel fulfilling its potential.

The world at large has certainly been opposed to modern Israel for the most part—first, to Israel again becoming a nation, and then at every turn while it has negotiated its way amongst the sea of nations.

The following is a brief overview of Israel's help from the United States and its opposition from antagonists which include, sadly, a seemingly schizophrenic America.

America was against Israel's 1949 declaration of Jerusalem as its capital. The US also opposed Jordan's plan, as announced in 1950, to make Jerusalem its second capital. This country, following the 1967 War, opposed Israel's annexation of East Jerusalem. It proposed that a negotiated settlement be at the heart of the future of Jerusalem.

American presidential administrations have insisted that Jerusalem's future not be the subject of unilateral actions that could adversely affect negotiations, for example, by moving the US embassy from Tel Aviv to Jerusalem. President George H. W. Bush held that the US does not believe that new settlements should be built in East Jerusalem. He also believed America does not want to see Jerusalem "divided."

Congress passed the Jerusalem Embassy Act in 1995, which declared the American policy that "Jerusalem should be recognized as the capital of the State of Israel." Democratic candidate Barack Obama in 2008 called Jerusalem the "capital of Israel." On June 4, 2008, he told the American Israel Public Affairs Committee (AIPAC), in his first foreign policy speech after capturing the Democratic nomination on the previous day, that "Jerusalem will remain the capital of Israel, and it must remain undivided." However, the then-senator and presidential hopeful reversed his opinion almost immediately.

In 2010, the Obama administration condemned evictions and house demolitions affecting Palestinians living in East Jerusalem. The Foreign Relations Authorization Act of 2002 stipulated:

> For purposes of the registration of birth, certification of nationality, or issuance of a passport of a United States citizen born in the city of Jerusalem, the Secretary shall, upon the request of the citizen or the citizen's legal guardian, record the place of birth as Israel.

Neither President George W. Bush nor Barack Obama, however, complied with that act. A federal appeal court declared the 2002 law invalid on July 23, 2013. On June 8, 2015, the Supreme Court of the United States struck down Section 214(d) of the Foreign Relations Act 2003, citing the law as an overreach of congressional power into foreign policy.

The US operates through a consulate in Jerusalem that primarily handles matters dealing with the Palestinian Authority. The US Embassy in Tel Aviv handles relations with the government of Israel. The US consulate is not accredited to the Israeli cabinet.

Recognition of Jerusalem as the Capital of Israel

On December 6, 2017, President Donald Trump's administration officially recognized Jerusalem as the capital of Israel. Trump added that the State Department would initiate the process of building a new US Embassy in Jerusalem.

In one of many actions that seemed to run counter to what the president directed, the State Department issued, apparently, its own declaration of dealing with the Jewish state in regard to moving the embassy. Secretary of State Rex Tillerson later clarified that the president's statement "did not indicate any final status for Jerusalem" and "was very clear that the final status, including the borders, would be left to the two parties to negotiate and decide." State Department officials said on December 8 that there will not be any immediate practical changes in how the U.S. deals with Jerusalem. This includes the United States policy of not listing a country on the passports of citizens born in Jerusalem. On December 8, Assistant Secretary of State David M. Satterfield said, "There has been no change in our policy with respect to consular practice or passport issuance at this time." When asked what country the Western Wall is in, State Department spokeswoman Heather Nauert said, "We're not taking any position on the overall boundaries. We are recognizing Jerusalem as the capital of Israel."

Trump's decision to recognize Jerusalem as Israel's capital was opposed vigorously by the majority of world leaders. The United Nations Security Council held an emergency meeting on December 7, and fourteen out of fifteen members condemned Trump's decision. The Security Council said the decision to recognize Jerusalem was in violation of UN resolutions and international law, but was unable to issue a statement to that effect without the endorsement of the United States.

U.S. envoy Nikki Haley called the United Nations "one of the world's foremost centres of hostility towards Israel." Britain, France, Sweden, Italy, and Japan were among the countries that criticized Trump's decision at the emergency meeting. Shortly before Trump's announcement, in November 2017, 151 nations of the United Nations General Assembly voted to reject Israeli ties to Jerusalem. Six nations voted against the resolution, and nine abstained.

Federica Mogherini, the European Union's foreign policy chief, declared that all governments of European Union member states were united on the issue of Jerusalem, and reaffirmed their commitment to a Palestinian State with East Jerusalem as its capital. On December 9, Turkey announced that President Recep Tayyip Erdogan would be working with French president Emmanuel Macron in a joint effort to persuade the United States to reconsider its decision.

Palestinian officials have adamantly declared that the announcement disqualifies the United States from being part of peace talks, and Hamas demanded the start of a new intifada following Trump's declarations. Hard on the heels of the announcement, there were demonstrations in Iran, Jordan, Tunisia, Somalia, Yemen, Malaysia and Indonesia, and outside the US Embassy in Berlin.

Four people were killed in clashes following the announcement, including two Hamas members killed in an Israeli airstrike on December 9, on a Hamas military facility in response to a rocket attack from

Gaza. Two protesters were shot near Gaza's border fence on December 8, while the Israel Defense Forces claimed it had shot towards dozens of instigators of riots, where participants were involved in burning tires and stone-pelting.

Following Trump's announcement, American embassies in Turkey, Jordan, Germany, and Britain issued security alerts for Americans traveling or living abroad in those countries. The United States also issued a general warning for Americans abroad about the possibility of violent protests. The American consulate in Jerusalem restricted travel of government employees to Jerusalem's Old City. The US Embassy in Jordan banned employees from leaving the capital and children of embassy employees were told to stay home from school.

America Acknowledges Israel

America moved toward a strengthened recognition of Israel's nation status with the Jerusalem Act of 1995.

The Jerusalem Embassy Act of 1995 is a public law of the United States passed by the 104th Congress on October 23, 1995. The proposed law was adopted by the Senate (93–5), and the House (374–37). The Act became law without a presidential signature on November 8, 1995.

The Act recognized Jerusalem as the capital of the State of Israel and called for Jerusalem to remain an undivided city. Its purpose was to set aside funds for the relocation of the Embassy of the United States in Israel from Tel Aviv to Jerusalem, by May 31, 1999. For this purpose, it withheld 50% of the funds appropriated to the State Department specifically for "Acquisition and Maintenance of Buildings Abroad" as allocated in fiscal year 1999 until the United States Embassy in Jerusalem had officially opened. Israel's declared capital is Jerusalem, but this is not internationally recognized, pending final status talks in the Israeli-Palestinian conflict.

Despite passage, the law allowed the President to invoke a six-month waiver of the application of the law and reissue the waiver every six months on "national security" grounds. The waiver was repeatedly invoked by Presidents Clinton, Bush, and Obama. President Donald Trump signed a waiver in June 2017. On June 5, 2017, the U.S. Senate unanimously passed a resolution commemorating the 50th anniversary of reunification of Jerusalem by 90-0. The resolution reaffirmed the Jerusalem Embassy Act and called upon the President and all United States officials to abide by its provisions. On December 6, 2017, Trump recognized Jerusalem as Israel's capital, and ordered the planning of the relocation of the embassy. However, following the announcement, Trump signed an embassy waiver again, delaying the move, as mandated by the Act, by at least six months. Legally, however, the U.S. embassy can be moved at any time without reliance on the Act.

On February 23, 2018, President Trump announced that the US Embassy in Israel would reopen at the Arnona Counsular services site of the current U.S. Counslate-General in Jerusalem on May 14, 2018, to coincide with the 70th anniversary of the Israeli Declaration of Independence.[112]

America's position has been that its recognition of Israel doesn't imply a particular view on the status of Jerusalem.

The United States did not recognize Jerusalem as Israel's capital when it became a nation again in 1948. The US voted for the UN Partition Plan in November 1947, which provided for the establishment of an international regime for the city. The US position since then has been that final status of Jerusalem be resolved through negotiations. The American government didn't recognize Jerusalem as Israel's capital until

President Donald Trump's announcement on December 6, 2017.

A *Jerusalem Post* report explains.

> SEOUL—President Donald Trump on Wednesday said the
> US recognizes Jerusalem as Israel's capital and would move its
> embassy there, upending decades of a diplomatic consensus over
> the status of the city pioneered by his predecessors.
>
> Citing a 1995 law, the Jerusalem Embassy Act, compel-
> ling the president to make the move absent national security
> risks, Trump said the time had come to recognize what everyone
> already knows to be true. "Jerusalem is the capital the Jewish
> people established in ancient times," he said. "Today Jerusalem
> is the seat of Israel's government."[113]

Trump, taking into account that the international community insists
that any resolution to the Israeli-Palestinian matter must be determined
in direct negotiations between those two parties, endorsed a two-state
solution. He said, "The agreement is a great deal for the Israelis and a
great deal for the Palestinians." He said the US will support a two-state
solution, if agreed to by both sides.

The president stated that his actions to not determine the specific
boundaries of Israeli sovereignty would be "subject to final status negotiations between the parties."

The Israeli government insists that Jerusalem is its eternal, undivided
capital. The Palestinian Authority demands that any peace agreement
must guarantee a sovereign state and a capital in the eastern districts of
Jerusalem.

"We are not taking a position on any final status issues," the president said. UN Ambassador Nikki Haley insisted that the US would not
be "taking sides" on any issue involving the eastern districts of Jerusalem.

UN Secretary General Antonio Guterres indicated that the international community didn't interpret the US actions in this way. He spoke
to the press following the president's declaration and said in effect that

the decision by Trump to recognize Jerusalem as the capital of Israel and move the American Embassy there would likely cause rioting and other troubles for the region. He urged calm and indicated the decision should be reconsidered.

"Jerusalem is a final status issue that must be resolved in final status negotiations between the two parties," Guterres stated. "In this moment of great tension, I want to make it clear there is no alternative to the two-state solution. There is no Plan B."

France's president, Emmanuel Macron, also called the decision "regrettable" and said the status of Jerusalem was not for one country to decide, but a matter of international security, of consensus, and of law. And Britain's prime minister, Theresa May, characterized the move as "unhelpful" to the prospects for peace in the region.

"We disagree with the US decision to move its embassy to Jerusalem and recognize Jerusalem as the Israeli capital before a final status agreement," May said. "The British Embassy to Israel is based in Tel Aviv and we have no plans to move it."

"We encourage the US administration to now bring forward detailed proposals for an Israel-Palestinian settlement," she added. "To have the best chances of success, the peace process must be conducted in an atmosphere free from violence. We call on all parties to work together to maintain calm."[114]

Benjamin Netanyahu Weighs In

America's allies in the Mideast region registered strong condemnation for Trump's decision to move the embassy to Jerusalem. Turkey threatened to sever ties to Israel, and Egypt refused to recognize the decision by the president, warning of severe consequences that would develop as a result. Turkey implied there would be protests in all its major cities and that relationship with the American Embassy would be cut off.

Even with the blanket condemnation of the international community and the major players of the region threatening protests, US Secretary of State Rex Tillerson said that after consultation with its partners, the United States administration believed that his team "firmly believes there is an opportunity for a lasting peace."

The White House "peace team," which includes Trump's son-in-law Jared Kushner and special representative for international negotiations, Jason Greenblatt, had the president's full approval of the decision. The team was fully in the loop on all matters involved, according to the *Jerusalem Post* report, which attributed the information to a White House source.

The source said, "The peace team was fully aware of this and in the loop. Certain parties are going to react the way they need to react. We expect bumps along the way—but we believe there is an historic opportunity."

Greenblatt wrote on Twitter that Trump's speech was a "courageous" effort to recognize the current and historic reality of the city's status. His team is committed to pressing on, he continued, no matter how angrily parties react in the short term.

President Trump heavily criticized previous presidents as being cowardly because they failed to make the move earlier, "under the belief that delaying recognition of Jerusalem would advance the cause of peace."

"The record is in," he added. "After two decades of waivers, we are no closer to a lasting peace agreement between Israel and the Palestinians."

Trump announced from the White House diplomatic reception room, "Old challenges demand new approaches. My announcement today marks the beginning of a new approach." He made the announcement with Vice President Mike Pence, a long-time champion for the move.

Members of Israel's cabinet praised the decisions by the president as "destined" and "overdue." Prime Minister Benjamin Netanyahu praised the president in a video statement.

"We're profoundly grateful to the president for the courageous and just decision," He said. The prime minister called the decision one taken in furtherance of peace. He added, "because there is no peace that does not include Jerusalem as the capital of Israel," and concluded, "This decision reflects the president's commitment to an ancient and enduring truth."

But the Palestinians have warned in the tone of an angry promise that the move by Trump will be a potentially lethal stroke to the president's growing peace initiative. Hamas, the terrorist organization, called for a new intifada (a violent uprising) in response to the move.

Palestinian President Mahmoud Abbas, in a speech full of threats, denied Trump's claim that his move was in fact a step towards peace and said that, with the actions, the US had relinquished its historic role as broker.

Abbas said in a televised address: "The US administration with this statement has chosen to go against all the international and bilateral agreements, and to ignore the international consensus." He stated further, "The United States is withdrawing from the role it has played in the peace process."

Abbas gave a brief history on Christian and Muslim interaction in the contested city, known in the Arab world as al-Quds. He did so without acknowledging any Jewish history whatsoever as part of the city.

The militants of Islam in the area carried out *days of rage* as part of violent protests against the American president giving Israel the strong recognition that no other state within the world's nations would give.

Prophetic Scenario Shaping

The move of the American Embassy from Tel Aviv is indeed something to rivet the attention of the Bible prophecy student at this moment. There can be no doubt that Trump's decision to move the embassy on Israel's seventieth anniversary of rebirth into modernity has profound significance.

However, even such a powerful dynamic within the end-times stage-setting process pales by comparison to other elements within that activity. We have gone over some of these things before in this book and will later touch on them again. These matters of prophetic state-setting are so important as to possess almost infinite significance, because they portend eternal consequence for billions.

Tribulation Light

We are now seeing issues and events occur in this Age of Grace much like, but not as virulent as, those prophetically scheduled for the seven years of worldwide horror leading up to Christ's Second Advent.

Several specific prophecies in Jesus' Olivet Discourse can be examined as "Tribulation light" events in our headlines today.

> Then said he unto them, Nation shall rise against nation, and kingdom against kingdom: And great earthquakes shall be in divers places, and famines, and pestilences; and fearful sights and great signs shall there be from heaven. (Luke 21:20–21)

Jesus was foretelling that these troubles will be unprecedented in their ferocity during the Tribulation era. He exhorted that when these things begin to happen, we should know that His return is drawing near. Note that the Lord said when these things "begin" to come to pass, we are to "look up...for your redemption draws near" (Luke 21:28).

Jesus said, as recorded in other places and as we touched on earlier, that these issues and events will be like birth pangs, in that they will begin in a milder manner than they will become closer to the moment of birth.

1. Earthquakes

Earthquakes, Jesus said, will mark the beginning of "sorrows" (birth pangs). Staying within the birthing analogy, these earthquakes will be lighter in severity than they will become during the full-blown Tribulation when Christ's return is about to happen. We are told in Revelation an ultimate quake will occur as Christ is breaking through the black clouds of that terrible time. Every mountain will fall: a mighty event indeed!

Almost every geographical region of the planet is experiencing seismic activity on an increasing scale, it seems. All these tremors are mild when compared to the Revelation description of the final quake that will bring every tall structure on earth crashing down. However, the cumulative effects have prophetic significance. Just within a very short time-frame not long ago, as example, we had the following earthquake reports:

5.7-Magnitude Earthquake Felt in New Zealand Capital

New Zealand's capital city Wellington was rocked by 5.7-magnitude earthquake on Tuesday (Feb. 9), according to the country's earthquake monitoring service.

Massive Earthquake Hits Near Papua New Guinea Island of Bougainville

A 6.3 magnitude earthquake hit near the Papua New Guinea island of Bougainville early on Tuesday morning. The undersea quake struck at 3.19am local time.

Taiwan Quake Kills at Least 18 as Search for Missing Continues

A strong earthquake rocked a region of Taiwan that's a hub for chipmaking suppliers to the likes of Apple Inc. and Qualcomm Inc., killing at least 18 people.

Earthquake Shakes Tokyo, No Tsunami Risk

An earthquake has struck close to Tokyo, shaking much of the metropolitan region. There were no immediate reports of injuries or damage, and no tsunami.

Chile Earthquake: Strong Tremor Strikes Near Tongoy and La Serena

A strong earthquake with a preliminary magnitude of 6.4 has struck off the coast of central Chile, centered off Tongoy and La Serena, seismologists say.

Strong Earthquake Hits Solomon Islands

A magnitude 6.4 earthquakes hit the Solomon Islands at 12.19am today, according to the Malaysian Meteorological Department.

Such reports continue in never-ending headline crawls. The tremors are coming with increasing frequency and intensity.

2. Pestilence

Remember the Ebola scare of a few years ago. Think of the HIV natter that was on the front pages and growing, seemingly, uncontrollably. And recall the Zika virus that is apparently spread by mosquitoes and that has no medical defense. There is growing concern among the medical research community that many of the pestilences are in the process of developing resistance to antibiotics and other forms of combating disease.

The Tribulation era will see these diseases become full-blown. The toll in human life will be beyond comprehension.

The above-mentioned developments are but sidebars to the real story regarding signals that show how near this generation is to the Tribulation era.

3. Nation Rising against Nation and Kingdom Rising against Kingdom

This is the real scriptural crux of proof of where we stand on God's prophetic timeline. As stated earlier, "nation" in the Greek language, as used here, is *ethnos* or "ethnic" in English. Jesus was predicting that the very end of the age would produce great ethnic upheaval. People will be raging against each other for reasons of race. Likewise, the Lord said that "kingdom against kingdom" will mark the era leading up to His Second Advent.

Is there any doubt whatsoever that these indicators have been in our headlines recently? In the very streets of America, the ethnic rage sometimes boils to the uncontrollable level. The rioting in places like Ferguson, Missouri, and Baltimore, Maryland, leap instantly to mind. Such rage is at the heart of problems around the world. Religious fervor, inciting ethnic hatreds, mark this generation as the one Jesus must have had in His omniscient mind when giving this prophecy.

We are experiencing "Tribulation light" prophetic birth pangs on a moment-by-moment basis. It will be fascinating, as watchers on the wall, to see what the coming months will bring. We, as born-again believers, hope it brings the shout of the Lord Jesus: "Come up here!" (Revelation 4:1).

Red Lights Flashing!

Israel being at the heart of much of what is going on generates many inquiries by interested prophecy watchers. Things transpiring during recent times is like seeing the flashing, red lights at train tracks: Imminent danger exists! Time to pay close attention!

A key prophetic reality to consider is the world's treatment of God's chosen nation within recent times. Seventy-two nations (an interesting number tied to the fallen Watchers/angels)—most overtly antagonistic to Israel—gathered during the inaugural week of 2017, ostensibly to determine the Jewish nation's fate. Their intent, in the opinion of many, was to force Israel into giving up all claims to the land upon which the nation resides.

Intervention by the incoming Trump administration preempted full implementation of the anti-Israel agenda. Great Britain also added its conference-dampening input.

Israel, with its constant vigilance against ever-present attempts to destroy the nation, managed to thwart much of its UN enemy efforts in the Paris conference matter.

United Nations globalists' agenda, under the Resolution 2334 rubric they want to establish, is to declare Israel an occupier—the oppressor of the Palestinians who, the Israel antagonists say, have legitimate claim to the land.

While even now angry losers in America's presidential election continue to sniffle and sob, and in some cases rage, that Donald J. Trump is illegitimate occupier of Obama's White House, the UN Israel-haters go through their own sort of whining and moaning. We have witnessed a constant diatribe of antics orchestrated by Satan himself, no doubt, in order to try to rearrange the geopolitical and socioeconomic landscape. Pope Francis, in meeting with Palestinian Authority President Mahmoud Abbas, intruding into the Israeli-Palestinian land-for-peace thrust by the UN, also demonstrated Satan's hand being inserted into the religious arena in his attempt to set the international stage for Antichrist's eventual rule (a point many conservative Catholics agree with).

Israeli Prime Minister Benjamin Netanyahu called the Paris peace conference, devised by the Palestinian Authority and hosted by France, a "fraud." He said the conference was "anti-Israel." He warned that the phony summit "will further lead to the adoption of anti-Israel positions." Critics of the so-called Paris summit for peace between Israel and the Palestinians say that the conference and UN R2334 constituted an effort to lock Israel into the borders as they were in 1949. A document produced as a result of the meetings might, it was feared, have meant that Israel would have no claim to the Temple Mount, Mount Olivet, and all other of the sites revered as holy by Jews and Christians. Such a document would, it was thought, be designed to give the territory to the new Palestinian state if the so-called two-state solution were to come to fruition. Representatives of Israel weren't part of the conference. Netanyahu has vowed to ignore anything coming out of the "summit." The ramifications of this attempted globalist grab in Middle East politics remain to be seen.

Immediately upon release of information about R2334, then US Secretary of State John Kerry made his now infamous, obviously anti-Israel statement as part of his speech. Kerry said that Israel could be either Jewish or Democratic; it cannot be both.

The Trump administration continues to have much to say in changing America's course as stated by Kerry. However, the former secretary of state's audacious declaration thus laid out for the world the fact that the Obama administration viewed Israel as an oppressive regime intent upon treating Palestinians cruelly if the Jewish state doesn't go along with allowing the Palestinians all they want.

Ignoring all the atrocities and terrorism spawned daily by enemies who are vowed to destroy Israel, Kerry, at the time, went on to imply America would recommend punitive repercussions for Israel's refusal to make peace under terms of the Paris meetings.

Even though the conference in France seems to have been neutralized in large part, such statements by America's (now former) top representative on the world diplomatic stage raises red flags—and sets the red lights flashing, to be sure. Thoughts immediately go to Genesis 12 about those who bless Israel and those who curse it.

Zechariah 12 and 14, Joel 3:2, and many other prophetic passages involving God's pronouncements about Israel at the end of the age leap at us. The red lights flash brightly. There are no more powerful signals in Scripture on the nearness of Christ's return at Armageddon following the Tribulation period.

Israel, the false peace process, all nations being turned against God's chosen nation…these are flashing red lights to be sure. However, like the Lord's obvious intervention into so much of the globalist agenda, for the moment, His mighty hand has again interceded in this matter of the deck being stacked in favor of the Palestinians against God's chosen people.

Third-Temple Tension

The Trump administration's move of the American Embassy from Tel Aviv to Jerusalem has added to tensions surrounding Moriah. But, this is likely the destiny of the process that will produce the Third Temple—the *Tribulation* Temple.

The new president seems overwhelmingly in Israel's corner, despite still considering a two-state solution to the Israeli-Palestinian conflict. The fact that Trump has deemed to locate the embassy in God's touch-stone city seems to predestine a stronger tie than ever to influencing matters in Jerusalem, Israel, and the region.

This can be either a good thing or a deadly mistake.

nine

Temple End-Times Intrigue

WILL BUILDING THE Third Temple atop Moriah necessitate the destruction of the Dome of the Rock?

Such an action seems impossible at present. To destroy that shrine of Islam would bring immediate, worldwide, Muslim rage and, likely, war against Israel. The question has also been raised: Will the Dome fall as the result of an act of God—i.e., an earthquake or some other even more dramatic event?

A principal authority within the organization said the following:

> "God's Holy Mountain Vision" project hopes to defuse religious strife by showing that Jews' end-of-days vision could harmoniously accommodate Islam's present architectural hegemony on the Temple Mount…. This vision of religious shrines in peaceful proximity can transform the Temple Mount from a place of contention to its original sacred role as a place of worship shared by Jews, Muslims and Christians.[115]

The program, including interfaith studies and educational programs of various sorts, is sponsored by the Interfaith Encounter Association at the Mishkenot Sha'ananim's Konrad Adenauer Conference Center in Jerusalem.

The Dome of the Rock, according to Islam, covers the rock from which Muhammed ascended to Heaven. Jewish tradition has it that the Dome of the Rock now covers the stone on Mount Moriah where the First and Second Temples' Holy of Holies sat.

Until recently, Jewish tradition held that the Dome of the Rock would have to be somehow removed in order to construct a Third and final Temple in its proper location. However, an alternative position emerged when a young scholar named Frankel presented the idea that Jewish doctrine regarding the rebuilding of the Temple emphasizes the role of a prophet, which puts forth a different option than the traditional. His work was presented in an article that appeared in 2007 in *Tehumin*, an influential journal of Jewish law.

This prophet would have almost supernatural authority, including the discretion to stipulate exactly where the Temple will be situated. The prophet would have this authority no matter what other Jewish tradition involved in the matter of Temple reconstruction might specify.

Frankel formed this belief based upon a supernatural, holy revelation being given to a genuine prophet saying that the Temple will be rebuilt on the present Temple Mount or extended area that is in peaceful proximity to the Dome of the Rock and other structures of prayer, such as the Aksa Mosque and nearby Christian shrines. Muslims and Jews alike have raised opposition to the idea, however. Founder of the Islamic Movement in Israel, Sheikh Abdulla Nimar Darwish, stated that it was pointless to conjecture about things that would take place when the Mahdi, the Muslim messiah, comes upon the scene (you can learn the important facts regarding Mahdi's connection to the return of Jesus and the Third Temple in our book *The Final Roman Emperor, the Islamic Antichrist, and the Vatican's Last Crusade*).

Darwish said in a telephone interview with the *Jerusalem Post*: "Why are we taking upon ourselves the responsibility to decide such things? Even Jews believe that it is prohibited to rebuild the Temple until the messiah comes. So what is there to talk about. The mahdi will decide whether or not to rebuild the Temple. If he decides that it should be rebuilt, I will go out to the Temple Mount and help carry the rocks."

He warned that any attempt to rebuild the Temple before the coming of the Mahdi would mean trouble. "As long as there is a Muslim alive, no Jewish Temple will be built on Al-Haram Al-Sharif [the Temple Mount]. The status quo must be maintained, otherwise there will be bloodshed."

Perhaps presaging such trouble that would almost certainly arise, Baruch Ben-Yosef, chairman of the Movement to Restore the Temple, minced no words in expressing that the Temple had to be built where the Dome of the Rock presently stands. "Anybody who says anything else simply does not know what he is talking about," he said. "A prophet does not have the power to change the law which explicitly states the location of the Temple."

Ben-Yosef rejected the notion that rebuilding of the Temple had to be done by a prophet. "All you need is a Sanhedrin," he said.

The Temple Mount came under Israeli control in 1967 following the 1967 Six Day War. Mainstream Orthodox rabbis have opposed attempts to rebuild the Temple since that time. A decree prohibiting Jews from entering the area because of matters involving purity was issued by the Chief Rabbinate of Israel. Nonetheless, a number of fervently dedicated organizations have called to take steps to renew the sacrifices on the Temple Mount and rebuild the Temple.

These include such organizations as the Movement to Restore the Temple and outspoken rabbis, like Rabbi Israel Ariel, head of the capital's Temple Institute and a top cleric within the revived Sanhedrin, whose leader is Rabbi Adin Steinsaltz.

Temple Temperament Grows

Temple intrigues continue to manifest while this generation moves more deeply into times nearer Christ's return. Conditions surrounding God's chosen people and His chosen nation are changing moment by moment. Attention of the entire world is drawn on an hourly basis toward the one spot on earth most focal in considering Bible prophecy.

This being the case, it is appropriate to ask: Do the Jewish people notice the lateness of the prophetic hour?

A remnant does, it seems. The following news report makes the point:

> On Tuesday, the holiday of the Ninth of Av, a record-breaking 1,300 Jews ascended to the Temple Mount, turning a day of deepest mourning for the destruction of the Temples into a catalyst to bring the beginnings of the Third Temple.
>
> "I know that if there had been an announcement on the radio to go up and build, thousands more Jews were ready for that," Rabbi Yisrael Ariel, the Chief Rabbi of Hebron told *Breaking Israel News* of the awe-filled atmosphere on the Mount.[116]

ten

Gog-Magog Temple Ties

EZEKIEL THE PROPHET foretold a coming attack on the nation Israel. Such an assault would have been impossible for the period from AD 70 until 1948. There was no nation called Israel. The Jewish people were once again scattered into the many nations of the world, where they were horrendously persecuted and murdered by the millions.

The matter of this prophesied assault from Israel's enemies from its north is no longer impossible. As a matter of fact, it is not only *possible*, it is becoming more *probable* by the hour. Here again is what Ezekiel predicted for the attack that looks to be shaping up in our time.

> And the word of the LORD came unto me, saying,
>
> Son of man, set thy face against Gog, the land of Magog, the chief prince of Meshech and Tubal, and prophesy against him,
>
> And say, Thus saith the Lord GOD; Behold I am against thee, O Gog, the chief prince of Meshech and Tubal:
>
> And I will turn thee back, and put hooks into thy jaws, and

I will bring thee forth, and all thine army, horses and horsemen, all of them clothed with all sorts of armour, even a great company with bucklers and shields, all of them handling swords:

Persia, Ethiopia, and Libya with them; all of them with shield and helmet:

Gomer, and all his bands; the house of Togarmah of the north quarters, and all his bands: and many people with thee.

Be thou prepared, and prepare for thyself, thou, and all thy company that are assembled unto thee, and be thou a guard unto them.

After many days thou shalt be visited: in the latter years thou shalt come into the land that is brought back from the sword, and is gathered out of many people, against the mountains of Israel, which have been always waste: but it is brought forth out of the nations, and they shall dwell safely all of them. (Ezekiel 38:1–8)

Today's headlines are filled with descriptions of formidable forces gathering due north of Israel. These forces are almost precisely those given by the Old Testament prophet. The names of antiquity are different, but they are the same nations, populated by Israel-hating people who are progeny of the ancient people about which Ezekiel wrote.

Repeating the Gog-Magog coalition prophesied by Ezekiel, a recent commentary gives some perspective about just how these forces are coming together.

A major leg of the Ezekiel 38–39 Gog-Magog coalition is coming into view. The Turkey leg is now, undeniably in the estimation of many students of prophecy, on the end-times table of Bible prophecy….

Modern-day Turkey covers most of the territory that made up ancient *Togarmah*. Ezekiel was told to prophesy that the *house of Togarmah* will be among the horde from the north of Jerusalem that will assault Israel near the time of Christ's return….

Russia is pared down from its configuration as the nucleus of the former Soviet Union. It more or less once again covers territory that it encompassed during the time of Ezekiel's giving the Gog-Magog prophecy…

Iran, which is the central-most territory today that once was called Persia, has joined Russia as a close ally–again, just to Israel's north. Russia's and Iran's military assets co-mingle in the region to influence Syria, another end-times player.[117]

The stage for the Gog-Magog invasion is certainly in the process of being set. Exactly when can't be determined at this point. God, Himself, indicates that He will be the One who sets the "hook in the jaw" of the demon-driven leader Ezekiel calls Gog.

Ezekiel, it is more than interesting to note, is the very prophet who gives phenomenal details of the Temple that will sit atop Moriah as the end of human history prior to Christ's Second Advent nears.

This book presents a look at Ezekiel's Third, and even Fourth Temples, especially in the last chapter. We will review here Israel's history a bit more deeply.

Israel's story is unique in all of human history. No nation has come close to enduring the vicissitudes the Jewish people have been subjected to. It has been overrun by enemies and destroyed many times—to the point that today some antagonists say that it never really even existed, at least not in places surrounding the Temple Mount.

The Jews have been killed in the most vicious ways imaginable throughout the centuries and removed from their land. Yet they have returned time after time to reclaim that land—always in the face of enemies vowed to murder and remove them again.

The Hebrew way of life should have long ago gone extinct, the people having been absorbed by most every culture on earth. Ancient empires arose to power and either caused them to assimilate or attempted to destroy them entirely. All other such people coming under such maltreatment have disappeared forever. But, the eternal Jew remains indestructible as a race.

Survival of the Jewish culture into modernity has been nothing less than miraculous. The Jews should have been wiped from the face of the earth more than two thousand years ago.

Moses led them from Egyptian bondage about 1447 BC. Any stretch of logic says they should have been eliminated by the powerful Egyptian military forces. If not that, the harsh wilderness life, devoid of any sustenance for human life, should have wiped them out. But, we know the story. God provided and they are again a nation—and, just as prophesied, they are the focus nation and people of the world today in hourly headlines.

Despite seemingly everything God's enemies had to throw against His chosen people, Israel ultimately regained the land from which they had been scattered. Led by Joshua, they proved God's promises to Abraham were unbreakable. They were forced to fight enemies blood-vowed to wipe them out for the next four hundred years. The Hittites, Philistines, Amorites, and others had to be defeated in order to bring Israel's kingdom to its full glory. Their rule became a time of much prosperity, an era during Solomon's reign about which the Queen of Sheba said that not even half of its magnificence had been told.

Following Solomon's death, Israel split into two kingdoms, and the people engaged in idolatry and the most egregious types of sinful activity. Eventually, the Assyrian Empire invaded from the north and destroyed Israel, the Northern Kingdom. The final defeat came in 722 BC. The Babylonian Empire assaulted from the west and destroyed the Southern Kingdom of Judah in 587 BC. The Babylonians took captive many Israelites while destroying Jerusalem and ultimately the Temple Solomon built. The Jews remained captive in Babylon for more than seventy years.

Again, logic would have it that the Jews, totally absorbed into the wicked Assyrian and Babylonian cultures, should have assimilated, never to be a distinct people again. God's promises, however, are never broken.

He faithfully preserved His people through their time of captivity and slavery.

The Babylonian Empire finally fell to the Medo-Persian Empire, and the Jews were allowed to return to Jerusalem and rebuild the Temple. Alexander the Great of the Greek Empire conquered the Medo-Persian Empire in 330 BC. Following Alexander's death, his four generals— Seleucus, Cassander, Lycimachus, and Ptolomy—divided the Greek Empire amongst themselves.

The kingdoms of General Seleucus (Syria) and General Ptolemy (Egypt) fought mightily against each other for greater parts of Alexander's empire. Israel was caught between these feuding generals. The Greek persecution of the Jews came to a head when General Antiochus Epiphanes, who eventually emerged from the feud, assaulted Jerusalem in 170 BC. He butchered thousands of Jews and defiled the Second Temple by smearing swine blood on the alter and committing other blasphemous atrocities.

The Jews were allowed to resume Temple worship atop Moriah when the Romans conquered the Greek Empire. That ended when the city of Jerusalem and the Temple were destroyed in AD 70 exactly as Daniel the prophet and Jesus had prophesied. The destruction was the result of the Jewish revolt when Roman Emperor Vespasian sent his son, General Titus, to put down the uprising.

God's chosen people were scattered into places in other parts of the world, where they suffered the most terrible sorts of persecution for 1,848 years.

Again, the Jewish people should have disappeared from history, never again to reappear. Their suffering included the terrors of Islam, the Crusades, the Inquisition, the Russian pogroms, the Nazi Holocaust, and other atrocities. But, as noted numerous times, the God of Heaven never reneges on a promise. His faithfulness—and the proof that His prophetic Word is absolute truth—was manifest for all the world to witness when, in 1948, the Jews, who had begun returning in the nineteenth century, reestablished their homeland. The nation was reborn in a single day, just as prophesied in Isaiah 66:7, on May 15, 1948!

History Since Rebirth

Israel has been attacked incessantly by its enemy neighbors since then. These enraged forces are constituted primarily of Arab Islamists. Gamal Abdel Nasser, leader of Egypt, led a coalition against Israel in 1956. He again was leader in 1967, when he gathered forces to attack again. Israel struck preemptively in an action that initiated the Six Day War.

Egypt's Anwar El Sadat led yet another coalition of Arab nations against Israel in the 1973 Yom Kippur War. Israel totally defeated those forces in every case—forces that outnumbered the Jewish military by millions. Truthful observers of those conflicts must acknowledge that the victories were nothing short of miraculous. Israel won tremendous chunks of territory. The United Nations tried in every case to interfere as Israel's victories became more and more overwhelming. The UN insisted time after time that Israel give back the land they won. That organization is still populated by nations that hate Israel and consider it an "occupier" of land that doesn't belong to it. It still insists Israel must return land they don't rightly own.

But, the God who gave it to His chosen people sees it differently. Israel will one day legitimately reside upon vastly greater portions of that Middle Eastern region. Supernatural power has assured the survival of Israel to this point, despite enemies surrounding it who openly declare they will wipe it from the land.

The Gog-Magog Attack

One fascinating point to consider is that the prophet Ezekiel is the same servant given special connection to both the Gog-Magog attack and to the Temples that will occupy the Mt. Moriah site at a time yet future. There must be profound reason the two factors are given to this one Old Testament prophet. The reason may be tied inextricably to the one who most hates both God and his chosen people.

Some scholars believe that Lucifer once had rule over a perfect, earth-type planet. He lost that dominion, as they would have it, when he led the rebellion against God in Heaven. Lucifer, some scholars believe, then came to a recreated Planet Earth to spoil it, causing man's fall in the Garden of Eden, bringing death and the separation of God from the human race. Lucifer's choice to rebel sealed his fate. Now known as "Satan," he hates with a vengeance that cannot be measured.

The Lord made a way for lost mankind to be saved from their sin and instead be reconciled to Himself. He promised a redeemer who would one day come to offer salvation—but, not to Lucifer and the one-third of the angels who rebelled with him.

Satan now seeks to thwart God's plan of salvation. He apparently thought he could do so by destroying God's Son, who came to Earth as Israel's Messiah. Satan worked through the Jews and all of mankind to have the Redeemer murdered.

Of course, Jesus resurrected from death on the third day after His crucifixion. Rather than God's plan to redeem mankind being thwarted, it was sealed and delivered by the Lord Jesus Christ. When He said, "It is finished," the redemption of all who would believe Christ and His resurrection would be saved from separation from God forever (Romans 10:9–10).

Satan's hatred for the Jews—the people through whom the Savior came into the world—has grown more virulent with each passing century. He apparently, within his super-intelligent yet reprobate mind—thinks he can yet win, thus reverse God's plan. If he can make God out to be a liar and a betrayer of truth, he, himself, can get out of the doom that awaits him.

Israel is at the center of his target. If he can destroy the Jews, he will have made God to be a liar, thus not God—for God has said He cannot lie.

This brings us to the reason for the Ezekiel tie to both the Gog-Magog attack and the Third Temple that is on the end-times drawing board. Satan's plan is to destroy Israel once and for all. This plan has been formulated by God, Himself, who says He will put "hooks into the jaws" of Satan's leader of the attack on Israel Ezekiel predicts. God will bring Satan's forces against Israel in order for all but one-sixth of them to be destroyed. God will again prove that He, not Lucifer, is indeed God!

The Gog-Magog attack is aimed at Jerusalem, at the heart of which sits the Temple Mount. This, as said many times before, is God's touchstone to humanity, His most sacred place. Taking control of that Third Temple—the Tribulation Temple— is Lucifer's objective. He couldn't usurp God's heavenly throne like he claimed (Isaiah 14:14), but he still thinks he can usurp the holy place from where Jesus Christ will rule and reign in Jerusalem. It is where Satan will indwell his man of sin, Antichrist, when that last terrible tyrant enters the Third Temple and declares himself God and demands to be worshipped.

Again, the Temple is the focus of Ezekiel, who meticulously laid out the blueprint for that Jewish house of worship, just as is the Gog-Magog assault from the north of Jerusalem, which he describes in great detail. The congruency cannot be missed. Ezekiel's prophetic thrust is undeniable. The forces arrayed against God's chosen nation at the end of the current dispensation will be drawn by God, Himself, toward Mount Moriah, where the Third Temple will be placed.

Let us look closer at this force that, as we have seen, is even now beginning to coalesce to the north of Jerusalem. Those who study Bible prophecy have long anticipated an attack on Israel by forces from the north led by Russia. The attack, it is believed, will come when Israel seems at peace, with no fear of such an assault.

Dr. Jack Van Impe writes:

Early in the 20th century, Dr. Ironside wrote: In the last days, the final head of the Russian people will look with covetous eyes upon the great developments in the land of Palestine. They will determine that Russia must have her part of the wealth there produced. Consequently, we have the picture of a vast army, augmented by warriors from Persia, Cush, Phut, marching down toward Palestine.[118]

How can we know with such certainty that Russia is the nation the prophet Ezekiel pointed to in God's indictment? The questions must be addressed:

- Who are Gog and all the players mentioned in Ezekiel's prophecy?
- Where are the exact regions these players reside, in modern terms?
- Who is this leader called Gog?
- Where is the land of Magog?
- Where on a map can we find the cities of Meshech and Tubal?
- What nations was Ezekiel writing about when he stipulated Gomer and Togarmah as consort nations with the Gog-Magog coalition?

Genesis 10 presents a list of nations to begin with our investigation. Here we find the key names in Ezekiel's prophecy:

Now these are the generations of the sons of Noah, Shem, Ham, and Japheth: and unto them were sons born after the flood. The sons of Japheth; Gomer, and Magog, and Madai, and Javan, and Tubal, and Meshech, and Tiras. (Genesis 10:1, 2)

Employing the system that was the custom of the time, the editors of the *Scofield Reference Bible* presented the following information about the names we wish to examine in the table of nations. Customs of ancient times included a man's descendants adopting his name as the name of their tribe. Historians and Bible students have thus been able to trace the movements of some of the tribes and can know with some certainty where their descendants can be found today. The following helps in considering these nations that will be part of the Gog-Magog attack.

- Magog – From Magog are descended the ancient Scythians or Tarters, whose descendents predominate in modern Russia.
- Tubal – Tubal's descendents peopled the region south of the Black Sea from whence they spread north and south. It is probable that Tobolsk perpetuates the tribal name.
- Meshech – Progenitor of a race mentioned in connection with Tubal, Magog, and other northern nations. Broadly speaking, Russia, excluding the conquests of Peter the Great and his successors, is the modern land of Magog, Tubal, and Meshech.

Notes from the *Scofield Reference Bible*, published in 1909, indicate that Russia will be the main aggressor in Ezekiel's end-time battle.

In the Oriental tongue, the name of the Caucasus Mountains that run through Russia means "Fort of Gog" or "Gog's last stand." If you were to ask a Russian what he calls the heights of the Caucasus Mountains, he would say, "the Gogh."

The evidence builds.

The word that is translated "chief" in Ezekiel 38:3 is "Rosh" in the Hebrew language. For centuries, prophetic scholars have generally agreed that the word "Rosh" is a proper name. Allowing this long-accepted conclusion in the translation of this verse would make it read, "And say, Thus saith the Lord God; Behold, I am against thee, O Gog, the Rosh prince of Meshech and Tubal."

But who is Rosh?

"Rosh" was the name of the tribe dwelling in the area of the Volga. And "Rosh" is the word for "Russia" today in some languages of the world. In Belgium and Holland, it is "Rus." Here, abbreviated, it's "Russ," and often appears in that form in the headlines of newspapers.

An understanding of this moved Robert Lowth, bishop of London two hundred years ago, to write: "Rosh, taken as a proper name in Ezekiel signifies the inhabitants of Scythia from whom the modern Russians derive their modern name. The name 'Russia' dates only from the seventeenth century and was formed from the ancient name 'Russ.'"

It is obvious to some, then, that Ezekiel was issuing a warning to the Russian prince (leader) of Meshech and Tubal.

We have already seen from Scofield's notes of 1909 that Tubal is the root of the name "Tobolsk," but what about Meshech? In his note on Ezekiel 38:2, Scofield continues his identification, stating: "That the primary reference is to the northern European powers headed by Russia, all agree.... Gog is the prince, Magog his land, the reference to Meshech and Tubal (Moscow and Tobolsk) is a clear mark of identification."

As has been already shown, Dr. Scofield was by no means the first to come to this conclusion. In 1890, Arno C. Gaebelein wrote a book on Ezekiel. Commenting on chapters 38 and 39, he declared: "This is Russia, Moscow, and Tobolsk."

Another important voice of the past is that of Josephus. In Book I, Chapter VI of his work, this historian who lived almost two thousand years ago stated that the Scythians were called Magogites by the Greeks.

Why is that important?

The Scythians populated Russia.

Little wonder then that the weight of prophetic scholarship has gone with the conclusion that Russia is the chief aggressor named by Ezekiel in this end-time war with Israel. The allies of Russia in that fierce conflict will be Persia (Iran and Iraq), Ethiopia, Libya, Gomer (Eastern Germany and Slovakia), and Togarmah (Turkey).

It is interesting that Daniel adds Egypt to the names of nations coming against Israel and the final world dictator so that the invasion includes attacks from the north and the south, as well as the prospect of trouble from the east (see Daniel 11:40–44).

There is no need to marshal the scholars of the past to confirm the place or purpose of this war. Ezekiel explained:

After many days thou shalt be visited: in the latter years thou shalt come into the land that is brought back from the sword, and is gathered out of many people, against the mountains of Israel, which have been always waste: but it is brought forth out of the nations, and they shall dwell safely all of them. (Ezekiel 38:8)

What a clear and up-to-date description of Israel! It is certainly the land that is brought back from the sword, a former wasteland, gathered out of many people, and brought forth out of the nations.

The invaders of Israel will come with immense air power:

Thou shalt ascend and come like a storm, thou shalt be like a cloud to cover the land, thou, and all thy bands, and many people with thee. (Ezekiel 38:9)

They will also come in full confidence of victory:

And thou shalt say, I will go up to the land of unwalled villages; I will go to them that are at rest, that dwell safely, all of them dwelling without walls, and having neither bars nor gates, To take a spoil, and to take a prey; to turn thine hand upon the desolate places that are now inhabited, and upon the people that are gathered out of the nations, which have gotten cattle and goods, that dwell in the midst of the land. (Ezekiel 38:11, 12)

The allies of Russia in that fierce conflict will be Persia (Iran and Iraq), Ethiopia, Libya, Gomer (Eastern Germany and Slovakia), and Togarmah (Turkey).

Those curious about the Gog-Magog attack must ask some interesting questions, such as the following:

Question: What could cause the Gog-Magog force to attack?

Answer: First, Islam hates Israel passionately. The forces will be mostly Islamic, with Russia and Germany being the exceptions. These nations have vowed to wipe Israel off the face of the earth for millennia. They will join the attack with glee. Satanic hatred and rage will be the primary motivation.

Second, Israel is the doorway to Middle Eastern oil riches. Oil and gas finds within the Jewish state's territory continue to grow. There is well-placed speculation that there could be vast quantities of petroleum beneath the land. Tremendous gas fields lay beneath the Mediterranean within Israel's territorial waters. Russia would be in complete control of the oil of the region if it succeeded in conquering the area.

Third, Israel being the crossroads between three continents, Russia could, by conquering the region, construct a railroad connecting Moscow to the Sinai Peninsula. It might then take the Gulf of Suez Canal. It could then have sway over Mediterranean and Persian Gulf shipping, then extend its railroad into Egypt and on into all of Africa and control Africa's many resources.

Fourth, Russia's longtime desire to establish warm-water ports for expansion southward has made great strides by inserting itself into Syria. It has its warm-water port. But, a successful invasion of Israel could greatly expand its warm-water capability, thus securing it complete control of Mediterranean shipping.

And fifth, the mineral riches of the Dead Sea have long thought to be a prize worthy of capture by the Gog-Magog forces. This doesn't seem as important as it once did in eschatological thinking, but the riches are there and would certainly add to the spoils of conquest. The trillions of dollars it might provide could provide funding for greater military power.

Question: Could Russia carry out this assault at present?

Answer: Such an attack would bring Israel's nuclear weaponry into play. The Israeli Defense Force would almost certainly employ whatsoever weapon systems at their disposal to defeat such an attack.

The Gog-Magog attack will most likely take place following a disarmament by the prophesied covenant of peace confirmed by Antichrist. The Gog leader will then see that Israel can be assaulted with little fear of major resistance.

Question: Why are a number of nations, such as Saudi Arabia, Jordan, Egypt, and others, not mentioned as part of the Gog-Magog coalition?

Answer: Not long ago, these would certainly have eagerly joined the Gog-Magog forces. But we have watched as forces within the Arab-Islamist regions have transformed. They have made new alliances because of, for example, the dangers presented by an increasingly threatening Iran.

Saudi has become much more Western-oriented, wanting protection from the Persian threat. It has been amazing to see the prophetic landscape changing in such dramatic fashion.

Overwhelming Gog-Magog Factor

Despite all the factors listed above, there is one overwhelming issue to consider in thinking on why God will determine to attack the Jewish state. That involves Lucifer's rage against God's people. His hatred of the Jewish people has been front and center for all the world to see throughout the ages and is ratcheting up at the present hour.

To repeat: Satan intends to usurp Christ's earthly throne that will sit atop the supernaturally elevated and topographically altered Mount Moriah. The Gog-Magog forces, even if unknowingly, will earlier be drawn toward that spot and all but one-sixth of those forces will meet their doom. The fire of judgment—whether supernatural or nuclear—will fall upon the nations from which the Gog-Magog forces come.

The Third Temple—the one in which Antichrist will sit, declaring himself to be God and demanding worship—will likely sit atop Moriah at the time of the Gog-Magog attack. We get this idea because Ezekiel's prophecy says Israel will be "at rest, in unwalled villages" when the attack comes. This means that Antichrist will likely have confirmed the covenant of peace and given his assurance that his forces will protect Israel.

It will, however, be Israel's omnipotent God who does the protecting. Israel is invincible forever, because God cannot lie.

> And it shall come to pass at the same time when Gog shall come against the land of Israel, saith the Lord GOD, that my fury shall come up in my face.
>
> For in my jealousy and in the fire of my wrath have I spoken, Surely in that day there shall be a great shaking in the land of Israel;
>
> So that the fishes of the sea, and the fowls of the heaven, and the beasts of the field, and all creeping things that creep upon the earth, and all the men that are upon the face of the earth, shall shake at my presence, and the mountains shall be thrown down, and the steep places shall fall, and every wall shall fall to the ground.
>
> And I will call for a sword against him throughout all my mountains, saith the Lord GOD: every man's sword shall be against his brother.
>
> And I will plead against him with pestilence and with blood; and I will rain upon him, and upon his bands, and upon the many people that are with him, an overflowing rain, and great hailstones, fire, and brimstone.
>
> Thus will I magnify myself, and sanctify myself; and I will be known in the eyes of many nations, and they shall know that I am the LORD. (Ezekiel 38:18–23)

eleven

Trump's Triumphal Entry

IT IS ALL so eerily similar to 1948. A president of the United States opposed by much of Washington, DC, the State Department, the news media, and the world, for that matter. The issue is the same: the recognition of Israel's legitimacy.

The president was Harry S. Truman in 1948. Today, seventy years later, the president is Donald J. Trump. Both men have bucked the rants and ravings of their day. Both were triumphant in their political careers. Truman defeated Thomas Dewey in 1948 to secure reelection. Most say it was a miraculous victory. The photo still stands as one of American news journalism's most famous: Harry Truman holding up the *Chicago Tribune* the day after the election and grinning broadly. The headline, of course, read "Dewy Defeats Truman."

It seemed the forces of the Western diplomatic and governmental world were arrayed against Truman in his decision to recognize the new state of Israel on May 14, 1948. When a meeting was requested by the US State Department leading up to the decision, Truman listened to the argument against recognizing the Jewish state. He listened also to an advisor, Clark Clifford, a proponent for supporting Israel's nationhood.

Secretary of State George C. Marshall—whom Truman greatly respected—was livid that Clifford was allowed to present his case. Marshall told Truman in that meeting, with all in attendance watching, that if Truman decided to support Israel, he, Marshall, would vote for his opponent in the upcoming election.

Truman decided to support Israel rather than kowtow to his famous secretary of state. Thereby Truman "blessed" Israel.

Many believe this is primary reason for the famous photo of the smiling president holding up the newspaper with the famous headline. It was made obvious that Truman had been blessed with a miracle in being reelected against what many saw as overwhelming odds. Thus, Genesis 12:1–3 was proven true for the whole world to see.

Many of those same people are convinced that Donald Trump's victory against overwhelming odds are in part due to his outspoken support for Israel. He promised to move the American Embassy to Jerusalem from Tel Aviv in full recognition of Jerusalem as Israel's capital. He followed through and is one of very few leaders on the international scene who champions the Jewish state.

The Israel miracle continues to unfold during its post-seventieth birthday into modern times. President Trump's triumphs seem to coincide with those miracles.

Intrigues involving the status of Jerusalem are profound beyond any in recent times. A strange setting of the prophetic stage is in process, with Saudi and Israel engaging in unprecedented overtures to each other. A key prophetic player is the chief cause of the strange bedfellows climbing between the geopolitical diplomatic sheets. We get a flavor of this from the following news excerpt:

> Imagine an Israeli taking a direct flight on El Al airlines to Riyadh, or the House of Saud establishing an embassy in Jerusalem. Previously unthinkable, rumors abound of a desire by Crown Prince Mohammad bin Salman (MBS) to normalize ties between the two countries....

Israel's relationship with the Saudis appears to be warming, with the countries allied in the struggle against a common enemy, Iran....

There are a number of reasons Riyadh and Jerusalem may be cozying up, outside of the desire to stop Iran's expansionism. Both countries agree, for example, that the "Arab Spring" revolutions were destabilizing and unleashed dangerous forces. They likewise believe that a reduction in American influence in the Middle East left a power vacuum that risks being filled by enemies.[119]

Many prophetic observers believe that Sheba and Dedan of Ezekiel 38:13 likely refers to the area possessed by present-day Saudi and surrounding territory. These will not be part of the Gog-Magog assault against Israel given by the prophet Ezekiel.

Instead, they will apparently stand on the sideline and issue a note of diplomatic protest, along with others. Certainly, recent developments, with Iran (ancient Persia) being the chief nemesis of both Israel and Saudi, have the Jews and Arabs coming together. They are doing so, at least, in their desire to promote their common defense.

At the same time, the Arab/Muslim world as a conglomerate body is making sounds of war. The reason: rumors that American President Donald J. Trump has moved the US embassy from Tel Aviv to Jerusalem.

Another excerpt framed the situation as it began developing into present circumstance.

The Trump administration has notified U.S. embassies around the world that it plans to formally recognize Jerusalem as the undivided capital of Israel, according to a report published Thursday by the *Wall Street Journal.* The plan includes the future relocation of the U.S. Embassy from Tel Aviv to Jerusalem.

According to the report, the plan has not been finalized, but envoys were being notified so that they can inform their host governments and prepare for possible protests....

"The president has always said it is a matter of when, not
if, [the embassy will relocate to Jerusalem]," a White House
spokesperson said.[120]

It seems that we are about to witness the world's geopolitical players
take a sip from that cup prophesied by Zechariah (12:3). Giving Jerusalem validation as the rightful capital of Israel was a thing that should
be done. The president was right to do so. But, doing so almost without a doubt will bring consequences—ones that no American president
has been willing to risk since Congress declared Jerusalem the capital of
Israel with The Jerusalem Embassy and Recognition Act of 1995.

Despite blessings that will flow from Trump's love for and support
of Israel, there are prophetic matters of consequence to consider. God
said He Himself will make Jerusalem a "cup of trembling" to those who
deal treacherously with His chosen city and people. The world today
is drunk with hatred for God and the nation of Israel. Perhaps it is this
American president who is chosen to be God's instrument for leading
the world to take a sip from that prophesied deadly cup.

Trump Prophetically Enlightened?

Presidents of the recent past have made statements that seemed to have
Bible prophecy in view.

Jimmy Carter, despite his seeming dislike for the Jewish state,
referred to the Holy Land as having biblical and historical importance
according to Israel's prophets. Ronald Reagan sometimes would refer
to the Second Coming of Christ and the reality of Armageddon. Bill
Clinton once said that his pastor, Dr. W. O. Vaught, told him when
Clinton was governor of Arkansas that if Bill ever became president, he
had better treat Israel according to Genesis 12 regarding the blessings or
cursing to be given by the Lord depending upon whether one blessed or
cursed Israel.

President Donald Trump, in talking about his decision declaring Jerusalem as Israel's eternal capital and announcing he was going to move the U.S. Embassy from Tel Aviv to Jerusalem announced several important reasons for his decision. Then he said: "It is reality, And, it's the right thing to do."

One must wonder how much of this president's declaration is based upon true understanding of why it's "the right thing to do."

A considerable amount of the criticism about Trump's decision comes from a specific, leftist diatribe. These say it's the crazy evangelical Zionists who base Israel's right to the land they "occupy" upon the Bible. The word "Bible" is dripping with vitriol, even when read rather than heard. It's like they are saying "the Bible!... *Ugh!*"

"Trump is listening to the Bible thumpers and doing it for their votes" has been the rant. Yet, the following is exactly what makes Mr. Trump's decision the "right thing to do":

> But I have chosen Jerusalem, that my name might be there; and have chosen David to be over my people Israel.
>
> Now it was in the heart of David my father to build an house for the name of the LORD God of Israel.
>
> But the LORD said to David my father, Forasmuch as it was in thine heart to build an house for my name, thou didst well in that it was in thine heart:
>
> Notwithstanding thou shalt not build the house; but thy son which shall come forth out of thy loins, he shall build the house for my name.
>
> The LORD, therefore, hath performed his word that he hath spoken: for I am risen up in the room of David my father, and am set on the throne of Israel, as the LORD promised, and have built the house for the name of the LORD God of Israel.
>
> And in it have I put the ark, wherein is the covenant of the LORD, that he made with the children of Israel. (2 Chronicles 6:6–11)

As stated previously, almost every leader on the world stage is against the decision. Even our closest allies, like British Prime Minister Theresa May, are adamantly against the declaration and the move. Yet this president is unmoved. He seems determined to carry out the promise that presidents preceding him didn't have the political will or courage to honor. Trump has proven that he keeps promises, even bucking the heavy resistance of opposition from outside his own political party and from within. He forges ahead, despite the world's opposition to this decision. He doesn't wither under the fire of the fanaticism of the Islamic world that rages with hatred for Israel.

It is not possible to know for certain, Christian counsel from people such as Dr. Robert Jeffress, pastor of First Baptist Church of Dallas, may have made it known to the president the truth about Israel from God's perspective. Thankfully, Mr. Trump has wisely listened to such counsel, it appears. America stands in much better stead with the Almighty with this fulfilled, presidential promise.

How Near?

One of the prophetic Scriptures most studied by those who hold the premillennial view of end-times matters is the following:

> Now learn a parable of the fig tree; When his branch is yet tender, and putteth forth leaves, ye know that summer is nigh: So likewise ye, when ye shall see all these things, know that it is near, even at the doors. Verily I say unto you, This generation shall not pass, till all these things be fulfilled. Heaven and earth shall pass away, but my words shall not pass away. (Matthew 24:32–35)

Despite the seminaries often teaching that Jesus, in the Olivet Discourse, addresses only the Jews (Israel), many believe Jesus is speaking not just to Israel but to all, Jews and Gentiles alike, who will accept Christ for salvation down through the ages.

Although there are differences of opinion in precisely what the prophecy means, most agree that the fig tree in Scripture refers most often to the nation Israel. This prophecy is thought by many to be among the strongest scriptural reasons to believe that this present generation will experience Christ's return Israel, as is said, is God's prophetic timepiece. The view holds that this generation will see the prophecy fulfilled within the definitive timeline framed by Israel being back in the land God gave them.

Certainly, recent history in combination with current events presents a strong case that gives this view credibility. Consider the following:

1) In Psalm 90, the Bible defines a generation as seventy years.
2) The nation Israel was reborn in a single day, as prophesied, in 1948.
3) We are in the year 2018—seventy years since Israel came back into the land as a nation following World War II.
4) America moved its embassy from Tel Aviv to Jerusalem, letting all the world know that we consider Jerusalem the Jewish state's capital.
5) This happened on May 14, the exact anniversary of the month and day of Israel's rebirth into modernity.

These factors are not all to consider in thinking about Jesus' prophecy. Immediately after He talked about the generation that would see all the prophecies fulfilled, He spoke of several conditions that will mark the last generation before His Second Coming. His "days of Noah, days of Lot" prophecy outlines with precision how that generation will be carrying on life in general when He catastrophically intervenes into human affairs. This is all outlined immediately after Jesus said that no one knows the day or hour when His next intervention will take place.

Jesus indicated that life will be going along as usual, with buying, selling, building, etc. Then He would be "revealed," and the result would be God's judgment that very day.

America's quick movement into the global order seemed assured as the 2016 presidential election loomed. Many Christians feared that liberty, especially for the Christian way of life, would be all but ended if the election went as expected. It would be anything but a time like Jesus described in the "days of Noah, days of Lot" prophecy.

Then came Trump. He came out of the prayers of those called by the Name of Jesus Christ who implored the Lord to act leading up to that election. The miracle occurred. The nation was given not necessarily a godly man, but without a doubt, God's man for the hour, a president who has put in place policies and structure for a profound economic uptick.

Third Temple Talk

President Trump's involvement brings great expectations to the Jews who look with prophetic anticipation to the future. The following explains:

> On Monday, the US Embassy was officially opened in Jerusalem as per the orders of President Donald Trump in what many believe was an integral part of the Messianic process that will culminate in another architectural landmark: the building of the Third Temple....
>
> Rabbi Jeremy Gimpel, the founder of the Land of Israel Network, sees the US Embassy opening in Jerusalem as part of Prophecy and an answer to Jewish prayers.
>
> "The Jewish People have been praying and working toward the day that Jerusalem becomes a praise among the nations," Rabbi Gimpel told *Breaking Israel News*, citing a verse in Isaiah to illustrate his point.[121]

Rabbi Zimble said: "Now, we are seeing just the beginning of this prophecy as nations begin moving their embassies from Tel-Aviv to Jerusalem." He continued, "This is a step in the prophetic process of redemption."

Rabbi Kimble offered thoughts on those religious people who were skeptical about a religious basis for Trump's political decision to move the embassy. "I would encourage those who say that President Trump is not a holy man and therefore can have no place in this Godly process to look to the book of Isaiah and Ezra where the divine plan of restoration was done through a man named Cyrus," he said. "It would be a tragic mistake to view this historic move as unintentional or a coincidence, coming, as it does, on Israel's 70th anniversary."

Rabbi Hillel Weiss, spokesman for the nascent Sanhedrin, an initiative to reestablish the biblically mandated court of seventy-one elders, said Trump's decision, as part of the "redemptive process, is key to the president's success." But, he added a precautionary thought: "The opening of the US Embassy in Jerusalem is not the end; it is a means…. It is one step in the Geula process that is moving towards the Temple, which must, by necessity, involve all the nations and even the Temple is merely a means for sanctifying all of creation."

The following article further elucidates:

Rabbi Shimon Apisdorf, a noted Torah teacher and author, believes the opening of the embassy is explicitly described in Jewish sources as part of the end-of-days process. The rabbi cited Kol Hatur (Cry of the Turtle Dove), written in the 18th century by Rabbi Hillel Rivlin of Shklov, a close disciple of Rabbi Elijah ben Solomon Zalman, the leading rabbi of the generation known as the Vilna Gaon.

The Kol Hatur laid out 156 steps in the process of Moshiach. One of the steps is called Koresh Meshichi based on King Cyrus allowing and even enabling the Jews to come back to Israel and build the Temple.

This step is the role non-Jews and their leaders play in the
Moshiach. It is specifically for non-Jews and as such, is not a
mitzvah that Jews are commanded to perform.[122]

Trump and Third Temple

There is intensifying chatter among religious elements in Israel that
everything that has transpired from Trump's election portends the
soon rebuilding of the Third Temple. The electrifying decision by this
unusual president to move the American Embassy to Jerusalem is just
part of what has ignited the Temple talk. Again, we can best understand
the excitement and all it entails through ongoing Israeli news reports
such the following:

> US President Donald Trump's unabashed support for the Jewish
> state and his public recognition of Jerusalem as its capital have
> many Israelis electrified.
>
> The current American leader's positive attitude toward Israel
> seems nearly illogical, especially after decades of far more hostile
> trends.
>
> A prominent Israeli rabbi believes the reason for this unprec-
> edented (at least in modern times) shift is that Trump has a big
> role to play in the building of the Third Temple and the coming
> of Messiah.[123]

twelve

Tribulation and the Third Temple

ACCUSATIONS COME IN hot and heavy diatribe that those who hold to a literal interpretation of Bible prophecy want a Third Temple built on Moriah to bring on Armageddon and the return of Christ. This, of course, is nonsense. No true students of biblical eschatology from the literalist viewpoint have any these ambitions. Those who hold such a prophetic worldview simply watch with studied interest the developments leading toward Christ's Second Advent. They understand that what has been given by the Old Testament and New Testament prophets will come to pass. The question is only *when.*

There is no wish on the part of these observers for suffering to begin and Armageddon to come. But, it will all happen exactly as God's prophetic Word has foretold. The faithful Bible student's heavenly firective is to faithfully and accurately do his or her best to discern the signs of the times during these—as the late Dr. Chuck Missler once put it—"times of the signs."

Nevertheless, the truth of God's Word cannot be changed. The Third Temple will be the edifice the most despicable tyrant of history—Antichrist—will invade and desecrate as he declares himself to be God.

This will begin the most terrible time in Jewish—and human—history, according to Jeremiah the prophet (Jeremiah 30:7) and the Lord Jesus Christ (Matthew 24:21).

It is the Christian's purpose to lift the holy name of Jesus Christ so that men, women, and children of all races will be drawn to him by the Holy Spirit for salvation. This must never be lost on us while things prophesied unfold during these times so near Christ's return to make all things right on Planet Earth. The Tribulation is something all Christians should warn the world against being a part of, regardless of whether Gentile or Jew. As has clearly been established, the Tribulation—the last seven years of human history also known as "Daniel's seventieth week"—is prophesied to be the most terrible time that human beings will ever endure. The event is based on the prophet Daniel's prophecy of 490 years that will culminate with Christ's Second Advent (Second Coming). Israel (the remaining Israelites who believe in Messiah, Jesus Christ), will then enter the Millennial Kingdom and a thousand-year period of rest and plenty.

The seventy weeks are actually based upon 490 years divided by seventy. Each of the seventy weeks contains seven 360-day Jewish calendar years. The last seven years are a time of unprecedented trouble.

Dr. Thomas Ice writes the following:

We know from the beginning of chapter 9 (verse 2) that Daniel had read about "the number of years which was revealed as the word of the Lord to Jeremiah the prophet for the completion of the desolations of Jerusalem, namely, seventy years." The two passages which Daniel surely studied were Jeremiah 25:11–12 and 29:10–14. Both texts clearly speak of Israel's Babylonian captivity as limited to a 70-year period. Both passages also blend into their texts, statements that look forward to a time of ultimate fulfillment and blessing for the nation of Israel. This is why Daniel appears to think that when the nation returns to their land, then ultimate blessing (the millennial kingdom) will coincide with their return.

Ice goes on to write that Daniel's error was pointed out to the prophet.

> "Daniel appears to think that when the nation returns to their land, then ultimate blessing (the millennial kingdom) will coincide with their return. Daniel's errant thinking about the timing of God's plan for Israel occasioned the Lord's sending of Gabriel "to give you insight with understanding" (Dan. 9:22).
>
> God was not yet ready to bring history to its destined final climax. Thus, He told Daniel that He was going to stretch out history by seventy times seven years (i.e., 490 years).
>
> Study, and history proves to those who believe in these judgments as literal, and accept God's dealing dispensationally with Israel, in particular, and with mankind in general, that 69 of the prophetic weeks (483 years) have been fulfilled. The last week of 7 years will begin…with the confirming of the covenant by "the prince that shall come" (Dan. 9: 27).[124]

thirteen

From Moriah to Millennium

MOUNT MORIAH IS the centerpiece of the wrap-up of the age, according to Jesus Christ.

Before He sat upon the Mount of Olives, just prior to His crucifixion, the Lord told His disciples to "see all these things," meaning to look upon the Temple and its vastness and beauty. As they did so, He said that all of it would be torn down. Not one stone would be left upon another. He then launched into a series of end-times prophecies after answering their question: "Tell us, when shall these things be? and what shall be the sign of thy coming, and of the end of the world?" (Matthew 24:3).

Moriah was to become a barren surface. And, history shows that the Romans indeed inundated that surface with salt so that nothing would grow there. They intended for the Jews to never have a house of worship there again. They wanted to assure that no further rebellion would arise from that promontory.

Rome, for a time, looked at the Second Temple as a possession of the empire and as an asset of sorts. But, with Jewish rebellion, the Roman soldiers under Titus became enraged. The Temple was set on fire—some believe due to an accident—and the destruction began.

The Roman soldiers were allowed to take whatever booty they could find from victory, so they took the Temple apart stone by stone. This is because the Temple walls and nooks and crannies of the building was adorned with gold and silver, and in some places, with precious gemstones. Thus, the soldiers took the building apart to get every last bit of these materials they could find.

Jesus' words to His disciples were fulfilled in AD 70, thirty something years later.

Yet, in that same Olivet Discourse, Jesus indicated that the Temple Mount would one day be occupied by a Jewish Temple again:

> When ye therefore shall see the abomination of desolation, spoken of by Daniel the prophet, stand in the holy place, (whoso readeth, let him understand:)
> Then let them which be in Judaea flee into the mountains:
> Let him which is on the housetop not come down to take any thing out of his house:
> Neither let him which is in the field return back to take his clothes.
> And woe unto them that are with child, and to them that give suck in those days!
> But pray that your flight be not in the winter, neither on the sabbath day:
> For then shall be great tribulation, such as was not since the beginning of the world to this time, no, nor ever shall be. (Matthew 24:15–21)

Let us now look at what rolls out, prophetically, from that Olivet moment until the glorious, millennial reign of Christ comes into human history.

The Temple of Ezekiel

In that day shall the branch of the LORD be beautiful and glorious, and the fruit of the land shall be the excellent and splendid for those who are escaped of Israel.

And it shall come to pass, that he who is left in Zion, and he who remaineth in Jerusalem, shall be called holy, even every one that is written among the living in Jerusalem.

When the Lord shall have washed away the filth of the daughters of Zion and shall have purged the blood of Jerusalem from its midst by the spirit of justice, and by the spirit of burning.

And the LORD will create upon every dwelling place of Mount Zion, and upon her assemblies, a cloud and smoke by day, and the shining of a flaming fire by night; for upon all the glory shall be a defense.

And there shall be a tabernacle for a shadow in the daytime from the heat, and for a place of refuge, and for a covert from storm and from rain. (Isaiah 4:2–6)

Locations have been found of where two temples stood in the past on the Temple Mount. The "First Temple"—Solomon's Temple—was destroyed by Nebuchadnezzar's forces, the armies of Babylon. The destruction took place on the 9th of Av in 586 BC. Jewish exiles, approximately seventy years later, were allowed to return to Jerusalem to build an altar, the Second Jewish Temple, and finally the walls of the city.

The Second Temple, although much less grand, was later greatly enlarged and expanded by Herod the Great. This *Second* Temple was the one in which Jesus was dedicated, and where He taught and cast out the money-changers on two occasions.

The Day of Pentecost following the resurrection of Jesus found Jewish believers assembled for prayer in the Temple courts (Acts 2). There the Holy Spirit came from Heaven to begin the calling out of a new group of believers (both Jews and Gentiles)—a body now known as the church of Jesus Christ. Preaching by the apostles and public miracles recorded in the book of Acts took place in the courts just outside this structure. But the now-magnificent Second Temple was destroyed by General Titus and besieging Roman armies on the 9th of Av in AD 70. This destruction had been predicted by Jesus earlier (see Matthew 24 and Luke 21). Since that time, no Jewish temple has been built on the site, therefore no blood sacrifices for sin have been possible for religious Jews up to the present day.

There are three references to a Third Temple standing at some point on Mount Moriah. Additionally, there are scriptural references to a Fourth Temple that will one day be the edifice at which all people will pay homage to the King of all kings, Jesus Christ.

Jews have an intense interest in the place where the First and Second Temples stood because this is where they await the building of the Third Temple. That structure must be placed upon the hallowed ground where the Holy of Holies once sat. The problem, of course, is that the entire Temple Mount is under the control of the Muslim Waqf. This site has been under such control since it was allowed by Israeli General Moshe Dayan to go into Jordanian hands following Israel's victory in the 1967 Six Day War. It is still a mystery to many why Dayan agreed to such a thing.

The Third and Fourth Jewish Temples

Although the number is growing, only a small portion of Orthodox Jewish believers in Israel believe the Messiah will build the coming Third Temple. Groups like the Temple Institute, however, are dedicated to preparing for every aspect of Temple worship. They believe it can be restarted at first opportunity. Their constant planning, of course, causes great angst among those opposed to such an eventuation. And, the opposition comes from the Islamist factions in and around Jerusalem, Islam in general, and almost the entire so-called international community.

Christians, of course, believe that the Messiah who was promised to the Jewish people, Jesus the Christ (Yeshua), came to Earth already. He will come a second time to establish His millennial kingdom on the Earth, ruling for a thousand years in Jerusalem from the throne of His forefather, King David.

Although the New Testament speaks three times of the existence of a Third Jewish Temple in Jerusalem at the end of the present age, the fate of that Third Temple is not presented in the New Testament.

An immense and devastating earthquake is predicted for when Jesus' foot touches down on the Mount of Olives at His Second Coming. Most of Jerusalem will be destroyed when that quake occurs. There will be great topographical changes. A valley will rip through the region, and water will flow from the holy mountain to the Mediterranean and the Dead Sea. These changes in the entire land when Messiah comes are spoken of in numerous passages of the Bible.

> Comfort ye, comfort ye my people, saith your God.
>
> Speak ye tenderly to Jerusalem, and cry unto her, that her warfare is accomplished, that her iniquity is pardoned; for she hath received from the LORD's hand double for all her sins.
>
> The voice of him that crieth in the wilderness, Prepare ye the way of the LORD, make straight in the desert a highway for our God.
>
> **Every valley shall be exalted, and every mountain and hill be made low; and the crooked shall be made straight, and the rough places plain.**
>
> And the glory of the LORD shall be revealed, and all flesh shall see it together, for the mouth of the LORD hath spoken it. (Isaiah 40:1–5, quoted in Luke 3:5; emphasis added)

And it shall come to pass…saith the Lord GOD, that my fury shall come up in my face.

For in my jealousy and in the fire of my wrath have I spoken, **Surely in that day there shall be a great shaking in the land of Israel;**

So that the fish of the sea, and the fowls of the heavens,, and the beasts of the field, and all creeping things that creep on the earth, and all the men that are upon the face of the earth, shall quake at my presence, and **the mountains shall be thrown down, and the steep places shall fall, and every wall shall fall to the ground.** (Ezekiel 38:18–22, emphasis added)

And the seventh angel poured out his bowl into the air, and there came a great voice out of the temple of heaven, from the throne, saying, It is done.

And there were voices, and thunders, and lightnings; and there was a great earthquake, such as was not since men were upon the earth, so mighty an earthquake, and so great.

And the great city was divided into three parts, and the cities of the nations fell; and great Babylon came in remembrance before God, to give unto her the cup of the wine of the fierceness of his wrath.

And every island fled away, and the mountains were not found.

And there fell upon men a great hail out of heaven, every stone about the weight of a talent; and men blasphemed God because of the plague of the hail; for the plague was exceedingly great. (Revelation 16:17–21)

For I will gather all the nations against Jerusalem to battle; and the city shall be taken, and the houses rifled and the women ravished; half of the city shall go forth into captivity, and the residue of the people shall not be cut off from the city.

Then the LORD will go forth and fight against those nations as when he fights on a day of battle.

And his feet shall stand in that day upon the Mount of Olives, which is before Jerusalem on the east; and the Mount of Olives shall cleave in its midst toward the east and toward the west, and there shall be a very great valley; and half of the mountain shall remove toward the north, and half of it toward the south.

And ye shall flee to the valley of the mountains; for the valley of the mountains shall reach untio Azel; yea, ye shall flee, as ye fled from before the earthquake in the days Uzziah, king of Judah; and the LORD my God, shall come, and all the saints with thee.

And it shall come to pass, in that day, that the light shall not be clear, nor dark,

But it shall be one day which shall be known to the LORD, not day, nor night; but it shall come to pass that, at evening time, it shall be light.

And it shall be, in that day, that living waters shall go out from Jerusalem; half of them toward the former sea, and half of them toward the hinder sea; in summer and in winter shall it be.

And the LORD shall be king over all the earth; in that day shall there be one LORD, his name one.

All the land shall be turned like the Arabah from Geba to Rimmon south of Jerusalem; and it shall be lifted up, and inhabited in its place, from Benjamin's gate unto the place of the first gate, unto the corner gate, and from the towar of Hananel unto the king's winepresses. (Zechariah 14:2–10)

From all the carnage that will come from this devastation, it is easy to presume that the Third Temple sitting atop Moriah will be destroyed. When Christ's foot touches down, the land will be shaken so hard that the very mountains of the world will fall flat. The very topography will certainly have to be rearranged greatly. This is because the Fourth Temple—the one Jesus will Himself have constructed on the Temple site at that time, will be enormous—much larger than the previous structures.

The prophet Ezekiel, in chapters 40–48, presents in great detail a future Temple in Israel that is **much too expansive to fit on the present site that is believed to be where the Temples once sat.** The Temple of Ezekiel proper measures about 875 feet square, and it sits in the middle of a large consecrated area. Bible scholar Lambert Dolphin writes:

> Ezekiel's temple is also very different in many details from any previous temples that have existed in Israel (or elsewhere). Therefore most Bible scholars believe there will one day exist in the Holy Land a Fourth or "Millennial" Temple.
>
> Ezekiel also describes the reapportionment of the land in specific lots during the millennial kingdom. The temple and the temple district are not part of the rebuilt city of Jerusalem according to the details of this reapportionment. Note that the Temple area will be located to the North of rebuilt Jerusalem:
>
> "When you allot the land as a possession, you shall set apart for the Lord a portion of the land as a holy district, twenty-five thousand cubits long and twenty thousand cubits broad; it shall be holy throughout its whole extent. Of this a square plot of five hundred by five hundred cubits shall be for the sanctuary, with fifty cubits for an open space around it. And in the holy district you shall measure off a section twenty-five thousand cubits long and ten thousand broad, in which shall be the sanctuary, the most holy place. It shall be the holy portion of the land; it shall be for the priests, who minister in the sanctuary and approach the Lord to minister to him; and it shall be a place for their houses and a holy place for the sanctuary. Another section, twenty-five

thousand cubits long and ten thousand cubits broad, shall be for the Levites who minister at the temple, as their possession for cities to live in."

"Alongside the portion set apart as the holy district you shall assign for the possession of the city an area five thousand cubits broad, and twenty-five thousand cubits long it shall belong to the whole house of Israel."

"And to the prince shall belong the land on both sides of the holy district and the property of the city, on the west and on the east, corresponding in length to one of the tribal portions, and extending from the western to the eastern boundary of the land. It is to be his property in Israel. And my princes shall no more oppress my people; but they shall let the house of Israel have the land according to their tribes." (Ezekiel 45:1–8.)

Adjoining the territory of Judah, from the east side to the west, shall be the portion which you shall set apart, twenty-five thousand cubits in breadth, and in length equal to one of the tribal portions, from the east side to the west, with the sanctuary in the midst of it. The portion which you shall set apart for the Lord shall be twenty-five thousand cubits in length, and twenty thousand in breadth. (Ezekiel 48).[125]

Many Bible scholars hold that the purpose of the Fourth Jewish Temple (Ezekiel 40–45) will be to serve as a memorial to the holiness of God. It will apparently be a teaching center to instruct men about proper worship during Christ's millennial reign on earth.

Because the bloodline of humanity will still be tainted by the original sin from the Fall in the Garden of Eden, people born during the thousand-year reign of Christ will have to be redeemed from sin if they are to go to Heaven. The Temple will, in part, be in place to remind everyone of the substitutionary death of Jesus on the cross, as the "Lamb of God," more than two thousand years earlier.

Fourth Temple Thoughts

The following is excerpted from Lambert Dolphin's excellent essay, *The Temple of Ezekiel* (used by permission).

Mr. John W. Schmitt of Portland, Oregon (Ref. 3) has devoted many years to a study of Ezekiel's Temple, and to the construction of several fine scale models used for educational purposes.

Ezekiel had planned to enter the priestly service in the First Temple when he reached thirty years of age. His plans were cut short in 597 when King Nebuchadnezzar raided and captured Jerusalem after a brief siege, taking with him young king Jehoichin and "all the princes, and all the mighty men of valor, ten thousand captives, and all the craftsmen and smiths." (2 Kings 24:14). (By way of reference, Daniel and his three friends of the tribe of Judah plus others from Jerusalem had previously been taken to Babylon in a raid by General—soon to be King—Nebuchadnezzar after the battle of Carchemish in 605. That famous battle ended the rule of Egypt in the ancient world).

In the fifth year of his own exile from Jerusalem, that is in 593 BC, Ezekiel was called by God to exercise a prophetic ministry to the house of Israel which he continued until about the year 570. Ezekiel was married, in fact his wife died as a sign from God on the day the siege of Jerusalem began, (24:18).

Ezekiel's temple and the millennium occupies the last eight long chapters of his book. He gives 318 precise measurements of the temple using some 37 unique words that are architectural terms, such as "door-posts," "windows," etc. Ezekiel received this great wealth of information on the millennial temple in the year 573 BC in the form of a vision and a personally conducted tour of the temple by "a man whose appearance was like the appearance of bronze." (Evidently *the* Angel of the Lord). "He had a line of flax and a measuring rod in his hand and he stood in the gateway." (40:3) The tour began at the Eastern Gate—which was closed:

"Then he brought me back to the outer gate of the sanctuary, which faces east; and it was shut. And he said to me, "This gate shall remain shut; it shall not be opened, and no one shall enter by it; for the LORD, the God of Israel, has entered by it; therefore it shall remain shut. Only the prince may sit in it to eat bread before the LORD; he shall enter by way of the vestibule of the gate, and shall go out by the same way." (44:1–3)

The present Golden Gate in the Eastern Wall of the Temple Mount in Jerusalem is walled shut. Jewish and Arab tradition teaches—probably because of a misinterpretation of this passage in Ezekiel—that the Jewish Messiah is to enter the Golden Gate. For that reason the gate was walled up by the Arabs in the 11th Century after the Crusades, (if not earlier) or perhaps by Suleiman the Magnificent in AD 1539–1542—to prevent the Jewish Messiah from entering. The much older gate beneath the present Golden Gate, or else another (as yet undiscovered) gate in the Eastern wall could have been the one used by Jesus when He rode into Jerusalem on Palm Sunday riding on the foal of a donkey.

In addition to being a very large and complex structure Ezekiel's temple differs in several very important ways from any previously existing Jewish temple. These have been cataloged by researcher John Schmitt, a Portland, Oregon Bible scholar, as follows:

Features Unique to Ezekiel's Temple

- No wall of partition to exclude Gentiles (compare Ephesians 2:14) The Gentiles were previously welcome in the Outer Courts, but excluded from the inner courts on pain of death.
- No Court of Women (compare Galatians 3:28 (Outer Court and Inner Court only)

- No Laver (see Ezekiel 36:24–27, John 15:3)
- No Table of Shewbread (see Micah 5:4, John 6:35)
- No Lampstand or Menorah (see Isaiah 49:6, John 8:12)
- No Golden Altar of Incense (Zechariah 8:20–23, John 14:6)
- No Veil (Isaiah 25:6–8, Matthew 27:51)
- No Ark of the Covenant (Jeremiah 3:16, John 10:30–33)
- Major Changes to the Altar: The sacrificial Altar will be approached by a ramp from the East. Previous altars were all approached from the South. Now there will be stairs to the altar, not a ramp as previously. The top of the altar is now described by the Hebrew word "ariel" [Isaiah 29:1] meaning "hearth of God" or "lion of God." [Rev. 5:5].

If the previous temples, as well as the Tabernacle of Moses, are pictures for us of man as the dwelling place of God, then Ezekiel's temple may be intended to teach us about the marvelously new resurrection bodies waiting for every believer when he leaves this present life (2 Corinthians 5:1–5).

Believing saints from the Old Testament epoch, saints from the Christian era, and all those raised from the dead at the rapture and at the second coming of Christ in glory receive new resurrection bodies, like that of Jesus, as detailed in 1 Corinthians 15. Yet, after the Battle of Armageddon, Jesus will gather all the survivors of the nations outside Jerusalem and determine which individual sons and daughters of Adam are worthy to enter the Millennial Kingdom on earth. This is the famous judgment of the sheep and the goats described by our Lord in Matthew 25:31–46, and also given by the prophet Joel:

"For behold, in those days and at that time, when I restore the fortunes of Judah and Jerusalem, I will gather all the nations and bring them down to the valley of Jehoshaphat, and I will enter into judgment with them there, on account of my people and my heritage Israel, because they have scattered them among the nations, and have divided up my land, and have cast lots for my people, and have given a boy for a harlot, and have sold a girl for wine, and have drunk it. "What are you to me, O Tyre and Sidon, and all the regions of Philistia? Are you paying me back for something? If you are paying me back, I will requite your deed upon your own head swiftly and speedily. For you have taken my silver and my gold, and have carried my rich treasures into your temples. You have sold the people of Judah and Jerusalem to the Greeks, removing them far from their own border. But now I will stir them up from the place to which you have sold them, and I will requite your deed upon your own head. I will sell your sons and your daughters into the hand of the sons of Judah, and they will sell them to the Sabeans, to a nation far off; for the LORD has spoken." Proclaim this among the nations: Prepare war, stir up the mighty men. Let all the men of war draw near, let them come up. Beat your plowshares into swords, and your pruning hooks into spears; let the weak say, "I am a warrior."

Hasten and come, all you nations round about, gather yourselves there. Bring down thy warriors, O LORD. Let the nations bestir themselves, and come up to the valley of Jehoshaphat; for there I will sit to judge all the nations round about. Put in the sickle, for the harvest is ripe. Go in, tread, for the wine press is full. The vats overflow, for their wickedness is great. Multitudes, multitudes, in the valley of decision! For the day of the LORD is near in the valley of decision. The sun and the moon are darkened, and the stars withdraw their shining. And the LORD roars from Zion, and utters his voice from Jerusalem, and the heavens and the earth shake. But the LORD is a refuge to his people, a stronghold to the people of Israel. "So you shall know that I am the LORD your God, who dwell in Zion, my holy mountain. And Jerusalem shall be holy and strangers shall never again pass through it. "And in that day the mountains shall drip sweet wine, and the hills shall flow with milk, and all the stream beds of Judah shall flow with water; and a fountain shall come forth from the house of the LORD and water the valley of Shittim. "Egypt shall become a desolation and Edom a desolate wilderness, for the violence done to the people of Judah, because they have shed innocent blood in their land. But Judah shall be inhabited for ever, and Jerusalem to all generations. I will avenge their blood, and I will not clear the guilty, for the LORD dwells in Zion." (Joel 3)

The criterion for judgment at this time will be how individuals Gentiles have treated the Jews, especially believing Jews who constitute "true Israel." The "Sheep" category clearly represents those righteous gentiles whose hearts are right before the Lord, that is they are all regenerated men and women, but individuals who have not previously received their resurrection bodies. They will repopulate the earth, according to Christian belief, during the thousand year reign of Messiah under greatly improved living conditions:

"But be glad and rejoice for ever in that which I create; for behold, I create Jerusalem a rejoicing, and her people a joy. I will rejoice in Jerusalem, and be glad in my people; no more shall be heard in it the sound of weeping and the cry of distress. No more shall there be in it an infant that lives but a few days, or an old man who does not fill out his days, for the child shall die a hundred years old, and the sinner a hundred years old shall be accursed. They shall build houses and inhabit them; they shall plant vineyards and eat their fruit. They shall not build and another inhabit; they shall not plant and another eat; for like the days of a tree shall the days of my people be, and my chosen shall long enjoy the work of their hands. They shall not labor in vain, or bear children for calamity; for they shall be the offspring of the blessed of the LORD, and their children with them. Before they call I will answer, while they are yet speaking I will hear. The wolf and the lamb shall feed together, the lion shall eat straw like the ox; and dust shall be the serpent's food. They shall not hurt or destroy in all my holy mountain, says the LORD." (Isaiah 65:18–25)

During this thousand year reign of Yeshua over a restored earth, with Satan locked away in the abyss (Rev. 20:2), sinners will be born on the earth and will need to be instructed in matters of God's grace and mercy. For this reason most commentators on Ezekiel believe that the Fourth Temple will be Memorial in nature, looking back in time to the cross of Jesus Christ, just as the Tabernacle and First and Second Temples pointed ahead in time to the cross. The prescribed worship services of Ezekiel's temple are also described for us in great detail by the prophet. The priests presiding over the temple services will be of the line of Zadok (44:15) who proved faithful after the failure of the Levitical priests in the line of Eli (1 Samuel 2:35, 1 Kings 2:26–27, 35). The Millennial Temple will not have a separate High Priest. Instead the previously separate offices of King and Priest will be combined in the Messiah as noted, (See Zechariah 6:9–15)

Approximate Distribution of Land to the Twelve Tribes during Messiah's Coming Reign

In addition to the physical differences in Ezekiel's Temple a number of changes are made in the annual cycle of Jewish feasts. It is very clearly that the Millennial Temple sacrifices are definitely not a re-instatement of the Mosaic system.

Another feature of the Millennial Temple is the presence of a great stream of fresh water which issues from beneath the Southern wall of the Temple. Ezekiel describes this river, which divides into two branches and flows Westward into the Mediterranean Sea and also Eastward into the Northern end of the Dead Sea, freshening all the land South of Jericho,

Then he brought me back to the door of the temple; and behold, water was issuing from below the threshold of the temple toward the east (for the temple faced east); and the water was flowing down from below the south end of the threshold of the temple, south of the altar. Then he brought me out by way of the north gate, and led me round on the outside to the outer gate, that faces toward the east; and the water was coming out on the south side. Going on eastward with a line in his hand, the man measured a thousand cubits, and then led me through the water; and it was ankle-deep. Again he measured a thousand, and led me through the water; and it was knee-deep. Again he measured a thousand, and led me through the water; and it was up to the loins. Again he measured a thousand, and it was a river that I could not pass through, for the water had risen; it was deep enough to swim in, a river that could not be passed through.

And he said to me, "Son of man, have you seen this?" Then he led me back along the bank of the river. As I went back, I saw upon the bank of the river very many trees on the one side and on the other. And he said to me, "This water flows toward the eastern region and goes down into the Arabah; and when it enters the stagnant waters of the sea, the water will become fresh. And wherever the river goes every living creature which swarms will live, and there will be very many fish; for this water goes there, that the waters of the sea may become fresh; so everything will live where the river goes. Fishermen will stand beside the sea; from Engedi to Eneglaim it will be a place for the spreading of nets; its fish will be of very many kinds, like the fish of the Great Sea. But its swamps and marshes will not become fresh; they are to be left for salt. And on the banks, on both sides of the river, there will grow all kinds of trees for food. Their leaves will not wither nor their fruit fail, but they will bear fresh fruit every month, because the water for them flows from the sanctuary. Their fruit will be for food, and their leaves for healing." (47:1–12)

This same stream of water seems to be identical to that described in Zechariah 14:8 and Joel 3:18. If so then the site of the Fourth Temple would seem to be on or near the present Temple Mount in Jerusalem. If this is so, then the city of Jerusalem will evidently be rebuilt to the South since the temple holy district is specified in Ezekiel 48 as North of the rebuilt city of Jerusalem. Some commentators have suggested that the Millennial Temple will be located at Shiloh, 31 kilometers to the North of present day Jerusalem.

A second reason for believing that the site of Ezekiel's Temple may be near the present Temple Mount is found in Ezekiel's description of the return of the Lord to dwell forever with His people Israel. The Lord says the people will no longer defile the temple site with the dead bodies of their kings. Since there are so many cemeteries on and around the Temple Mount this would require a special ritual cleansing of the entire area (described by Ezekiel), and of course the relocation of the rebuilt City to the South of the Temple district as we have already noted:

Afterward he (the angel of the Lord brought me (Ezekiel) to the gate, the gate facing east. And behold, the glory of the God of Israel came from the east; and the sound of his coming was like the sound of many waters; and the earth shone with his glory. And the vision I saw was like the vision which I had seen when he came to destroy the city, and like the vision which I had seen by the river Chebar; and I fell upon my face. As the glory of the LORD entered the temple by the gate facing east, the Spirit lifted me up, and brought me into the inner court; and behold, the glory of the LORD filled the temple. While the man was standing beside me, I heard one speaking to me out of the temple; and he said to me, "Son of man, this is the place of my throne and the place of the soles of my feet, where I will dwell in the midst of the people of Israel for ever.

And the house of Israel shall no more defile my holy name, neither they, nor their kings, by their harlotry, and by the dead bodies of their kings, by setting their threshold by my threshold and their doorposts beside my doorposts, with only a wall between me and them. They have defiled my holy name by their abominations which they have committed, so I have consumed them in my anger. Now let them put away their idolatry and the dead bodies of their kings far from me, and I will dwell in their midst for ever. "And you, son of man, describe to the house of Israel the temple and its appearance and plan, that they may be ashamed of their iniquities. And if they are ashamed of all that they have done, portray the temple, its arrangement, its exits and its entrances, and its whole form; and make known to them all its ordinances and all its laws; and write it down in their sight, so that they may observe and perform all its laws and all its ordinances. This is the law of the temple: the whole territory round about upon the top of the mountain shall be most holy. Behold, this is the law of the temple. (Ezekiel 43:1–12)

Jerusalem, the rebuilt city in Israel, on earth, during the Millennium, should not be confused with the heavenly city known as "New Jerusalem," referred to in the New Testament, (Hebrews 11:16, 12:18–29, Revelation 21–22) which seems to take the form of a great orbiting or stationary satellite above the earth. This vast city whose dimensions are of the order of 1500 miles on a side, may be connected to the millennial temple by a space-time gate way. The New Jerusalem does not include a temple (Revelation 21:22, 23)—"The Lord God, the Almighty and the Lamb, are its temple."

During the millennial kingdom sin will continue to exist on

the earth, but all forms of defilement and sin are clearly excluded from the New Jerusalem, and guarded against by the complex rituals proscribed for the Temple of Ezekiel on the earth.

Ezekiel saw in a great vision the departure of the glory (the *Shekinah*) of God from the Temple of Solomon, (Ezekiel 9:1–11:25). In a subsequent vision of Jerusalem in 573 BC, eighteen years later, Ezekiel was shown the future return of the Shekinah to Israel and to the Temple (43:1–12). That future day had also been foreseen by the prophet Isaiah:

In that day the Branch of the LORD shall be beautiful and glorious; And the fruit of the earth shall be excellent and appealing For those of Israel who have escaped. And it shall come to pass that he who is left in Zion and remains in Jerusalem will be called holy—everyone who is recorded among the living in Jerusalem. When the Lord has washed away the filth of the daughters of Zion, and purged the blood of Jerusalem from her midst, by the spirit of judgment and by the spirit of burning, then the LORD will create above every dwelling place of Mount Zion, and above her assemblies, a cloud and smoke by day and the shining of a flaming fire by night. For over all the glory there will be a covering. And there will be a tabernacle for shade in the daytime from the heat, for a place of refuge, and for a shelter from storm and rain. (Isaiah 4:2–6)

Although we are given much information in the Bible on Tabernacle and Temples, the principal Biblical emphasis is not on buildings but on men and their character, scripture does not negate the use of shadows and symbols.

"Thus says the Lord: 'Heaven is my throne and the earth is my footstool; what is the house which you would build for me, and what is the place of my rest. All these things my hand has made, and so all these things are mine, says the Lord. But this is the man to whom I look, he that is humble and contrite in spirit and trembles at my word" (Isaiah 66:1, 2).[126]

As Christ's Millennial Kingdom Nears

Israel is the sure signal that Bible prophecy is on track to fulfillment.
The Third Temple will be built just as foretold and precisely on time
in bringing all things to fruition that are scheduled prior to the Second
Advent of Jesus Christ.

God's chief adversary, Satan, will do all he can to prevent fulfillment
of things to come. He must change history as predicted by God's Word.
To change that prophesied future would be to change his own fate—
being cast into the Lake of Fire.

> And the devil that deceived them was cast into the lake of fire
> and brimstone, where the beast and the false prophet are, and
> shall be tormented day and night for ever and ever. (Revelation
> 20:10)

The following article frames the battle being waged even now, while
things surrounding the Temple Mount are ramping up for the dénoue-
ment of human history.

Satan's Plan to Steal Jerusalem

On May 14, 2018, the U.S. moved its embassy from Tel Aviv to
Jerusalem. The Jews were rejoicing in Jerusalem (dancing, prais-
ing God, etc.) and the Palestinians were rioting in Gaza (about
60 killed, more than 2,000 wounded, etc.).

A Christian friend called and asked, "What is the big deal?"

The big deal is that God has a plan for Jerusalem and Satan
is using Turkey, Iran, Hezbollah, Hamas, the Palestinians and
others to try to stop it.

The Bible mentions Jerusalem more than any other city on
earth (over 800 times).

Prime Minister Netanyahu quoted Zech. 8:3 at the U.S.

embassy Dedication Service. Here is Zech. 8:2–8 and what I think God said.

"Thus saith the LORD of hosts; I was jealous for Zion with great jealousy, and I was jealous for her with great fury. Thus saith the LORD; I am returned unto Zion, and will dwell in the midst of Jerusalem: and Jerusalem shall be called a city of truth; and the mountain of the LORD of hosts the holy mountain. Thus saith the LORD of hosts; There shall yet old men and old women dwell in the streets of Jerusalem, and every man with his staff in his hand for very age. And the streets of the city shall be full of boys and girls playing in the streets thereof. Thus saith the LORD of hosts; If it be marvellous in the eyes of the remnant of this people in these days, should it also be marvellous in mine eyes? saith the LORD of hosts.

Thus saith the LORD of hosts; Behold, I will save my people from the east country, and from the west country; And I will bring them, and they shall dwell in the midst of Jerusalem: and they shall be my people, and I will be their God, in truth and in righteousness" (Zech. 8:2–8 KJV).

This has not been fulfilled. God's jealousy means God doesn't intend to let Satan have Jerusalem (Jesus was presented to God at Jerusalem; Jesus suffered and died at Jerusalem; Jesus ascended into heaven at Jerusalem; Jesus is coming back to Jerusalem; the Church began at Jerusalem and more).

God's plan calls for Jesus to dwell in Jerusalem (on the Temple Mount), for Him to rule and be worshiped there, and for His Word to go fourth out of Jerusalem during the Millennium (Isa. 2:1–2; Psa. 132:13; Isa. 2:3). Satan wants to stop this.

Satan wants to be worshipped. He doesn't want Jesus to dwell in Jerusalem, be worshipped and the Word of God to go all over the world. Satan doesn't want to be cast into the bottomless pit for a thousand years (Rev. 20:1–3).

To fulfil His plan, God said He would bring the Jews back

to Israel from other countries. He would cause Jerusalem to be rebuilt as a dwelling place for Jews of all ages. He said the return of the Jews and the rebuilding of Jerusalem will be marvelous in the eyes of the Jewish people (thus the rejoicing). But that is just a foretaste of the future because all Israel will be saved and He will be their God.

About 2% of the Jews are Messianic Jews and, as far as I know, they understand God's plan. Some of the Jews are religious, but they wrongly think they can go back under the Law (rebuild the Temple, resume the animal sacrifices, etc.) and fulfil God's plan. The remainder of the Jews are secular (not religious) and they have other ideas about what the nation should be doing.

Jerusalem occupies a unique position in two Bible timelines: the beginning and the end of the "times of the Gentiles" (Luke 21:24) and the beginning and the end of the "seventieth week of Daniel" (the Tribulation Period; Dan. 9:24–27).

The "times of the Gentiles" began with the destruction of Jerusalem by Babylon in Old Testament times (Dan. 1:1-2; 2:31–45) and they will end when Gentiles can no longer influence the events in Jerusalem (at the Second Coming of Jesus [Zech. 14:1–4; Luke 21:24]);

The "seventieth week of Daniel" (Tribulation Period) will begin when the Antichrist confirms a worthless treaty with Israel and many others for seven years of peace in Jerusalem and the Middle East (Dan. 9:27) and it will end when Jesus comes back to the Mount of Olives in Jerusalem (Zech. 14:1–4).

The existence of Jerusalem was necessary to fulfill all of these prophecies plus another very important one, "Behold, I will make Jerusalem a cup of trembling unto all the people round about, when they shall be in the siege both against Judah *and* against Jerusalem. And in that day will I make Jerusalem a burdensome stone for all people: all that burden themselves with it shall be cut in pieces, though all the people of the earth be gathered together against it" (Zech. 12:2–3).

Dr. John Hagee delivered the closing benediction at the U.S. embassy service. Among other things, he said, "It was You oh LORD who gathered the exiles from the nations and brought them home again. It was You who made statehood possible. It was You who gave a miraculous victory in 1967 when Jerusalem was reopened to worshipers of all faiths. Jerusalem is the city of God. Jerusalem is the heartbeat of Israel. Jerusalem is the place where Abraham placed his son on the altar of the Temple Mount and became the father of many nations. Jerusalem is where Isaiah and Jeremiah penned principles of righteousness that became the moral foundations of western civilization. Jerusalem is where Messiah will come and establish a kingdom that will never end."

He added, "Let the word go forth from Jerusalem today that 'Israel lives.'" Shout it from the housetops that 'Israel lives.' Let every Islamic terrorist hear this message: 'Israel lives.' Let it be heard in the halls of the United Nations: 'Israel lives.' Let it echo down the halls of the presidential palace in Iran: 'Israel lives.' Let it be known to all men that 'Israel lives' because He that keepeth Israel neither slumbers nor sleeps."

Just prior to Dr. Hagee's words, Prime Min. Netanyahu told the gathered dignitaries, they had come to Jerusalem "at a time when Israel is a rising power in the world."

That reminds me of something Jesus said, "Now learn a parable of the fig tree; When his branch is yet tender, and putteth forth leaves, ye know that summer *is* nigh: So likewise ye, when ye shall see all these things, know that it is near, *even* at the doors. Verily I say unto you, This generation shall not pass, till all these things be fulfilled" (Matt. 24:32–33).

The fig tree (Israel) is putting forth leaves. It is a rising power. The U.S. has moved its embassy to Jerusalem. Two more nations (Guatemala and Paraguay), followed suit before the week was over.

On Monday, May 14, 2018, Gaza was in turmoil. Hamas terrorists and Palestinians were being killed. Turkey's Pres. Erdogan recalled his ambassadors from the U.S. and Israel.

On Wednesday, Turkey's Pres. Erdogan said, "We will continue to be with our Palestinian siblings not only with our hearts, but with all our resources." He added, "We will never allow Jerusalem to be stolen by Israel."

On Thursday, a Turkish newspaper with ties to Mr. Erdogan was calling for the creation of an Islamic army to attack Israel, and Iran's Ayatollah Khameni said, "Palestine will be liberated from the enemies and Jerusalem will be its capital."

God's kingdom on earth is approaching. The Jews are rejoicing. Satan is raging. Israel's enemies are deceived. Jerusalem is a burdensome stone.

Israel is not trying to steal Jerusalem from the Palestinians. Satan is trying to steal Jerusalem from God. And He has already assured us that we win.[127]

fourteen

Jacob's Trouble Temple

JOYFUL EXCITEMENT ABOUNDS among some today over prospects for the rebuilding of a Jewish Temple. This variety of excitement, however, displays a profound lack of understanding about what God's Word has to say about the Third Temple that will certainly, without a shadow of doubt, be constructed atop Mount Moriah. And, as I said at the start of this book, I predict US President Donald Trump will, as the rabbis in Israel hold, soon speak in favor of its construction. *This will be the single most important and prophetic event in our lifetime!* And when it happens, those who find great joy in the Temple's recreation will shortly thereafter experience exuberance turning to terror. From that Temple will flow the very source of all the hatred that has existed since the third part of the angelic throng rebelled in Heaven.

Its construction and establishment as the first Temple Mount place of worship for the Jews since the destruction of the Second Temple in AD 70 will indeed produce elation. It will be the answer to the desire most religious Jews have clung to down through the centuries.

Many believe the Temple again being built atop Moriah will be the result of a peace agreement between Israel and its enemies—between Israel and the rest of the world, for that matter.

When the announcement allowing that Temple construction is made, there will be celebrations like nothing that has been seen in the streets of Jerusalem since the time of King David. Not only the Jews, but most people around the globe who are aware of matters involved in the peace agreement, will be ecstatic. Cessation of hostilities will at last have come to this one place on Earth where World War III could have broken out at any moment.

Diplomats of the international community, of the United Nations and all other such august geopolitical bodies, will congratulate themselves for such a master stroke of genius, guaranteeing the peace of the Middle East, and of the world. And, it will, indeed, be a genius at the heart of confirming such a brilliant covenant, as that coming document will appear to be.

As has been pointed out several times before in this book, everything is already in preparation for the moment the Temple is built and the Temple worship is again established. The priests and their attire, all the vessels, and other items of Temple activity are in place. The sacrifices and oblations will begin in earnest. The sons and daughters of Abraham will have returned to the most holy place of their Mosaic system. No longer will it be: *"Next year in Jerusalem!"*

It is easy to imagine that even the totally secular, that is, the non-religious Jewish populations of the world, will feel their Jewishness. They will feel victorious as they sense their biological ties to Abraham, Isaac, and Jacob surging within.

They have been outcasts throughout the millennia. They have been hated, hunted, and hounded in practically every nation into which they have been scattered. Now…now…they can cry with a loud voice as one, *"Peace and safety at last!"*

All who have hated, hunted, and hounded them will now be governed by a personage like no other in memory. His sense of fairness and his passionate and compassionate championing of the Jewish race that has been so persecuted throughout the centuries will no doubt bring tears of love and adulation for the leader who has stepped forth from the nations to set all things right to give them a respectful place among their fellow man.

His preternatural ability to convince Israel's most hate-filled antagonists to allow the Jews to establish their Temple upon its holy place where the Ark of the Covenant once sat will move many within Judaism to declare him their long-awaited Messiah. This leader of unprecedented abilities will appear to have answers to not only the problems of the Jews, but to all the world's problems.

Those who hold to the literalist view of end-time matters believe there is first coming a an event that will bring the world into chaos, anarchy, and great trouble—socially, geopolitically, economically, and religiously. When it occurs, normal life will be turned upside down. People will clamor for a savior—one who will make things right. But, they will not seek the true Savior. They will look to the one the apostle John called "Antichrist."

This man who will seem to have the answers to the great dilemmas of mankind will step onto the stage of human history for his prophesied destiny as earth's last and most terrible despot. He will be the man of the hour ready to step forward and take control.

At first, Antichrist will seem to restore sensibility to a world gone mad. He will start the process that appears to bring world peace through the covenant that Israel will accept. That covenant will almost certainly include the guarantee of Israel's security and will allow the building of the Third Temple on Mount Moriah.

This will happen because Antichrist's irresistible presence will be the result of an invisible network of thousands of years of collective knowledge. He will be the embodiment of a very old, super-intelligent spirit. As Jesus Christ was the "seed of the woman" (Genesis 3:15), this man will be the "seed of the serpent." Moreover, though his arrival in the form of a man is foretold by numerous Scriptures, the broad masses will not immediately recognize him for what he actually is—paganism's ultimate incarnation: the "beast" of Revelation 13:1.

It's been assumed for centuries that a prerequisite for the coming of Antichrist would be a disturbance in the world order—such as we've witnessed with the election of Donald Trump—following which national boundaries would dissolve and ethnic groups, ideologies, religions, and economics from around the world would grow to orchestrate a single and dominant sovereignty. At the head of the utopian administration, a single personality will surface. He will appear to be a man of distinguished character, but will ultimately become "a king of fierce countenance" (Daniel 8:23). With imperious decree, he will facilitate a one-world government, universal religion, and global socialism. Those who refuse his New World Order will inevitably be imprisoned or destroyed until at last he exalts himself "above all that is called God, or that is worshiped, so that he, as God, sitteth in the temple of God, showing himself that he is God" (2 Thessalonians 2:4).

The question arises for those unfamiliar with the subject of the building of the Third Temple, the one that Antichrist will be instrumental in getting built: Where in the Bible do we find the fact that the Temple will be built? On top of that, where in the Bible do we read where that Temple will be placed?

Bible prophecy doesn't divulge precisely *when* the Temple will be built. However, we have four passages as proof texts that there will be a Temple atop the Temple Mount.

1. **Daniel 9:20–21, 24–27** The first proof text is found in the book of Daniel, in a message delivered to the prophet by the angel Gabriel, one of the Lord's mightiest messengers:

> And while I was speaking, and praying, and confessing my sin and the sin of my people, Israel, and presenting my supplication before the LORD, my God, for the holy mountain of my God;
> Yea, while I was speaking in prayer, even the man Gabriel, whom I had seen in the vision at the beginning, being caused to

fly swiftly, touched me about the time of the evening oblation. (Daniel 9:20–21)

The prophet had his mind, heart, and prayers, directed toward the one place on Earth considered the Most Holy: the Temple Mount, Mount Moriah. Daniel prayed that God would restore that place of worship to his people, the the Jews. The dumbfounded prophet could barely take in the breathtaking words of the angel:

Seventy weeks are determined upon thy people and upon thy holy city, to finish the transgression, and to make an end of sins, and to make reconciliation for iniquity, and to bring in everlasting righteousness, and to seal up the vision and prophecy, and to anoint the most Holy.

Know, therefore, and understand, that from the going forth of the commandment to restore and to build Jerusalem unto the Messiah, the Prince, shall be seven weeks, and threescore and two weeks: the street shall be built again, and the wall, even in troublous times.

And after threescore and two weeks shall Messiah be cut off, but not for himself: and the people of the prince that shall come shall destroy the city and the sanctuary; and the end thereof shall be with a flood, and unto the end of the war desolations are determined.

And he shall confirm the covenant with many for one week: and in the midst of the week he shall cause the sacrifice and the oblation to cease, and for the overspreading of abominations he shall make it desolate, even until the consummation, and that determined shall be poured upon the desolate. (Daniel 9:24–27)

Gabriel laid out the entire plan from the time the prophet sat praying toward Jerusalem and the Temple Mount. The angel said everything was set to put an end to the miserable mess Satan had made of his creation and man's part in the rebellion against the Lord.

The Messiah would come to offer Himself as Israel's Savior, but would be "cut off"—that is, would die…be crucified.

Gabriel's message from the Lord jumped forward quickly, telling that the city—Jerusalem—and the sanctuary—the Temple on Moriah—would be destroyed. This, of course, happened in AD 70 when the Roman legion did just as the prophecy foretold.

There was no Temple at the time Daniel sat dumbfounded before Gabriel as he took in the prophecy, but obviously one would be built.. But, that one yet to be built would be destroyed—again—in AD 70 by General Titus and the Roman soldiers, as covered earlier.

Gabriel indicated that the people who would destroy the city and sanctuary (the Romans, as it turned out) would produce the "prince that shall come" who would at some point "confirm the covenant with many." Then the rest of human history leading up to the end of the age would gush upon the world like a flood.

This whole prophetic process would encompass seventy prophetic weeks, which adds up to 490 prophetic years. The Messiah being "cut off"—crucified—happened at the sixty-ninth prophetic week mark. The last of the seventy weeks won't begin until the "prince that shall come" "confirms the covenant with many." This is when Antichrist assures the peace and safety of the Jewish people.[128]

2. **Matthew 24:15–21 and Mark 13:14–19** The second scriptural proof text that a Third Temple will be built is given by the Lord Jesus Christ Himself and recorded in two books of the Gospel.

> When ye, therefore, shall see the abomination of desolation, spoken of by Daniel the prophet, stand in the holy place, (whoso readeth, let him understand:)
> Then let them which be in Judaea flee into the mountains:

Let him which is on the housetop not come down to take any thing out of his house:

Neither let him which is in the field return back to take his clothes.

And woe unto them that are with child, and to them that give suck in those days!

But pray ye that your flight be not in the winter, neither on the sabbath day:

For then shall be great tribulation, such as was not since the beginning of the world to this time, no, nor ever shall be. (Matthew 24:15–21)

But when ye shall see the abomination of desolation, spoken of by Daniel the prophet, standing where it ought not, (let him that readeth understand,) then let them that be in Judaea flee to the mountains:

And let him that is on the housetop not go down into the house, neither enter therein, to take any thing out of his house:

And let him that is in the field not turn back again for to take up his garment.

But woe to them that are with child, and to them that give suck in those days!

And pray ye that your flight be not in the winter.

For in those days shall be affliction, such as was not from the beginning of the creation which God created unto this time, neither shall be. (Mark 13:14–19)

Jesus plainly prophesied that the "desolation of abomination" was spoken of by "Daniel the prophet." This would be the "prince that will come" Daniel was told about by Gabriel. This "abomination of desolation"—Antichrist, according to the apostle John (1 John 2:18)—will declare himself to be God while standing in the "holy place."

Jesus and Daniel tell us that the worse time of human history will unfold from this point. The time when Antichrist stands in the "holy place," the Temple atop Moriah, will be especially bad for the Jewish people, whom Jesus warns to flee into the mountains. They are not to even gather clothing. "Just go" is the command.

Antichrist will begin his reign of absolute terror in the middle of Daniel's seventieth prophetic week, according to Jesus. Three and one-half years into the Tribulation, this abomination of a man will declare himself to be God, demand worship, and immediately begin genocide against the Jewish people worse than anything Hitler, Himmler, and Goering could have imagined. As mentioned throughout this book, Jeremiah the prophet called this period "the time of Jacob's trouble." More about that prophecy later.

3. **2 Thessalonians 2:3–4** The third scriptural proof text of a Third Temple being constructed is given by the apostle Paul:

> Let no man deceive you by any means: for that day shall not come, except there come a falling away first, and that man of sin be revealed, the son of perdition;
>
> Who opposeth and exalteth himself above all that is called God, or that is worshipped; so that he as God sitteth in the temple of God, shewing himself that he is God. (2 Thessalonians 2:3–4)

Daniel calls him "the prince that shall come." Jesus calls him "the abomination of desolation." Paul calls him "the son of perdition [Apollo (see the must-watch new documentary *"Belly of the Beast"* for the chilling truth around this)]." Regardless of the names by which he is called, he will sit in the Third Temple—the *Tribulation* Temple—and declare himself to be God. He will demand that all on earth worship him. He will have a hatred for the Jewish people that is directly from the mind of Lucifer the fallen one —Satan.

As a matter of fact, this man will be indwelt at this point by the devil himself, who has always wanted the worship reserved exclusively for Jehovah. John the apostle calls him "Antichrist":

> Little children, it is the last time: and as ye have heard that anti-christ shall come, even now are there many antichrists; whereby we know that it is the last time. (1 John 2:18)

4. **Revelation 11:1–2** It is John, as "the revelator," who gives us the fourth scriptural proof text of a Third Temple atop Mount Moriah:

> And there was given me a reed like unto a rod: and the angel stood, saying, Rise, and measure the temple of God, and the altar, and them that worship therein.
> But the court which is without the temple leave out, and measure it not; for it is given unto the Gentiles: and the holy city shall they tread under foot forty and two months. (Revelation 11:1–2)

This, of course, describes how the non-Jewish people will move about the outside of the Temple while Jews worship within. The reference to forty-two months has to be the first three and one-half years of Daniel's seventieth week—the seven-year Tribulation period. This means, it is very likely that the Tribulation Temple will be standing atop Mount Moriah almost at the very beginning of this last seven years before Christ's Second Advent.

The Jews are worshiping, according to John's description, in a rebuilt Temple until the halfway mark of the seven years, and then Antichrist desecrates the Temple and declares himself to be god. He then begins slaughtering every Jewish person he can lay hands on. So, this reference is to the first half of the seventieth week described by Daniel.

The point is that this is yet another proof that a Temple—the *Third Temple*—will stand on top of the Temple Mount at some point. It will be, again, a Temple, not of joy, but for carrying out Antichrist's genocide against the house of Israel. It will be set up to carry out the time of *Jacob's trouble.*

Here are Jeremiah's words about Daniel's seventieth week—the last three and one-half years of that era, which the Lord called "great Tribulation":

> For, lo, the days come, saith the LORD, that I will bring again the captivity of my people Israel and Judah, saith the LORD: and I will cause them to return to the land that I gave to their fathers, and they shall possess it.
>
> And these *are* the words that the LORD spake concerning Israel and concerning Judah. For thus saith the LORD; We have heard a voice of trembling, of fear, and not of peace. Ask ye now, and see whether a man doth travail with child? wherefore do I see every man with his hands on his loins, as a woman in travail, and all faces are turned into paleness? Alas! for that day is great, so that none is like it: it is even the time of Jacob's trouble; but he shall be saved out of it. (Jeremiah 30:3–7)

Just as Jesus in the Olivet Discourse likened the Tribulation to a woman about to give birth, Jeremiah also likens all of Israel under Antichrist's evil persecution to a woman in labor pain. The end-times scenario above is one that many early Church Fathers agreed with. The late Grant Jeffrey once noted:

> Lactantius wrote about a rebuilt Temple that would stand in the last days prior to Christ's return. In his book *The Divine Institutes*, he described the seven-year Tribulation period and the persecution that will be brought about by the Antichrist: "Then he will attempt to destroy the temple of God and persecute the righteous people; and there will be distress and tribulation, such as there never has been from the beginning of the world."

Another early church theologian, Victorinus, also wrote about the Third Temple. His *Commentary on the Apocalypse* explored the prophecies found in the book of Revelation. Victorinus wrote about the False Prophet, the partner of the coming Antichrist, saying the False Prophet will place an image, or statue, of the Antichrist in the rebuilt Temple.…"

One of the greatest of the early church writers, Irenaeus, taught that the new Temple would be a genuine Temple built by the religious Jews…and in his book *Against Heresies* [he] affirmed his understanding of the Scripture's prophecies about animal sacrifice being reinstated in the future Temple.[129]

Israel Saved

The last seven words of this Tribulation prophecy in Jeremiah constitute God's bottom line in dealing with His chosen people. They are wonderful words promising a magnificent future for all of *believing* Israel: "he shall be saved out of it."

Jacob is the "he" of this passage—the father of the twelve tribes named after him, representing all of the nation Israel. We see the promise of that Jeremiah 30:7 prophecy fulfilled in the following.

And I will pour upon the house of David, and upon the inhabitants of Jerusalem, the spirit of grace and of supplications: and they shall look upon me whom they have pierced, and they shall mourn for him, as one mourneth for his only son, and shall be in bitterness for him, as one that is in bitterness for his firstborn. (Zechariah 12:10)

A remnant of the Jewish people, those who will recognize the returning King Jesus as their Messiah, will thus be "saved" and will form the Israel that will be greatly blessed by God during the Millennium and beyond.

God's Prophetic Timeline

The building of the Third Temple is out there in the hazy future of things to come. While the student of Bible prophecy cannot say for sure at this point exactly *when* that edifice will be built, knowing how Bible prophecy is scheduled to unfold provides an idea of how close the building of that Temple—and all other prophecies scheduled—might be to coming to pass.

World Leader Comes Forth

The nations of earth will be in chaos. The turmoil will cause severe ramifications while governments seek to restore civil order and regain governmental and economic equilibrium. According to prophecy, one man will step forward to proffer a plan to quell the fears of war in the Middle East (Daniel 9:27). This prophecy correlates to Revelation 6:2, with the rider on the white horse coming forth.

Peace Covenant Confirmed

The great world leader will arrive just in time to look like the shining knight on the white horse. He will have the answer to the looming all-out war in the Middle East. He will be able to sell a seven-year peace plan that is already available, apparently. Israel will agree to the covenant, as will her enemies, and, in effect, the whole world will accept the (European?) leader's masterful sales pitch. But Israel's acceptance will fly in the face of God. This "covenant made with death and Hell," as it is called in Isaiah 28 will cause God's judgmental wrath to begin to fall.

Attack on Israel

The Gog-Magog attack prophesied by Ezekiel is controversial, as far as where it will fit into the end-times timeline is concerned. Some have the event just before or in conjunction with a Rapture, while others believe it will happen right after a Rapture or nearer the mid point of the Tribulation period. Russia is destined to present some of the most fearsome trials and tribulations for Israel. Gog, "chief prince of Rosh," is the leader of Russia described in Ezekiel 38 and 39. In ancient language, Gog means "leader." "Rosh" is the ancient name for the land of Russia. In the last days, Russia will be the leading nation of the Gog-Magog coalition of nations that will make a move against Israel and be defeated by a supernatural act of God. Persia (Iran) comes right along beside Russia, in prophetic parlance. According to Ezekiel 38:5, Iran will aid Russia in attacking Israel before or during the Tribulation. Even now, Iran acts as a destabilizing force in the world.

144,000 Evangelists

The Lord will not allow the dark, satanic realm to go unchallenged. He will seal (protect from Satan and his minions) 144,000 Jewish men with the gospel message of Jesus Christ, the only way to salvation, redemption, and reconciliation to God, the Father. (Read Revelation 7:3–8.) These will proclaim that message throughout the world, and millions upon millions of people will hear it and become Christians of the Tribulation period.

Two Old Testament-Type Prophets Preach

Two Jewish men will be placed during this period to preach the gospel and to point the finger of judgment if repentance doesn't occur. No one knows for sure who these men will be, but there seems good evidence that at least one of them will be Elijah, the Old Testament prophet whom God took up from earth in a fiery whirlwind. The satanic governmental regime will seek to kill these men, but won't be able to until God allows. Anyone who tries to kill them will, in like manner, be killed.

Finally, the regime will be able to kill them. Their dead bodies will lie in the streets of Jerusalem for three days, then they will be resurrected to life and will lift into the sky before the astonished eyes of their murderers and of the whole world.

Antichrist Revealed

The great world leader who confirmed the seven-year peace covenant, convincing Israel and its enemies to rely on him and his regime to keep the peace, will be struck with a deadly head wound. But he will be "resurrected" from death (see Revelation 13). *The astonishing new documentary film,* Belly of the Beast, *reveals when and where this event will take place, and even points to the exact (shocking) location where the "raising" ceremony will unfold!* This revived man of sin will, following this, suddenly appear in the new Jewish temple atop Mount Moriah at Jerusalem and declare himself to be God. He will demand worship from all the world's inhabitants. (Read 2 Thessalonians 2 and Revelation 13.) He is then revealed as Antichrist, the son of perdition, the man of sin. He will cause all to accept his mark or be cut out of the economic system—all buying and selling. He will order that all who do not worship him should be killed—chiefly by beheading. His partner in the satanic duo will point all worship to the beast, Antichrist. The false prophet will be Antichrist's John the Baptist figure.

Jews Flee

Jesus forewarned the Jews who will occupy Jerusalem at the time of Antichrist's revelation to flee to the mountains. (Read Matthew 24 and Revelation 12.) This era, as discussed earlier, the midpoint of the Tribulation era, will begin the time of Jacob's trouble (Jeremiah 30:7)—a time Jesus says will be the worst in all of history (Matthew 24:21). Antichrist will begin the greatest genocide ever to be visited upon the planet.

Antichrist Institutes Regime

Antichrist's regime will cause all to worship the beast, the Revelation 13 term for Antichrist. He will apparently set up some sort of idol, before which all must bow. This will likely be done by the image of himself being telecast in some way to all the world (Revelation 13.) His regime will consist of ten kingdoms, whose newly crowned kings (political leaders of the region) will give all their authority and power to Antichrist. We might be seeing the formative months and years of the formation of this ten-kingdom development with the various trading blocs beginning to form. The European Union seems to be the prototype for those that will follow. The North American Union (NAU) that seems to be underway in development, bringing America, Canada, and Mexico together in an economic trading bloc, appears to be one such "kingdom" in the making. Antichrist will bring together one world government, one world economy, and one world religion, to some extent—for a brief time, at least. This is a Babylonian-type system that will all but enslave the entire world.

Babylon System of Religion, Economy, Government Rules

The Babylonian system will be an extension of the revived Roman Empire. This was prophesied in Daniel 2, 7, 9, and 11, as well as in Revelation 13. Ancient Babylon and the Roman Empire's influence upon this end-time regime of hell on earth are described in Revelation 17 and 18. God will destroy the chief city of the end-time Babylon in one hour, the Bible prophesies in Revelation 18.

Kings of East Threaten, then Move

China, today, is a growing economic and military behemoth. It exerts hegemony over its neighbors of the Orient. The Bible predicts a day during the Tribulation when the "kings of the east" will march across the dried-up Euphrates River to do battle at Armageddon. This juggernaut will consist of two hundred million troops—all, prophecy seems to indicate, demon-possessed while they cross the area of the Euphrates. (Read Revelation 9 and 16.)

All Meet at Armageddon

The kings of the east march toward a rendezvous with all other nations of the world. God says this about this meeting:

> For, behold, in those days, and in that time, when I shall bring again the captivity of Judah and Jerusalem,
>
> I will also gather all nations, and will bring them down into the valley of Jehoshaphat, and will plead with them there for my people and for my heritage, Israel, whom they have scattered among the nations, and parted my land. (Joel 3:1–2). (Also read Revelation 16:16 and 19:17–18.)

Christ Returns

Just as the battle is becoming so violent that it threatens the end of all people and animals on earth, the black clouds of apocalypse will unroll like a scroll, and brilliant light from Heaven's core will break through, revealing the King of kings and His armies and myriad angelic hosts.

> And I saw heaven opened, and behold a white horse; and he that sat upon him was called Faithful and True, and in righteousness he doth judge and make war.
>
> His eyes were as a flame of fire, and on his head were many crowns; and he had a name written, that no man knew, but he himself.

And he was clothed with a vesture dipped in blood: and his name is called The Word of God.

And the armies which were in heaven followed him upon white horses, clothed in fine linen, white and clean.

And out of his mouth goeth a sharp sword, that with it he should smite the nations: and he shall rule them with a rod of iron: and he treadeth the winepress of the fierceness and wrath of Almighty God. (Revelation 19:11–15)

Christ Judges Nations

The conquering Creator of all things will establish His earthly throne atop Mount Moriah, which will be supernaturally reconfigured from topographical renovations made for the Millennium. All the nations of the world will come before the Lord Jesus Christ. (Read about the sheep-goats judgment in Matthew 25.) The people who have made it alive through the Tribulation will either be believers or unbelievers. Believers will be ushered into Christ's thousand-year reign on Earth while unbelievers will be cast into everlasting darkness.

Christ Sets Up Millennial Kingdom

The millennial reign of Christ will begin, a time during which the false prophet and the beast (Antichrist), the first to be thrown into the Lake of Fire, will begin to serve their eternal sentences. Satan will be confined in the bottomless pit, and none of his minions will be able to torment and tempt the millennial earth-dwellers. This period will be much like the times of Eden, with the Earth restored to its pristine beauty (Revelation 20–10). After the thousand years, the devil will be released from the pit for a short time. He will lead millions who will have been born during the Millennium in an assault on Christ at Jerusalem. God will send down fire and consume them all. Satan will be cast into the Lake of Fire. The lost dead will be resurrected (their eternal bodies joined to their souls), and all will stand before the great white throne of Christ to be judged. All will be cast into the Lake of Fire for eternity (Revelation 20:10–15). Jesus Christ will remake the heavens and the earth in preparation for everlasting, ever-growing ecstasy in God's presence. (Read Revelation 20:16–22:16.)

notes

1. Ray C. Stedman, *An Introduction to Daniel*, https://www.raystedman.org/old-testament/daniel, 58.
2. Abby Stevens, "Jewish Organization Opens Holy Temple Visitors' Center in Jerusalem," *Deseret News*, July 31, 2013, https://www.deseretnews.com/article/865583894/Jewish-organization-opens-Holy-Temple-Visitors-Center-in-Jerusalem.html.
3. Arutz Sheva staff, "Plans for Third Temple Have Begun," *Israel National News*, July 26, 2015, https://www.israelnationalnews.com/News/News.aspx/198621.
4. Adam Eliyahu Berkowitz, "Sanhedrin Urges Candidates for Jerusalem Mayor to Prepare for Third Temple," *Breaking Israel News*, November 8, 2018, https://www.breakingisraelnews.com/116619/sanhedrin-jerusalem-mayor-temple/.
5. "Sanhedrin Invites 70 Nations to Dedicate Altar for Third Temple," *Charisma News*, December 7, 2018, https://www.charismanews.com/opinion/standing-with-israel/74307-sanhedrin-invites-70-nations-to-dedicate-altar-for-third-temple.
6. Marissa Newman, "Rare Interfaith Temple Mount Confab Highlights a Christian Awakening," *Times of Israel*, December 5, 2018, https://www.timesofisrael.com/rare-interfaith-temple-mount-confab-highlights-a-christian-awakening/.
7. Adam Eliyahu Berkowitz, "Harbinger to Messiah: Red Heifer is Born," *Breaking Israel News*, September 5, 2018, https://www.breakingisraelnews.com/113476/temple-institute-certifies-red-heifer/.

8. Christina Maza, "Will Trump Hasten the Arrival of the Messiah? Jews and Evangelicals Think So," *Newsweek*, December 11, 2017, https://www.newsweek.com/jews-trump-persian-king-babylonian-exile-third-temple-judaism-744698/

9. Zia H Shah, "How Can We Build the Third Temple Together?" *Muslim Times*, December 6, 2017, https://themuslimtimes.info/2017/04/20/how-can-we-build-the-third-temple-together/.

10. Zafrir Rinat, "Earthquakes in Israel: Tenth Tremor in a Week Shakes North," *Haaretz*, July 8, 2018, https://www.haaretz.com/israel-news/.premium-earthquakes-in-israel-tenth-tremor-in-a-week-shakes-north-1.6248542.

11. Jason Keyser, "Jerusalem's Old City at Risk in Earthquake," Associated Press, updated January 19, 2004, http://www.msnbc.msn.com/id/3980139/.

12. Khaled Abu Toameh, "Abba's Fatah: Israel Planning to Destroy Al-Aqsa Mosque," *Jerusalem Post*, July 26, 2018, https://www.jpost.com/Israel-News/Abbass-Fatah-Israel-planning-to-destroy-Al-Aqsa-Mosque-563525.

13. Ohr Margalit, "A New Vision for God's Holy Mountain," http://newsweek.washingtonpost.com/onfaith/guestvoices/2009/06/a_new_vision_for_gods_holy_mountain.html.

14. Adam Eliyahu Berkowits, "Biblical Numerology Predicts Trump Will Usher in Messiah," *Breaking Israel News*, May 16 2016, https://www.breakingisraelnews.com/67748/biblical-numerology-predicts-trump-will-usher-messiah/#YpPoq8q60l05J0SD.97.

15. Bob Eschliman, "Rabbi Predicts Trump Will Win and Usher in the Second Coming," *Charisma News*, November 4, 2016, http://www.charismanews.com/politics/elections/61031-rabbi-predicts-trump-will-win-and-usher-in-the-second-coming.

16. Sam Kestenbaum, "Jewish Mystics Hope Trump's Israel Visit Might 'Raise the Temple,'" *Israel Forward*, May 22, 2017, http://forward.com/news/372256/for-jewish-mystics-trumps-israel-visit-part-of-messianic-process/.

17. Hillel Fendel, "Sanhedrin to Trump-Putin: Fulfill Cyrus-like Role in Jerusalem," November 15, 2016, http://www.israelnationalnews.com/News/News.aspx/220289.

18. Sam Kestenbaum, "Why These Jewish Mystics Think God Helped Trump Win," *Israel Forward*, November 15, 2016, http://forward.com/news/354530/why-these-jewish-mystics-think-god-helped-trump-win/.

19. Thomas Horn, *Saboteurs* (Crane, MO: Defender Publishing, 2017) 80–84.

20. Adam Eliyahu Berkowitz, "Sanhedrin Mints Silver Half-Shekel with Images of Trump and Cyrus," *Breaking Israel News*, February 15, 2018, https://www.breakingisraelnews.com/102784/sanhedrin-temple-movement-issue-silver-half-shekel-images-trump-cyrus/

21. "Islamic 'Messiah' al-Mahdi to Return by 2016, Followed By Jesus? Islamic 'Messiah' al-Mahdi to Return by 2016, Followed by Jesus?" *Israel, Islam and the End Times,* May 19, 2015, http://www.israelislamandendtimes.com/islamic-messiah-al-mahdi-to-return-by-2016-followed-by-jesus/. Accessed January 3, 2016.

22. MCD Admin, "Prominent Rabbi Warns Friends Not to Leave Israel; 'Messiah Is Here with Us Already,'" *My Christian Daily*, http://mychristiandaily.com/mcd/prominent-rabbi-warns-friends-not-to-leave-israel-messiah-is-here-with-us-already/.

23. J. R. Church, "The 800-Year-Old Prophecy of Rabbi Judah Ben Samuel," *Prophecy in the News,* February 2010, 14.

24. Clarence Goen, "Jonathan Edwards: A New Departure in Eschatology," *Church History 28*, March 1, 1959, 29, 25–40.

25. Kerry R. Bolton, "US Recognition of Jerusalem's Capital: A Travesty of History," *Foreign Policy Journal*, May 24, 2018, https://www.foreignpolicyjournal.com/2018/05/24/us-recognition-of-jerusalem-as-israels-capital-a-travesty-of-history/.

26. Ibid.

27. "Objectives of the Temple Mount Faithful," http://www.templemountfaithful.org/objectives.php.

28. Bolton, "US Recognition," https://www.foreignpolicyjournal.com/2018/05/24/us-recognition-of-jerusalem-as-israels-capital-a-travesty-of-history/.

29. Nancy LeTourneau, "Trump's Support for Israel Doesn't Negate His Anti-Semitic Dog Whistling," *Washington Monthly*, October 29,

2018, https://washingtonmonthly.com/2018/10/29/trumps-support-for-israel-doesnt-negate-his-anti-semitic-dog-whistling/.

30. Ziah H. Shah, "How Can We Build the Third Temple Together?" *Muslim Times*, April 20, 2017, https://themuslimtimes. info/2017/04/20/how-can-we-build-the-third-temple-together/.

31. Adam Eliyahu Berkowitz, "Will Brazil's New President Call to Build the Third Temple?" *Breaking Israel News*, October 29, 2018, https://www.breakingisraelnews.com/116040/brazils-election-signal-first-stage-temple/.

32. Tupac Pointu, "Evangelicals Wield Voting Power across Latin America, Including Brazil," *Times of Israel*, October 6, 2018, https://www.timesofisrael.com/evangelicals-wield-voting-power-across-latin-america-including-brazil/.

33. "Armageddon Predicted as Jews Call for Third Temple to Be Built," *Sputnik News*, November 11, 2018, https://sputniknews.com/middleeast/201811111069715673-armageddon-jews-jerusalem-temple/.

34. "Jerusalem Islamic Waqf," Wikipedia, https://en.wikipedia.org/wiki/Jerusalem_Islamic_Waqf.

35. "Temple Mount Entry Restrictions," Wikipedia, https://en.wikipedia.org/wiki/Temple_Mount_entry_restrictions

36. Derek Gilbert, *The Great Inception* (Crane, MO: Defender Publishing, 2017) 241.

37. Derek Gilbert, *Last Clash of the Titans* (Crane, MO: Defender Publishing, 2018) 179, 180.

38. Rasha Abou Jalal, "Is Ryadh Really Pushing for Control of Jerusalem Holy Sites?" July 2, 2018, *Al-Monitor*, https://www.al-monitor.com/pulse/originals/2018/07/saudi-arabia-holy-sites-jordan-jerusalem-pa-guardianship.html.

39. David A. Andelman, "One Man's Disappearance Risks Bringing Down the Saudi Crown Prince," *Channel News Asia*, October 18, 2018, https://www.channelnewsasia.com/news/commentary/jamal-khashoggi-journalist-saudi-arabia-crown-prince-mbs-10835902.

40. Ben Hubbard, "Saudi Prince Says Israelis Have Right to 'Their Own Land,'" *New York Times*, April 3, 2018, https://www.nytimes.

com/2018/04/03/world/middleeast/saudi-arabia-mohammed-bin-salman-israel.html

41. "Saudi Arabia Hosts Rare Visit of US Evangelical Christian Figures," Reuters, November 1, 2018, https://www.reuters.com/article/us-saudi-christians/saudi-arabia-hosts-rare-visit-of-u-s-evangelical-christian-figures-idUSKCN1N6675

42. Holly McKay, "Islamic Group Chief Calls for Muslims to Join Christians, Jews in Jerusalem Meeting," Fox News, October 5, 2018, https://www.foxnews.com/world/islamic-group-chief-calls-for-muslims-to-join-christians-jews-in-jerusalem-meeting.

43. Hezki Baruk, Gil Ronen, "Netanyahu Seeking to Give David's Tomb to Vatican?" *Israel National News*, January 5, 2014, http://www.israelnationalnews.com/News/News.aspx/180149.

44. Shimon Cohen, "Claim: Vatican Hoarding Second Temple Vessels," *Israel National News*, May 28, 2014, http://www.israelnationalnews.com/News/News.aspx/181146.

45. Aaron Klein, "US Plan Gives Jerusalem Holy Sites to Vatican," WND, December 15, 2013, https://www.wnd.com/2013/12/u-s-plan-gives-jerusalem-holy-sites-to-vatican/.

46. Peter Goodgame, "The Biblical False Prophet," *RedMoonRising*, last accessed November 11, 2011, http://www.redmoonrising.com/21Defense/biblicalFP.htm.

47. Ibid.

48. Hannah Roberts, "'Heretic' in the Vatican," *Politico*, May 28, 2018, https://www.politico.eu/article/pope-francis-heretic-vatican-liberal-conservative-war/.

49. "Minutes from Bilateral and Trilateral US-PAL-ISR Sessions Post Annapolis, Tuesday, 29th July 2008," viewable here: *Al Jazeera*, last accessed February 7, 2012, http://www.aljazeera.com/palestinepapers/.

50. Giulio Meotti, "Expose: The Vatican Wants to Lay Its Hands on Jerusalem," *Israel National News*, December 15, 2011, http://www.israelnationalnews.com/News/News.aspx/150757#.TzV9aORnDmd.

51. "Minutes from Bilateral and Trilateral US-PAL-ISR Sessions Post Annapolis, Tuesday, 29th July 2008," viewable here: *Al*

Jazeera, last accessed February 7, 2012, http://www.aljazeera.com/palestinepapers/. Please note that formatting *but none of the content* has been changed from the original source.

52. "Vatican Secretary of State Speaks with Condoleezza Rice about Christians in Middle East, Iraq," *Catholic News Agency*, last accessed February 13, 2012, http://www.catholicnewsagency.com/news/vatican_secretary_of_state_speaks_with_condoleezza_rice_about_christians_in_middle_east_iraq/.

53. Levitt Letter 21:2 (Feb 1999), 3, as cited in Randall Price, *The Coming Last Days' Temple* (Eugene, OR: Harvest House, 1999), 475.

54. Randall Price, *The Coming Last Days' Temple* (Eugene, OR: Harvest House, 1999), 481.

55. "History of Mid-East Peace Talks," BBC News, July 29, 2013, www.bbc.com/news/world-middle-east-11103745.

56. Dr. Randall Price, *World of the Bible.*

57. Dr. David Reagan, "The Third Temple: When Will It Be Built?" Lion and Lamb Ministries, christinprophecy.org/articles/the-third-temple/.

58. "Devarim," Chabad of the West Side, http://www.chabadwestside.org/templates/articlecco_cdo/aid/1257081/jewish/Devarim.htm.

59. "Has the Ark of the Covenant Been Discovered?" Israel Video Network, September 1, 2017, https://www.israelvideonetwork.com/has-the-ark-of-the-covenant-been-discovered/.

60. Talmud Yoma' v.2. Translated by Michael L. Rodkinson. (New York: New Talmud Pub. Co.1903).

61. *Mishnah*, in Tractate Shkalim, it is written: "A priest in the Second Temple saw a section the floor which was different from the other floors and he understood that in this place there was an entrance to an underground tunnel and he came and shared it with his friend. Before he could finish sharing what he had seen with his friends, he died. They then knew very clearly that that was the place where the Ark of the Covenant was hidden." According to Maimonides, Solomon knew that the Temple would be destroyed in the future and prepared a repository for the Ark underneath the Temple mount. Later King Josiah hid the Ark in Solomon's secret vault. Maimonides, The Book of Temple Service, 17. also Hilchot Beit HaBecheirah 4:1 and Tractate

Yoma, 53b. Translated by Michael L. Rodkinson. New York: New Talmud Pub. Co.1903.

62. Captain Charles W. Wilson, *Ordinance Survey of Jerusalem* (London: Palestine Exploration Fund, 1884).

63. Major Condor, *Our Work in Palestine* (London: Palestine Exploration Fund, 1866).

64. Kebra Nagast, Miguel F. Brooks, Ed., *Glory of Kings* (Lawrenceville, NJ: Red Sea Press, 1996) 46.

65. 1 Kings 11:9–12, KJV

66. 2 Chronicles12:9, KJV.

67. *Columbia Encyclopedia,* 3rd ed. (New York: Columbia University, 1963) 453.

68. Robert Jamieson, A. R. Fausset, and David Brown, *Commentary Critical and Explanatory on the Whole Bible, 1871* (Hendrickson Publishers, New Edition, March 1, 1997).

69. 2 Chronicles 26:24, KJV.

70. 2 Chronicles 35:3, KJV.

71. Jamieson, Fausset, and Brown, *Commentary Critical and Explanatory on the Whole Bible.*

72. 2 Chronicles 35:20, KJV.

73. Jamieson, Fausset, and Brown, *Commentary Critical and Explanatory on the Whole Bible.*

74. 2 Chronicles 35:22–24, KJV.

75. *Columbia Encyclopedia*, 213.The Apocryphal books were considered historically valuable enough to be included in the King James Bible from its formation in 1611 until 1885. Later, these fourteen books were officially removed from the English printings of the King James Bible by the Archbishop of Canterbury in 1885.

76. II Macabees 2:4 Bishop Challoner's 18th century revision of the Douay Rheims version Catholic Public Domain Version. 2005 Ronald L. Conte Jr., translator and editor.

77. R. H. Charles, *The Apocrypha and Pseudopigrapha of the Old Testament*, Vol. 2, 2 Baruch 6 (Oxford, UK: Oxford Press, 1913).

78. James Strong, *Strong's Exhaustive Concordance of the Bible, Hebrew Dictionary, Hebrew Lexicon,* # 5015 (Iowa Falls, IA: World Bible Publishers, 1986).

79. Ibid. # 5013.

80. Ibid. # 5011.

81. Deuteronomy 34:10, KJV.

82. Deuteronomy 34:5, KJV.

83. Strong's Hebrew Dictionary, # 5014.

84. Talmud (Sanhedrin XI. 109a) (Cf. Obermeyer, pp. 314, 327, 346). Translated by Michael L. Rodkinson. (New York: New Talmud Pub. Co., c1896–c1903).

85. Numbers 21:9, KJV.

86. 2 Kings 18:24, KJV.

87. The sculpture of the serpent on the pole was created by Italian artist Giovanni Fantoni. Wikipedia Mount Nebo.

88. 1 Kings 8:10, KJV.

89. Ezekiel 11:23, KJV.

90. Ezekiel 43:4, KJV.

91. Exodus 34:35, KJV.

92. 1 Samuel 4:22, KJV.

93. R. H. Charles, *The Apocrypha and Pseudopigrapha of the Old Testament.*.

94. Ibid., Ta'anit 29a and in Pesikta Rabbati 26:6.

95. Ibid., Talmud. Jalkut Shekalim 50a and B. on Isa. xxi.

96. *Columbia Encyclopedia*, 1080.

97. David Flynn, *Temple at the Center of Time*, Official Disclosure, First Edition, (Crane, MO: Defender Publishing, September 8, 2008) 129–144.

98. *Breaking Israel News*, https://www.breakingisraelnews.com/112216/temple-vessels-found/, used by permission.

99. Shelley Neese, *Copper Scroll Project* (New York: Morgan James Publishing, 2019) 26.

100. "Building the Third Temple," The Mitzvah Project, http://themitzvahproject.org/building-the-third-temple/.

101. Randall Price, "Is the Temple Mount the Hoax of the Millennium? An Answer to the Current Controversy, Part 1," worldofthebible.com.

102. Robert Cornuke, "Temple: Archeology," Koinonia House, January 1, 2015.

103. David Reagan, "The Jewish Temples—Where Were They Located?", http://christinprophecy.org/articles/the-jewish-temples/.
104. Price, "Is the Temple Mount the Hoax of the Millennium? An Answer to the Current Controversy, Part 1."
105. Ibid.
106. Cornuke, "Temple: Archeology."
107. Reagan, "The Jewish Temples—Where Were They Located?"
108. Randall Price, "Archaeological Evidence of the Destruction of the Temple and of Temple-related Structures from the Historic Temple Confirm the Modern Temple Mount as the location of the Temple(s)".
109. Adam Eliyahu Berkowitz, "Ancient Jewish Sources Indicate Trump Will Pave Way for Third Temple: Prominent Rabbi," *Breaking Israel News,* March 22, 2018, https://www.breakingisraelnews.com/104682/ancient-jewish-sources-indicate-trump-will-pave-way-for-third-temple-prominent-rabbi/.
110. "Trump's Jerusalem Declaration 'Enormous Step Towards Bringing Third Temple'" By Adam Eliyahu Berkowitz December 7, 2017, https://www.breakingisraelnews.com/99002/trumps-jerusalem-declaration-next-step-third-temple/#IQA44Phvblqt8RI2.9
111. Ibid.
112. "Jerusalem Embassy Act of 1995," Congress.gov, https://www.congress.gov/104/plaws/publ45/PLAW-104publ45.pdf.
113. Michael Wilner, "Trump Announces US Moving Embassy to Jerusalem, US President Told Regional Leaders He Intended to Declare the City the Capital of the Jewish State," *Jerusalem Post,* December 6, 2017.
114. Ibid.
115. Yoav Frankel, director of the initiative, The Interfaith Encounter Association at the Mishkenot Sha'ananim's Konrad Adenauer Conference Center in Jerusalem.
116. Adam Eliyaho Berkowitz, "Redemption in the Air as Record-Breaking 1,300 Jews Ascend Temple Mount on Ninth of Av," *Breaking Israel News,* https://www.breakingisraelnews.com/92586/1300-jews-temple-mount-signal-end-exile-beginning-joyous-redemption-ninth-av/#MJIWEWhrRedUDCWh.99.

117. Terry James, "Turkey on End-times Table," Raptureready.com, Terryjamesprophecyline.com.
118. Dr. Jack Van Impe, "A Message of Hope from Dr. Jack Van Impe: The Coming War with Russia," *Perhaps Today* magazine.
119. Ian May, "Inside the Prospective Israel-Saudi Arabia Rapprochement," *Israel News*, *Jerusalem Post.*
120. Hana Levi Julian, "White House Notifies US Embassies Around the World of Plan to Recognize Jerusalem as Capital of Israel," JewishPress.com, December 1, 2017.
121. Adam Eliyahu Berkowitz, "An End-of-Days Guide to the Embassy Move," *Breaking Israel News*, May 14, 2018.
122. Ibid.
123. Israel Today staff, "Top Israeli Rabbi Believes Trump Will Build Third Temple in Jerusalem," *Breaking Israel News*, March 29, 2018.
124. Dr. Thomas Ice, "Daniel's Seventieth Week."
125. Lambert Dolphin, "Ezekiel's Third Temple," lambert@ldolphin.org, Lambert Dolphin's Library, The Temple Mount Web Site, Revised May 31, 1995, April 19, 1996, January 18, 1997, November 7, 1997. March 1, 2000. December 4, 2001. July 14, 2002. July 13, 2004.
126. By permission of Lambert Dolphin, www.ldolphin.org, Lambert Dolphin wwwtemplemount.org.
127. Daymond Duck, Prophecy Plus Ministries, Inc., Raptureready.com, May 23, 2018.
128. There are many excellent studies on this prophecy given Daniel by Gabriel. There isn't space here to go into detail, but it's recommended that you look to Dr. John Walvoord, Dr. Chuck Missler, and other Bible prophecy scholars to get the profound implications of Daniel's prophecy. The point we are considering here is that a Third Temple will be built—t Temple that Antichrist will desecrate.
129. Grant Jeffrey, *The New Temple and the Second Coming*, (Colorado Springs, CO: WaterBrook Press, 2007) 18, 20.